FROM the BARREL of a GUN

Pergamon Titles of Related Interest

Collins U.S.–SOVIET MILITARY BALANCE 1980-1985
Hunt & Shultz LESSONS FROM AN UNCONVENTIONAL WAR
Record REVISING U.S. MILITARY STRATEGY
Suchlicki CUBA: FROM COLUMBUS TO CASTRO,
Second Revised Edition

Related Journals
(Free specimen copies available upon request)

DEFENSE ANALYSIS

FROM
the BARREL
of a GUN
Armies
and Revolutions

Anthony James Joes

PERGAMON-BRASSEY'S
International Defense Publishers

Washington New York London Oxford
Beijing Frankfurt São Paulo Sydney Tokyo Toronto

Pergamon Press Offices:

U.S.A. (Editorial)	Pergamon-Brassey's International Defense Publishers, 1340 Old Chain Bridge Road, McLean, Virginia 22101
(Orders & Inquiries)	Pergamon Press, Maxwell House, Fairview Park, Elmsford, New York 10523, U.S.A.
U.K. (Editorial)	Brassey's Defence Publishers, 24 Gray's Inn Road, London WC1X 8HR
(Orders & Enquiries)	Brassey's Defence Publishers, Headington Hill Hall, Oxford OX3 0BW, England
PEOPLE'S REPUBLIC OF CHINA	Pergamon Press, Qianmen Hotel, Beijing, People's Republic of China
FEDERAL REPUBLIC OF GERMANY	Pergamon Press, Hammerweg 6, D-6242 Kronberg, Federal Republic of Germany
BRAZIL	Pergamon Editora, Rua Eça de Queiros, 346, CEP 04011, São Paulo, Brazil
AUSTRALIA	Pergamon Press (Aust.) Pty., P.O. Box 544, Potts Point, NSW 2011, Australia
JAPAN	Pergamon Press, 8th Floor, Matsuoka Central Building, 1-7-1 Nishishinjuku, Shinjuku-ku, Tokyo 160, Japan
CANADA	Pergamon Press Canada, Suite 104, 150 Consumers Road, Willowdale, Ontario M2J 1P9, Canada

First printing 1986

Library of Congress Cataloging in Publication Data

Joes, Anthony James.
    From the barrel of a gun.

    Bibliography: p.
    Includes index.
1. Military history, Modern--20th century.
2. Revolutions. I. Title.
U42.J64   1986   321.09   86-4281
ISBN 0-08-034238-8
ISBN 0-08-034237-X (pbk)

Printed in the United States of America

For AJ and Vicky

Contents

Acknowledgements

In the writing of this book I have incurred large debts of gratitude. The Board on Faculty Research at Saint Joseph's University supported the initial stages with a timely grant. Several colleagues—David H. Burton, Elwyn F. Chase, and James E. Dougherty—provided useful criticism. Franklin D. Margiotta, president of Pergamon-Brassey's, Inc., made many invaluable suggestions. My wife, Chris, and our two children bore with much grace the fearsome trials of sharing a house with someone writing a book. All this good assistance accounts for whatever merit the book may possess; for its flaws, I alone bear the full responsibility.

PERMISSIONS

Harper and Row
   Excerpts from *The Cuban Revolution*, by Hugh Thomas. By permission of Harper and Row. Copyright 1977 by Harper and Row.

MIT Press
   Excerpts from *Lost Soldiers: The French Army and Empire in Crisis, 1947–1962*, by George T. Kelly. By permission of MIT Press. Copyright 1965 by MIT Press.

Introduction: From the Barrel of a Gun

The waning years of the twentieth century are an Age of Revolution, from Afghanistan to El Salvador; from Ethiopia to Nicaragua; from Burma, Kampuchea, and the Philippines to Mozambique, Angola, and South Africa. This book is about a particular, crucial aspect of revolution—how and why governments lose their military superiority over indigenous opponents and are overthrown.

Every government maintains armed forces, often quite elaborate and expensive ones, at least in part to protect itself against internal enemies. Every successful revolution, therefore, means that the country's army has failed to play its appointed role. Yet many studies of revolution fail to address this military dimension. This lack of attention to the military components of the overthrow of governments derives in part from the often implicit assumption that once the long-term and middle-term economic and sociological causes of revolution are in place, revolution is practically inevitable.[1] The collapse of military opposition to the revolutionaries is merely a predictable consequence of this inevitability. Sometimes such assumptions are quite explicit and reach the extremes of the following dictum suggested by a noted sociologist: "The truth is that green bands led by determined men, with peasants alongside them and a mountain nearby, can defeat organized battalions of tyrants equipped with everything up to the atom bomb."[2] In the minds of many, the American experience in Vietnam has confirmed this view or some more moderate version of it.

In sharp contrast, professional revolutionaries have always been intensely concerned with the relationship between political and military power. "No revolution of the masses," wrote Lenin, "can triumph without the help of a portion of the armed forces that sustained the old regime. . . ."[3] (The events in Manila in February 1986 resoundingly demonstrated the continuing relevance of this insight.) After the Bolsheviks seized power in Russia, they set 24 conditions that a foreign Communist party would have to meet in order to receive Moscow's recognition. Condition number four stated: The obligation to spread Communist ideas includes the special obligation to carry on systematic and energetic propaganda in the army. Where such agitation is prevented by emergency laws, it must be carried on illegally.[4] Years later, Mao observed: "The existence of a regular Red Army of adequate strength is a necessary condition for the existence of Red political power. . . . Unless we have regular armed forces of adequate strength, *even though we have won the mass support of the workers and peasants*, we certainly cannot create an independent regime, let alone an independent regime that lasts long and develops daily [italics added]."[5]

Leninists and others with a practical interest in revolution have long been preoccupied with its military factors because revolutionary success involves two questions: First, where did the revolution come from; and second, why did it succeed?[6] It is the latter question that brings us face to face with the role of a government's armed forces. Some recent students of revolution suggest that no revolution can succeed as long as the government possesses the loyalty of the armed forces.[7] It follows, therefore, that "an analysis of the political position of the armed forces always lies at the heart of any concrete study of a revolution."[8]

In writing this book, we have taken these views of both practitioners and students of revolution to heart. Our thesis is a simple one—the military aspects of the overthrow of a government, far from being merely residual or totally determined, are always critical and often primary. They therefore deserve study, reflection, and analysis; in other words, "the part played by the army is decisive in any revolution."[9] Our purpose is neither to test standard theories of revolution—that is, theories of why regimes reach a crisis—nor to advocate a new theory. Instead, our purpose is to analyze actual revolutions in order to arrive at some concrete conclusions about the role of armed forces in revolutionary situations. These conclusions may provide a much more realistic and practical understanding of the essential components of successful revolutions.

Clearly, the defeat or defection of a government's armed forces does not take place in a political vacuum. Even though they maintained large and adequately equipped armies, the governments of the tsar, the shah, and the Hungarian Communists were torn from power by crowds of unarmed civilians. Other regimes, such as those in Brazil, Portugal, and the French Fourth Republic, were overturned by the armed forces that were presumably intended to defend them. Such apparently incongruous outcomes suggest that governments sometimes fall more from their own weaknesses and errors than from the strength and cunning of their adversaries. Trying to answer why a revolution succeeded requires consideration of the leadership that influenced the readiness and reliability of the armed forces. Above all, one must evaluate the degree of intelligence with which government leaders used those forces during and just before the period of crisis.

These concerns are of more than mere academic importance. Consider, for example, that the U.S. government, in dealing with a violence-torn country such as El Salvador or the Philippines, often seeks to locate—or to create—a "moderate center" as an alternative to authoritarians of the right and totalitarians of the left. But no government, even a popular and democratic one, will prevail unless it possesses appropriately equipped and politically convinced armed forces and the will and competence to use them to effect. As chapter 1 will detail, an overwhelming majority of the Russian people preferred the democratic alternative represented by Alexander Kerensky to either tsarism or bolshevism. But Kerensky neglected to ensure himself of a reliable army, or even a reliable regiment, and so the Russian people did not get their choice.

We have devoted a separate section to the Russian revolutions and their aftermath because of the overpowering importance and interest of those events, but the Russian February Revolution could easily have been grouped with the chapters on Hungary and Iran as another example of the failure of regular troops to protect the regime from civilian uprisings. Along with revolutions in the usual sense of the word, we have included examples of other types of change in government in which armed force plays a major role, such as civil wars and coups d'état. The choice of cases is justified by their manifest magnitude (China) or their relative immediacy (Iran) or because, as in the case of French Algeria, they contain lessons still unlearned, like unexploded land mines in a forgotten field.

NOTES

1. Mark N. Hagopian, *The Phenomenon of Revolution* (New York: Dodd, Mead, 1974), chap. four.
2. C. Wright Mills, *Listen Yankee! The Revolution in Cuba* (New York: McGraw-Hill, 1960), p. 114.
3. Edwin Lieuwin, *Arms and Politics in Latin America* (New York: Praeger, 1960), p. 134.
4. Chalmers Johnson, *Revolutionary Change* (Boston: Little, Brown & Company, 1966), p. 158.
5. Geoffrey Fairbairn, *Revolutionary Guerrilla Warfare: The Countryside Version* (Harmondsworth, England: Penguin, 1974), p. 92n.
6. Stanislav Andreski, *Military Organization and Society* (Berkeley: University of California, 1968), p. 158.
7. Hannah Arendt, *On Revolution* (New York: Viking, 1963), p. 112; Katherine Chorley, *Armies and the Art of Revolution* (Boston: Beacon, 1973), p. 16.
8. Johnson, *Revolutionary Change*, p. 99.
9. Chorley, *Armies*, p. 23.

PART

1

The Russian Cataclysm

The fall of the Tsarist regime had been predicted for a long time, yet surprised everyone when it finally occurred. Key sectors of Russian society had for years grown more and more alienated from the imperial system, which nevertheless was able to cling to power with the support of the army. The destruction, during three years of world war, of this old and loyal army, and its replacement by a new and unreliable one, denuded tsarism of its one effective defense. In St. Petersburg, brain center of the empire, the security situation was absurdly perilous: aswarm with foreign agents, throbbing with revolutionary agitation, inadequately supplied with food, the capital city was nevertheless inexplicably garrisoned with troops of the poorest quality. When, during a prolonged bread riot, the inept authorities provoked some of these demoralized troops to mutiny, the whole Tsarist edifice suddenly tumbled down. Thus, through an accident—the government's inability to gather together a few thousand politically reliable soldiers in the capital—war-battered Russia was thrust into its first experiment with republican democracy.

Alexander Kerensky emerged as the new order's moving spirit. The continuation of the unpopular war and the disloyalty of the capital garrison, the very circumstances that had undone tsarism, soon rendered Kerensky's government vulnerable to any organized faction ready to seize power. The amateurish attack launched by a few thousand Bolsheviks against the Winter Palace defended by a few hundred loyal troops was thus able to overthrow Kerensky, throttle Russian democracy, and establish the world's first Communist dictatorship. When Kerensky led a counterattack against the Bolshevik-held capital, he managed to reach the outer precincts of the city before the Bolsheviks were able to turn him back; yet the forces under his command numbered fewer than 1,000.

The new Bolshevik regime in St. Petersburg was disorganized, lacked popular support in the country at large, and faced both a gathering counterrevolution and intervention by several foreign states. In the midst of these perils,

1

the Bolsheviks possessed nothing remotely resembling a real army. But the enemies of the Bolsheviks were also in disarray. Controlling only peripheral areas of the country and lacking the most elementary political skills, the counterrevolutionary Whites could neither mobilize adequate numbers of troops nor effectively govern the territories they occupied, whereas foreign intervention was haphazard and small-scale. For a while, the fate of Russia (and much else besides) hung in the balance as miniscule armies clashed inconclusively on the roads to Moscow. The Whites eventually discovered the politically astute leadership they had so sorely lacked but, by that time, Leon Trotsky, boldly using former Tsarist officers, had built up a serviceable Red Army and thus saved the Bolshevik regime.

1

February and October

Today the War, tomorrow the Revolution.

— Mussolini

In March 1917, after nearly three years of world war, the Romanov dynasty suddenly and unexpectedly collapsed. This was the beginning of what George Kennan has called "the greatest political event of the present century."[1]

No one who studies the fall of the Tsarist monarchy and the destruction of the short-lived republic that followed it can fail to marvel at the extent to which this "greatest political event" depended on the inability of political authorities to provide themselves, at even the most critical moments and places, with even the most miniscule number of reliable troops.

THE POLITICAL CRACKS IN THE STRUCTURE OF TSARISM

The Tsarist regime fell because its unpopularity reached a peak at the very moment when its security forces were least able to respond to a revolutionary outbreak.

The unpopularity of the monarchy stemmed from the sullen detachment of much of the peasantry from the government and the educated classes; the revolutionary proclivities of Russia's still-infant but rapidly growing industrial proletariat; the seething discontent, often amounting to passionate hatred of the system, on the part of Russia's numerous national minorities, such as Jews and Ukrainians; the alienation of much of the middle class, especially the intelligentsia; and the personal inadequacies of the last tsar, Nicholas II.

Russia's peasant masses were withdrawn, superstitious, impoverished, and dirty. By 1914, the great nobility owned less than one-quarter of the land, and this proportion was steadily decreasing, but "deep in the heart of many of the peasants" was "the conviction that they had been cheated at the time of the emancipation" in 1861.[2] Cheated or not, the peasants had been left by the emancipation under the control of their own village communities.

3

Periodic redistribution of village lands and the ultimate authority of the community over crops prevented the emergence of private ownership and discouraged initiative; what was the sense of working hard to improve a holding that would soon enough be handed over to someone else?

The number of industrial workers in Russia had more than doubled between 1890 and 1913, from 1,425,000 to 2,931,000.[3] This was at once a sign of progress for the country and a source of peril for the regime. In Western Europe, working class parties could fight for what they wanted inside long-established middle-class and liberal traditions; freedom of speech and freedom of assembly ensured that the entry of the working class into the political arena would generally be an orderly one. But owing partly to the relative absence of a middle class and partly to the requirements of military defense, Russia was in 1914 what she had been for centuries, a centralized autocracy, in which the role of the citizen was not to participate but to comply. Thus, to many in the working class movement, it seemed that the only way to achieve real labor reforms, much less the socialist republic to which most of their leaders aspired, was through revolution.

Russia's ethnic minorities, taken together, probably constituted close to a majority of the empire's population in 1914. Many of them were bitterly hostile to the Tsarist regime, and with reason. Ukrainians, Poles, Georgians, and others were subjected periodically to "Russification" campaigns, which sought to impose upon them the Russian Orthodox faith and the Russian language. The large Jewish population was often the object of outrageous "pogroms": brutal communal attacks rendered even more scandalous by the complicity of government agents. The principal effect of this harsh policy against minorities was to create revolutionaries: Trotsky (Jewish) and Stalin (Georgian) are only the most prominent of the revolutionary leaders drawn from the national and religious minorities. At the same time that the regime offended its minorities by its Great Russian chauvinism, it failed to compensate for this by making itself popular with the Great Russian majority, by offering it, for instance, a real parliament and a real constitution.[4]

Many of the intelligentsia identified all that was modern and enlightened with parliamentary government, and longed to see Russia possess a truly effective legislative body. The elective national assembly, the Duma, girded about with restrictions and laboring under the hostility of the tsar, was ineffective. Nicholas II's ideas concerning government could be summarized as the concentration of power in the hands of the monarch, the primacy of the Holy Orthodox Church, and the political and cultural subordination of all the empire's many ethnic groups to the Russians—in a famous slogan: "Orthodoxy, Autocracy, Nationality." The failure to give the Russian intelligentsia a real parliament meant that by 1914 literally thousands of educated and patriotic persons who wanted to contribute to the building of a modern Russia were forced to regard their own government as at best an obstacle to the realization of their ideas and at worst an enemy to be destroyed. Progressive elements throughout the country assumed that the day of autocracy was finished and that therefore all that was needed to achieve true parliamentary democracy in Russia was to get rid of the tsar. Ironically, Nicholas II, "who fought so tenaciously against the granting of a constitution, had many of the qualities that would have fitted him excellently for the position of a constitutional monarch and practically none of those that were needed for the exercise of that absolute power to which he stubbornly clung."[5]

Years ago, Crane Brinton wrote:

> A mixture of the military virtues, of respect for established ways of thinking and behaving, of willingness to compromise and, if necessary, to innovate, and a willingness to recruit new members from the properly gifted of the other classes, is probably an adequate rough approximation of the qualities of a successful ruling class.[6]

The Tsarist system fell considerably short of these criteria in 1914. Yet we should not exaggerate either the repression or the stagnation of the Tsarist regime in the twentieth century. Educated travelers to the West presented a very negative picture of life in Imperial Russia, but the truth is more complex. Concomitant with a cultural life that displayed great vitality were a high rate of industrial development, progress in general education, considerable social legislation, and improvements in the system of justice. Florinsky rightly observes that Russia as a modern state was very young, really dating only from the emancipation of the serfs in 1861. And in 1905, Prime Minister Piotr Stolypin launched a fundamental attack on Russia's greatest social and economic weakness. Aware that a landowning peasantry is the most conservative class in the world, Stolypin determined to create just such a class by encouraging the breakup of peasant communes and the institution of widespread private ownership. Lenin grasped the profound significance of Stolypin's reforms; he believed that the destiny of Russia lay in a race between Stolypin's program and the next upheaval. Several times before Stolypin's death, Lenin remarked that he did not expect to live to see the revolution.[7] If the Russia of 1914 could have had another ten years of peace, another ten years of Stolypin's peasant reforms, Russia—and the world—would be unrecognizably different today. (Lenin, at the very least, probably would have died before any serious upheaval had had a chance to develop.) But the outbreak of the Great War changed everything. It was not the inadequacy of Stolypin's plans but the coming of a world war that provided the crisis needed by Lenin.[8]

And so we arrive at the most necessary cause of the Russian revolutions of 1917: the entrance of the country into the Great War. Not only did the war put a complete stop to Stolypin's program of creating a large class of conservative supporters of the regime; even more decisively, it brought about the destruction of the army, on which the regime ultimately relied for protection against its many disloyal subjects. Trotsky was absolutely correct when he wrote that "the Revolution grew directly out of the war."

THE DESTRUCTION OF THE TSARIST ARMY

Liberal elements within Russia were enthusiastically in favor of the war; they were sure that close alliance with the Western democracies would generate irresistible pressures for reform at home. (Many of the most extreme conservatives within Russia also held this view, and therefore opposed the war or favored an alliance with Germany.) The Tsarist government, for its part, plunged its backward country into the maelstrom in the first instance to honor its treaty obligations but more fundamentally because it was thought absolutely necessary to fight in order to preserve Russia's position as a Great Power. Nicholas II and his advisers saw in the battlefields of the Great War a refuge from problems foreign and domestic, instead of a graveyard for the system and even for the royal family itself. Similarly the Habsburgs sought, through precipitating the long-dreaded world war, to give their fragmenting multinational empire a new lease on life; only to see Austria–Hungary totally shattered by the pressures of war. In like manner, half a century before, the aristocrats of the American South had unleashed civil war in order to preserve their slave society; instead they saw their cherished institutions pulled up by the roots. War is a fearfully unreliable instrument of conservative statecraft.

A solid phalanx of Germany, Austria–Hungary, Bulgaria, and Turkey confronted Russia and effectively isolated her from her Western allies. It was to break through this cordon that Winston Churchill launched the Gallipoli campaign. From March 1915 to January 1916, thousands of British, French, and British–Imperial troops were killed in a fruitless effort to punch through Russia's encirclement and open a supply route to her that was as important psychologically as it was materially. The failure of this great effort besmirched the reputation of Churchill, its principal patron; it also established the reputation of Kemal Pasha, the Turkish Empire's only successful wartime commander, soon to emerge as the father-dictator of modern Turkey. Most of all, the bloody failure at Gallipoli confirmed the physical and psychological isolation of Tsarist Russia.

In September 1915, the tsar left St. Petersburg to take command of the front. This was a tragic error from many viewpoints. The tsar was totally unfitted for modern military command. Worse, it left the machinery of the imperial government too much in the hands of Empress Alexandra, widely believed to be secretly sympathetic to the German enemy and more and more under the scandalous sway of the sinister Rasputin. The influence of Alexandra on the operations of the wartime government was disastrous: largely due to her meddling, in the two years before March 1917 Russia had four prime ministers, six ministers of the interior, and four ministers of war—this during the supreme war crisis.

The professional military leadership, on the other hand, offered no consoling contrasts to this civilian ineptitude. In the spring of 1915, the Russian general staff began its "Retreat of 1812," a scorched-earth policy that in its brutality created a surge of millions of refugees to the interior of Russia and to its already turbulent great cities. This "criminal absurdity," as Florinsky called it, reached a point at which the Russian army prepared to abandon the city of Warsaw, a metropolis of 1 million, after blowing up its gas, water, and electricity supply centers. This insanity was cancelled only at the last moment.

Said Florinsky: "A ship without a captain, manned by an unskilled and undisciplined crew, Russia drifted along an uncharted course."[9] To revolution.

> The supreme solvent for the disintegration of the rank and file [of an army] is an unsuccessful war. . . . [Hence] [t]here can be little doubt that under modern conditions the last stages of an unsuccessful war provide the surest combination of circumstances for a successful revolutionary outbreak.[10]

Although defeat in war is propitious for revolution, it is no guarantee of it. The calamitous conflict with Japan in 1904–1905 resulted in serious outbreaks of revolutionary violence in the major cities of Russia, but the regime did not fall. During that crisis, the government had used some intelligent tactics: keeping the troops that were most politically reliable home from the front to deal with possible disturbances; using rural troops in urban areas; deploying, where feasible, soldiers who were ethnically different from the rioters they were to curb; and improving the treatment and the pay of soldiers used to defend the regime from civil unrest.[11] The failure of the government to repeat these intelligent and successful tactics will be considered below. But the greatest difference by far between the situation of 1905 and that of 1917, from the point of view of the government, was in the *composition* of the army. The allegiance of the pre-world war army to the Tsarist system was based on the mystique of loyalty to a God-appointed emperor and, most of all, on the seclusion of the professional military from the general population. By 1917, these circumstances, and indeed this army, had completely disappeared. During the Great War, Russia called up 15 million men, equal to more than one-third of the entire adult male population. This enormous draft of men not only caused severe economic and social dislocations, but created a vast and largely ungovernable army, which not only could not defend the regime but would actually topple it.

The conscripts of this vast new army were soon appalled and offended by a lack of supplies, even of such fundamentals as shoes and ammunition, by the needlessly degrading treatment accorded enlisted men by officers, and most of all by the obvious incompetence and military failure of their leaders. Still more damaging was the upheaval that the war caused among the officer corps. The enormous bloodletting of 1914 and 1915 affected the officers even more than it did the rank and file. Most of the replacements for the thousands of officers killed or badly wounded came from the nonaristocratic strata of Russian society; by 1916, fully 70 percent of officer trainees were of peasant origin, and another 26 percent were from the bourgeoisie, many of the latter indeed being members of the pre-war radical intelligentsia. After two and a half years of modern war, the army of the tsar was poorly equipped and badly trained, with inadequate leadership and low morale. Many of the rank and file were of poor intellectual and physical quality, and numerous officers were professionally incompetent, politically disloyal, or both.[12] Yet even this doomed army, this "army of the damned," had managed not only to withstand three winters of major war, but also to defeat the Austro-Hungarians. By early 1917, however, the sands had almost run out.

THE OUTBREAK OF THE FEBRUARY REVOLUTION

The epicenter of revolution, in February as in October, was the capital city of St. Petersburg (Russianized during the war to Petrograd). Built from scratch on the orders of Peter the Great, French and Italian architects had given it wide boulevards, magnificent public buildings, and an impressive spaciousness. A center for literature, music, theater, and ballet, St. Petersburg was one of the most brilliant and glittering of the world's capitals. It was also a nest of revolutionaries.

The government had long laid plans for meeting strikes and civilian outbreaks in the major urban areas, but no plans at all for countering military mutiny. Yet by 1917, many of the country's soldiers were really no more than unwilling civilians in military greatcoats.

Plans for the defense of the capital against civil upheaval included the deployment of from 6,700 to 12,000 police and mounted Cossacks.[13] There were more than 200,000 troops in the general vicinity of the capital, with the city garrison itself numbering about 150,000. All of these forces were more than adequate to deal with any disturbance—on paper. Closer inspection reveals how frail the government's defenses were. The original guards regiments of the capital, professional and loyal, had early been dispatched to the front lines; consequently the city garrison was largely composed of young boys or of men in their forties, those recuperating from wounds, or even criminals and strikers sent into the army as punishment. High casualty rates among the pre-war officer corps reduced the number of professionals among the officers in the St. Petersburg garrison to *less than one in ten*. Many of these capital troops had been demoralized by years of harsh treatment and very long periods of garrison duty. Their morale, and the control over them by their officers, had been further undermined by both true and false reports about the activities of Rasputin within the royal family and the latter's reputed pro-German sympathies.[14] Finally, the garrison was much too big to be kept in isolation from revolutionary agitators and German agents (sometimes the same people) who swarmed in the city streets and cafés; these troops should never have been stationed in the city proper, or close to it, in the first place.

Thus, the stage was set.

The civilian demonstrations that broke out in St. Petersburg late in February 1917, were provoked to some extent by German agents.[15] But there was plenty of flammable material lying about for them to work with. St. Petersburg was in the third winter of war, and long bread lines and intermittent strikes made everyone miserable and jittery. A lockout of workers at a large metal factory on February 22 (Old Style) was followed the next day (Thursday) by great numbers of women in mass demonstrations demanding bread; these manifestations were large in the working-class Viborg district of the city. Mounted Cossacks showed little energy in breaking up these crowds and by Saturday, February 25, most of the police in Viborg were barricaded in their stations.

The size and unexpected stubbornness of the demonstrations, the reluctance of Cossacks and troops to suppress them, and the incredibly inept responses of the authorities were the main elements of the short and explosive drama that followed.

In the beginning of the demonstrations, the government had forbidden the troops to fire on the populace. This policy permitted the crowds, and the professional agitators among them, to approach the troops and talk with them, undermining their willingness to take repressive action. Troops that may be called upon to confront civilian demonstrators should in no instance be permitted to mingle with them beforehand. Leaders of the demonstrations, for their part, vigorously discouraged the use of weapons by their side in order not to frighten, provoke, or infuriate the soldiers.

On Saturday, February 25, the city authorities received a stern telegram from the tsar, all this time away at the front: "Suppress the disorders." The next day, in several serious incidents, soldiers (who, of course, lacked modern riot control equipment) fired into the crowds under orders to shoot to kill. During these crucial days, whatever little morale the troops still had was destroyed by simple, bad leadership. Troops would be called out for action, then left standing in the squares for hours on end, without orders and without food. The soldiers perceived that their officers were very reluctant to order shooting; when the government later demanded that demonstrators be fired upon, many of the troops were aghast, because the demonstrators they were now to shoot at were not acting very differently from those who in previous days had been permitted to approach and mingle with them. From this time began the disaffection and mutinies that would spread so rapidly from one military unit to another; the first notable garrison rebellions began during the evening of Sunday, February 26.

Monday, February 27, was decisive for the regime and for history. Those units that had done the most firing on the crowds suddenly refused to shoot any more. Many soldiers, especially in working-class Viborg, began openly to fraternize with the demonstrators. That same day, an unpopular officer of the Volynsky Regiment, one Major Lashkevich, was murdered by one of his own soldiers. Fearing reprisals, the entire regiment mutinied and went around to the barracks of other units, pleading with or forcing the soldiers there to join them. During these momentous events, many officers throughout the city had been afraid to exercise leadership over their men, partly because of the great gap that had deliberately been created in the Tsarist army between officers and men, but also because agitators among the crowds had taken up the practice of killing individual officers in the streets while studiously avoiding injury to the enlisted men.

Here and there, the government still had opportunities to make a stand, but frittered them away. More than two thousand loyal troops with good morale had been gathered into the grounds of the Winter Palace on Monday, February 27. Hours passed. No action was taken. No effort was made even to feed the patrols. After dusk, these units were dispersed back to their own barracks for supper; along the way, they mingled with the crowds and dispersed.[16] The Bicycle Battalion, a city-based unit, put up fierce resistance against disloyal troops, but no one came to its aid; the battalion surrendered on February 28, and soon thereafter many of its officers were murdered. The police, meanwhile, had ceased to exist as a cohesive force; scattered around the city, however, were numerous and still loyal units of police and troops. Although with effective communications and proper leadership they could have made much trouble for the insurrection,[17] nothing was done to unify these elements and, as February 28 progressed, more and more of them either dispersed or joined the insurgents. These events were accompanied by the brutal murders of many officers, no fewer than 900, according to some authorities.[18] Estimates of casualties during these days include 700 soldiers, 500 civilians, and 73 policemen.[19]

On March 2, the general staff and commanders of outlying garrisons joined in asking the tsar to bring the disorders to an end and save the army from further disintegration by announcing his abdication. The tsar complied with this request the same day, renouncing the throne both for himself and for his son. A few days later, he was taken into custody by troops of the new provisional government.

In this way, the thousand-year-old Romanov dynasty came to its end.

The actions, or failures to take action, on the part of the tsar and the authorities on the scene in St. Petersburg have occasioned much bitter criticism. The distinguished historian Riasanovsky, for example, declares that "resolute action, such as promptly bringing in loyal forces from elsewhere, might have saved the imperial government."[20] But it is not clear that this would have been the case. Some units had indeed been sent into the city from outlying areas, but when they encountered disaffected elements from the city garrison, they began to waver. It might have been better, indeed the tsar's only real chance, to have withdrawn the St. Petersburg garrison entirely from the city as soon as the degree of disaffection began to be apparent, on the principle of "Lose the capital, but save the army." This tactic had been used with complete success by the government of Adolphe Thiers against revolutionary Paris in 1871.[21] But the collapse of authority among the St. Petersburg troops came so suddenly that there was probably no time to execute such a maneuver. The crux of the situation was that within St. Petersburg, the heart and brain of the whole empire, the garrison was rotten to the core, politically speaking, by February 1917, and the condition of the capital garrison was a metaphor for the condition of Russian society. Government leaders with the common sense and energy to make sure that the forces of order there were well-paid, well-trained, well-fed, with good officers and good morale, would have had the common sense and energy to avoid many of the mistakes of the previous three years, which had culminated in the demonstrations and mutinies of February 1917. In mitigation of this perhaps too harsh criticism of the Tsarist government, one must point out that the succeeding provisional government failed utterly either to remove the mutinous garrison or to whip it into shape (see below). Even more than that of the tsar, Kerensky's failure to discipline the St. Petersburg garrison was to have earthshaking consequences for the Russians and for the whole world.

The Tsarist system was in trouble by 1914, but we gain nothing by painting a completely dismal picture of it. A great deal of progress was being made in the economy and in education, and there was considerable freedom of expression and movement. But the Great War multiplied all the strains in the system to the breaking point, and magnified the personal inadequacies of the tsar. It also killed off a very large proportion of the professional officer corps.

But the immediate cause of the collapse of the Tsarist government is to be found in the deplorable condition of the St. Petersburg garrison.

> The tsar fell because some soldiers, impulsively and unexpectedly to themselves, disobeyed the command of their officers to fire on a demonstrating crowd. It was fear of punishment for their violation of discipline that frightened the demoralized soldiery, causing them to appeal to other regiments, give up their rifles and seek to lose themselves in the crowds. And the same fear caused the mutineers to look eagerly for larger justifications and meaning for their first impulsive act.[22]

Thus, although the overthrow of the Russian Empire was the long-postponed payment for years of misguided policies and ineffective leadership, it was also, in a real sense, an accident, avoidable even at the last hour.

THE PROVISIONAL GOVERNMENT AND THE ARMY

It is not hyperbole to say that "the Revolution came as a surprise to both the liberal and revolutionary leaders of Russia."[22] Lenin, for example, was in Switzerland on the day that the tsar abdicated, and Trotsky was in New

York City. The February insurrection had actually been in progress for four days before the Duma formed a provisional committee and tried to take over the leadership of the revolt. What almost all of the liberals of the Duma had desired was a change of monarch and a constitution; what they got instead was the collapse of the dynasty and a power vacuum—in wartime. There was no precedent whatsoever for the filling of that vacuum. The provisional government slapped together by the Duma had no legitimacy. The liberals, who dominated the provisional government, had only a very slender base of support in the country as a whole (owing to suffrage restrictions in Duma elections). Power in Russia was up for grabs. Everything hinged on the election of a constituent assembly that could settle the "institutional question" and set the new republic on a firm legal foundation. All this was to be done in a country waging a major war and suffering a partial foreign occupation. The seemingly endless delays in convening this constituent assembly worked against the provisional government: the army might have rallied to a democratically elected assembly—the embodiment of the will of the Russian people—and protected it against the rising Bolshevik power. But no one was very keen to protect the existing Duma and its provisional government, which represented hardly more than Russia's small middle class.

The essence of any concrete study of a revolution is an examination of the political condition within the army.[23] What was the position of the Russian armed forces after the fall of the tsar? The army, and above all, the St. Petersburg garrison (and from the point of view of taking and holding power, this was the key) fell almost immediately under the control not of the Duma but of the St. Petersburg Workers' and Soldiers' Council, the "Soviet." After February 1917, nominal power in the country was in the hands of the Duma and its dominant middle-class elements; real power in the capital city was exercised more and more by this extra-legal, self-appointed Soviet, a body that initially was moderate enough but that fell increasingly under the direction of the Bolsheviks. *What gave the St. Petersburg Soviet supreme importance was its control over the St. Petersburg garrison.* It had obtained this control by issuing the famous Order Number One, on March 1, 1917, which forbade the garrison to follow anybody's orders except those of the Soviet, and especially forbade it to move out of the city, an order that the garrison was more than eager to obey. Thus, the Duma and its provisional government, with questionable legitimacy and negligible support, exercised power side by side with the Petersburg Soviet, which had no legitimacy at all but had the garrison under its control. This is the essential fact that explains the final destruction of the provisional government and the imposition upon Russia of a Bolshevik dictatorship. "The ultimate complete loss by the Provisional Government of control over its armed forces predetermined and made possible the scope and success of the social upheaval throughout the country,"[24] an upheaval that had its culmination in the seizure of power in the capital by the Leninists.

It was not just the St. Petersburg garrison that escaped control of the provisional government; in a short time, the whole army was in such total disarray that when the supreme crisis arrived in October there were hardly any soldiers available to defend the provisional government from a coup d' état. What happened to the Russian army between March and October of 1917?

> The sudden relaxation of the old disciplinary bonds [after] two and a half years of mainly unsuccessful fighting under conditions of extreme physical hardship [resulted in] the evaporation of fighting capacity and a growing impatience of the peasant soldiers with the Government which gave them neither peace nor land.[25]

Eventually this army would engage in "the greatest mutiny in history."[26]

Would not the Russian army have disintegrated even if the February Revolution had never occurred? One can, of course, never be certain whether the battered Russian army would have fallen apart in 1917 even with the Tsarist system still in place.

> But the abrupt revolutionary change; the disappearance of the tsar; the new flood of talk and discussion; the assurance that the new government stood for liberty, a conception that to the average peasant soldier was inseparably associated with peace and land — all this made the loss of the fighting capacity of the army quite inevitable.[27]

The disintegration process was urged along by the Germans; after the February Revolution, Berlin forbade any attacks along the Russian front, waiting to see if the Russian army would continue to fall apart on its own.

The provisional government has been often and bitterly reproached for not having made peace with the Central Powers: "by refusing to give up the utopian formula 'war to the victorious end' the Russian propertied and middle classes assured themselves of revolution to the bitter end."[28] This is not an entirely realistic criticism. The men of the provisional government and most of their supporters in the Duma were culturally and emotionally admirers of the West. They knew that to make peace would enable the Germans to turn with their full force and fury on the Western Allies, and this they could not bring themselves to permit. Besides, what would have been the fate of Russia once the Germans had been victorious in the West? Therefore, Russia stayed in the war.

Nevertheless, the provisional government was not guiltless in the matter of the destruction of the army. One of its first acts was to decree the abolition of the death penalty. This supposedly enlightened and humanitarian act immediately made desertion from the army more attractive. After all, you could get shot at the front, but not if you were captured as a deserter. Neither did the idealistic liberals of the Duma prevent the introduction into the army of the committee system, which held officers accountable to an elected group of common soldiers and subjected every order to interminable discussion and debate. Army morale and discipline were already in a very low state before the February Revolution; the committee system destroyed both completely. Officers were the particular victims of this breakdown.

> They were made the immediate scapegoats for all the hardships and sufferings of the War which they themselves had so largely shared. The impossibility for the majority of the officers' corps to back the demand of their men for immediate peace and their desperate attempts to restore discipline singled them out as supporters of the old regime and exposed them to the worst insults and indignities.[29]

General Denikin (who would play a great role in the fast-approaching civil war) expressed his outrage at conditions to the provisional government:

> Disobedience, debauchery, and robberies prevail among the troops. . . . The officers are in a terrible position . . . they are insulted, beaten, murdered. There is only one honest way out for the officer, and that is death. [Finally] You have dragged our glorious banners in the mud. Now raise them up if you have any conscience.[30]

Stung by such reproofs, and unable to deny that its well-intentioned humanitarianism had produced chaos in the army and danger for the nation, the provisional government after a time attempted to restore some discipline. The reintroduction of the death penalty, erection of new military courts, the use of armed forces against recalcitrant units, the creation of shock units and national battalions (Polish, Muslim, etc.) were all intelligent measures, but they were not nearly enough to stem the rising tide of chaos and collapse.

KERENSKY IN POWER

The premiership of the provisional government fell in July 1917 to Alexander Kerensky, a 36-year-old lawyer and member of the peasant-based Socialist Revolutionary party. Believing himself the man of the hour, Kerensky thought he could revive and restore the failing Russian army by speechmaking campaigns. Chamberlin has left us a devastatingly unflattering picture of him:

> [His] quickness of movement and gesture, which created an external impression of strength and character [masked an] inability to think coldly and realistically outside the haze of his own glowing phrases. [A] wordy, gesticulating lawyer [with a] capacity for self-hypnotism, [his] banalities alternated with flights of hysterical rodomontade.[31]

Hardly had Kerensky, the former minister of war, become premier when the long-awaited July offensive of the Russian army began. Greeted by some local successes at first, the offensive soon ran into German reinforcements; defeat turned into rout, accompanied by much pillaging and burning, unmistakable symptoms of the rock-bottom level of morale within the army.

The coup de grace was dealt this suffering, dismembered army by the famous Kornilov affair. General Lavr Kornilov, believing it his duty and mission to establish order in the capital, put backbone into the government, and restore discipline to the fast-deteriorating army, led his troops toward the capital in late August. But as his forces approached closer to St. Petersburg, they were surrounded and infiltrated by swarms of propagandists, who broke the discipline of first one unit and then another. Before Kornilov had entered the near suburbs, his troops "simply melted away." The almost totally bloodless defeat of the attempted coup sealed the fate of Kerensky and of Russia's experiment with republican government. "Quite probably," writes Chamberlin, "an ultimate victory of Bolshevism was predetermined by the entire political, economic and social condition of Russia in 1917." Clearly this is a judgment with which many would take issue. But Chamberlin is undoubtedly correct when he goes on to observe that "Kornilov's futile, clumsy thrust for power facilitated and expedited this victory [of bolshevism]."[32] The Kerensky government had driven the Bolsheviks underground for their part in some disturbances in the capital a short time earlier, but the Kornilov affair allowed them to stage a dramatic comeback. They had been tireless in organizing a working-class defense of the city, sending agitators to melt away Kornilov's recruits and creating those armed bands that would soon achieve immortality as the "Red Guards." On the other hand, Kerensky's siding with the Bolsheviks against Kornilov completely deprived him of any support from conservatives, the significance of which would manifest itself when the Bolsheviks made their own play for total power. Finally, the "complete and ignominious collapse of the Kornilov-attempted coup" completely destroyed what was left of the prestige of the officer corps; most enlisted men saw the coup as counterrevolutionary and suspected every officer of sympathizing with it, that is, of treason against the people's revolution.[33]

THE SITUATION IN SEPTEMBER 1917

The provisional government was at the end of its rope. Not only had the prolongation of the war produced despair among the peasant soldiers and thus utterly gutted the army of any cohesiveness,[34] but the impatience of the peasants both in and out of uniform for a "solution" to the land question was wrecking the regime's slender political base as well. Land seizures, often accompanied by the killing of blooded stock and the destruction of many fine libraries, began to reach a crescendo as the year of 1917 staggered into its final months. The dark peasant masses were rising.

> The very fierceness and brutality which marked their upsurge are in some measure an indictment of the social and economic system which they swept away. It had built no adequate protective dikes; it had not given the peasantry enough education, enough sense of a stake in the land, enough feeling for property to insure itself against a violent collapse.[35]

One might add that the Tsarist regime had also failed to act against its enemies when it had the chance.

Yet neither the disintegration of the army nor the uprising of the peasants would necessarily have spelled the overthrow of the provisional government: after all, the peasant cared only for his village, and the soldier wanted only to get back to the land, not to march on the capital. The real physical threat to the provisional government came from the revolutionary proletariat of the great cities, especially St. Petersburg. In almost every other country in Europe, any government, no matter how little popular, could count on the support of the peasantry and the urban middle class against city extremists. But the weakness and disorganization of the middle-class elements in Russia were made evident by their total failure either to win any place of influence in the soviets or to build other organizations, including formations for self-defense, on their own, whereas the peasantry was busy burning up the very fabric of the society. This was the real significance of the peasant land seizures, the real price to be paid for the interruption of the Stolypin reforms: the Kerensky government found itself, in effect, left alone in the capital city to face a revolutionary proletariat more and more under the influence of bolshevism.

Meanwhile, due to the disappointing harvest of 1917, the government had to cut the bread ration in St. Petersburg to half a pound a day. And in late September, the Bolsheviks, having won a majority in the St. Petersburg Soviet, elected Leon Trotsky its president.

The eleventh hour had struck.

LENIN AND THE BOLSHEVIKS

It was Lenin who made the October Revolution; "no one else would have quite had the nerve."[36] Vladimir Ilyich Ulyanov, born in 1870 and a revolutionary from adolescence, began using the name Lenin continuously in 1901. Living much of the time in exile, eschewing music because it softened the character, never appearing in public without a three-piece suit, Lenin had but one interest, but one passion: revolutionary politics. He strove incessantly, by the tactics of splitting and secession, to create out of the intellectual and organizational chaos of Russian Marxism a monolithic party. He presented his vision of the party as a sort of revolutionary monastic order in the tracts *What is to be Done?* (1902) and *One Step Forward, Two Steps Back* (1904). Always preferring a rigid maintenance of his own position on any subject to even slight concessions in the interest of unity,[37] Lenin finally broke the Russian Social Democratic party wide open, into its Bolshevik (majority) and Menshevik (minority) elements over this question of the necessity of a spearhead party of professional revolutionaries, based on unyielding ideological uniformity and iron central control. To many Russian Marxists, this kind of vanguard party seemed quintessentially un-Marxist. Had not Marx and

Engels themselves written that "the emancipation of the working class is the work of the working class itself?" Of Lenin's project, Trotsky said in 1904: "The organization of the party would take the place of the party itself, the central committee would take the place of the organization, and finally the dictator would take the place of the central committee." Even Lenin himself once stated that "whoever wants to approach socialism by any other path than that of political democracy will inevitably arrive at the most absurd and reactionary conclusions . . . " (Thus, we see that Marxists *really can* predict the future.)

By the time of the outbreak of the Great War, after a lifetime of fighting, splitting, disrupting, expelling, organizing, and purging, Lenin was hardly more than the exiled leader of a small revolutionary sect.

> Few of the solid Swiss burghers of Berne and Zurich [where he lived in exile] knew of the existence of the bald little Russian who spent his days looking up statistics on the development of colonial empires, composing theses about turning international wars into civil wars, carrying on polemics with other isolated socialists who did not share his viewpoint. Had they known of him they probably would have regarded him as a man more pitiable and ludicrous than dangerous. Had anyone suggested toward the end of 1916 that within a year this obscure emigrant would rule the empire of the tsars the suggestion would have seemed incredibly fantastic.[38]

Both Bolsheviks and Mensheviks had spent most of their time since 1905 engaged in bitter mutual polemics; both were taken totally by surprise by the collapse of tsardom. Aware of Lenin's insistence that the Great War was not a war for the defense of the Russian motherland but merely an imperialistic brawl, the German high command soon after the February Revolution sent Lenin into Russia, firing him like a bullet at the heart of the pro-Ally provisional government. The German army also provided his party with financial support.[39] On returning to his own country, Lenin began to expound his "April Theses," in which he in effect accepted Trotsky's theory of permanent revolution. This stance stupefied most members of his own party. Until then, Bolsheviks and Mensheviks had agreed, in orthodox Marxist fashion, that backward Russia was in no way ready for a working-class government. The obvious next historical stage after the fall of "feudal" tsarism was a bourgeois–liberal regime. Lenin cast this impeccable Marxist analysis aside, declaring that the proletariat must come to power "now," and carry out the "historical tasks of the bourgeoisie." The order of the day according to Lenin was simply to seize power and then to wait for the proletariat in the West to follow the Russian example. Lenin thus transformed the traditional Marxist understanding of the relationship between economics and politics. Not Marx but Blanqui would be the guiding *geist* of the Bolshevik coup.[40] Lenin's determination to take and cling to power against all Marxist theory and prescription eventually would lead him to sacrifice at Brest-Litovsk even the *possibility* of a Western revolution, the alleged *imminence* of which had been the justification for the seizure of power by the Bolsheviks in the first place.

Lenin's demand that the Bolsheviks grab power had nothing to do with Marxist theory; he wanted an immediate insurrection because he feared another and more effective Kornilov-type coup and because he believed Kerensky was getting ready to abandon St. Petersburg, stronghold of bolshevism, to the German army. No doubt, it was the need to deal with these immediate problems at home that led Lenin to see everywhere in Europe signs of unrest that would erupt into revolution if Russia but gave the signal, if the St. Petersburg proletariat would but ring the revolutionary fire bell in the night. Thus, many theoretical and practical difficulties were solved, temporarily, by Lenin's cleverness; and (not least) if a Bolshevik coup in St. Petersburg was successful, the center of gravity of the world Marxist movement would shift from the industrialized West to Russia, Lenin's Russia.

Whatever the theoretical difficulties and contradictions of Lenin's position in 1917, his tactics were masterful, and during the summer and fall of that year certain principles of Communist activity were developed that would soon come to be considered as fundamental for all times and places. One of those principles, in the words of a distinguished student of Leninism, is as follows: "by disguising the ultimate Communist aim of total power for the small revolutionary party behind the 'simple idea' of providing equality and ending poverty, the masses could be involved in political activities of the required kind."[41] The Bolshevik promise of land to the peasant is an excellent example of this tactic; the Bolsheviks had no intention of permitting a class of land-owning peasants to be set up in Russia, and the land question would one day be settled along collectivist lines (with colossal loss of human life). At the time, however, the slogan "Land to the peasants!" enlisted the land hunger of most Russians on the side of the party that utterly repudiated the whole concept of private ownership of land. A second tactic is the instrumentalization of noncommunist groups for Communist aims: this is accomplished "by the penetration of existing associations or through the creation of associations for purposes ostensibly having aims unconnected with the ultimate aims of their Communist creators."[42] Thus, when rumors arose that Kerensky was preparing to flee from St. Petersburg and abandon "the cradle of the revolution" to the Germans, Trotsky took advantage of the situation to cover preparations for a Communist takeover. The arming of the workers' militia, for example, was done under the rubric not of preparing a Bolshevik coup but of preparing the defense of the city from the advancing Germans.

The Bolsheviks had been making themselves powerful in St. Petersburg by opposing Kornilov, and by shouting for "All power to the Soviets!" The followers of Lenin promised "Peace, bread, land"; the liberals of the provisional government promised "Constituent assembly" and "War to victory." It was no contest.

PRECOUP MANEUVERINGS

The spearhead of the Bolshevik seizure of power was the Red Guard. Numbering about 15,000 by October 1917, the Red Guard was neither well organized nor well armed, and could have been easily scattered by a much smaller number of regular soldiers. "But it was effective enough as a force for the achievement of the Bolshevik Revolution because it had only the feeblest opposition to encounter."[43] The government had few reliable troops to call upon: almost the whole St. Petersburg garrison was either pro-Bolshevik, anti-Kerensky, or neutral, whereas the middle-class liberals of the capital had built no armed force of their own. There was a city militia, but this body decided to consider itself under the command not of the provisional government but of the St. Petersburg Soviet. Clothed in this convenient interpretation of its duty, the militia would studiously ignore the coming insurrection.

The Kerensky government was well aware by mid-October that some major Bolshevik attack was in the offing, and made public statements to the effect that the Bolsheviks were doomed to defeat. Kerensky even told others that he wanted the Bolsheviks to try something, so that he could crush them once and for all.[44]

But this was all for show. Actually, Kerensky feared that an unsuccessful Bolshevik uprising would be the signal for another coup attempt from conservative forces; this fear partially paralyzed him. Believing that the real danger to his government came from the right, his actions against the Bolshevik danger up to the last hour were vacillating and ineffective; thus, he deprived himself of any conservative support he might otherwise have expected. (The principal conservative force in St. Petersburg then consisted of about 10,000 army officers, more than a match for the Red Guards, but these of course were hardly anxious to take any risks to save Kerensky, the man who had sided with the Bolsheviks against Kornilov.)

Many Russians, especially the conservatives, wanted to smother the impending Bolshevik coup by abandoning the city to the Germans. Kerensky sought instead to reestablish some kind of authority over the St. Petersburg garrison. But on October 16, the garrison decided to ignore Kerensky's order to move out of the city. Thus, the outcome of the Bolshevik uprising was actually determined a week before it began.

The key to this particular aspect of the unfolding drama lay in the garrison's dread of being sent out of the capital and into the front lines, as well as the lingering fear of punishment for the murders of officers during the events of February. The loyalty, therefore, of the troops in the capital was to anyone who would promise to protect them from these twin calamities, and that meant the St. Petersburg Soviet, in which the Bolsheviks had become the dominant element.[45]

It may be that in theory the replacement of the garrison by the better disciplined and more loyal troops from the area of the front could have saved the provisional government; the question is academic, since the government rejected any such moves in the first days of its existence. Subsequently, even if it had desired to take such action, it was too late.[46]

"And so," writes Trotsky, "the whole conflict in Petrograd came to a head over the question of the fate of its garrison."[47]

By the evening of October 22, Kerensky had indeed sent for loyal troops from the front; but the French ambassador wrote that Kerensky really seemed to be relying more on luck than on action.[48] The next day, after an address by Trotsky, the troops in the Fortress of Peter and Paul went over to the Bolsheviks without so much as a shot being fired, and the arms in that historic citadel soon found their way into the hands of thousands of Red Guards.[49] On October 24, the day before the Bolshevik uprising, which by now everyone knew was coming, the officers of the Cossack detachments, firm bulwark of state authority from days of old, voted to observe *neutrality* in the event of fighting in the city. And the military committee of the St. Petersburg Soviet reiterated its instructions to the garrison that it must not obey any orders from the provisional government. The president of the St. Petersburg Soviet, it will be recalled, was Leon Trotsky.

INSURRECTION IN ST. PETERSBURG

On the night of October 23, the Kerensky cabinet moved with unwonted briskness. It voted to suppress certain Bolshevik newspapers; ordered the arrest of leading Bolshevik agitators; called for criminal proceedings against certain members of the military revolutionary committee of the St. Petersburg Soviet; sent for military units on the city outskirts believed to be reliable (officer cadets, commando units, artillery); ordered the cruiser *Aurora*, anchored in the Neva river and known to be a hotbed of bolshevism, away from the city; cut off the telephone lines linking the Smolny Institute (a private girls' school used as Bolshevik headquarters) to the rest of the city; and ordered that the bridges be raised that connected the Viborg district with the downtown areas and that loyal troops be stationed at those bridges. These furious attempts to beat the Bolsheviks continued into the early morning of October 24, when the cabinet gave orders to arrest the leaders of the military revolutionary committee. Meanwhile, army commanders were still calling loyal troops to the city. None arrived. (The Bolsheviks also had difficulty in bringing in reinforcements. At about 8:00 P.M. on October 24, the Bolsheviks sent word to the revolutionary sailors at Helsingfors to come to St. Petersburg. Some of these sailors set off by small craft, and many took trains, but none arrived in time to be of help.)

Kerensky's strategy was to hold onto key government buildings and public utilities until outside help appeared. The plan to isolate the downtown area from pro-Bolshevik worker suburbs was a smart one, and military cadets were sent to raise the bridges across the Neva on the afternoon of October 24; most of the bridges, however, could not be raised, owing to the opposition of crowds or garrison troops or both.

During these hours, the Smolny Institute was fortified and well guarded. Nevertheless, Sukhanov, who left an extensive eyewitness account of these days, observed that the provisional government might have bagged the entire Bolshevik leadership at the school by sending a force of five hundred men. But, as Trotsky maliciously taunts: "*What* five hundred men?"[49] Lenin himself had been in hiding, and did not arrive at Smolny until midnight, October 24/25. Until then, the whole affair had been planned and directed by Trotsky, the "monumental partner in the monumental plan."[50] Before Lenin's arrival, the Bolshevik command had mainly been reacting to what it considered well-calculated government moves and had not yet given orders for a direct and complete seizure of the city. The Bolsheviks had been understandably but grossly overestimating the support of the Kerensky government, whose cadets would in fact yield everywhere, whose Cossacks would desert, and whose principal military commander was perhaps betraying it.[51] The Bolsheviks were taking over the city piecemeal, and almost by accident. But with the arrival of Lenin at Smolny Institute, the real revolution began, the assault on the very citadel of the provisional government: the Winter Palace.

THE ATTACK ON THE WINTER PALACE

The Winter Palace was directly across the Neva from, and thus directly under the guns of, the Fortress of Peter and Paul which had been in Bolshevik hands for several days. The palace guard had been strengthened during October 24 by the Bicycle Battalion and the "Women's Battalion of Death," a bourgeois unit with almost no training, recruited for the purpose of shaming the male troops. But at about 4:00 P.M., on October 24, the bicycle troops left the palace grounds, never to return.

The attack on the Winter Palace began only after almost all of the rest of the city had fallen into Bolshevik hands with unexpected, ridiculous ease. Kerensky's orders to the *Aurora* to sail away had been successfully countermanded, and Red Guards with armored cars had chased government cadets away from the bridges. On the night of October 24, Bolsheviks seized the two main railway stations in the city and occupied the State Bank building. They also took over the central telephone exchange, hooked up the Smolny telephones again and disconnected those of the Winter Palace. At about 3:30 A.M. on October 25, the *Aurora* put a detachment ashore and retook the Nikolaevsky bridge, the last stronghold of the government outside the palace grounds. The cabinet was now almost isolated inside the Winter Palace.

All of these movements had been relatively free of bloodshed, and life in St. Petersburg displayed a deceptive normality. Movies, restaurants, and theaters remained open; on the evening of October 25, Shaliapin was singing *Boris Gudonov* at the Opera.

Early in the morning of October 25, the Cossacks, three regiments strong, announced their neutrality. They did not like the Bolsheviks, but these horsemen were afraid to go into action on the city streets without infantry support; they also believed that Kerensky was a sure loser. This desertion was a calamitous blow to Kerensky, who had counted upon the Cossacks above all. Learning of these reverses, about which military headquarters was doing absolutely nothing, Kerensky confronted his military commander, one Colonel Polkovnikov, who continued to assure him that all was in readiness. Concluding that Polkovnikov had been deceiving him in the hopes that a Bolshevik success would signal a rightist countercoup, Kerensky fired him on the spot. Meanwhile, the cadets in armored cars whom Kerensky had sent out to retake the telegraph agency and the Baltic Railway Station returned and reported that they had been turned back by large Bolshevik forces. The palace itself was supposed to house approximately 700 of these officer cadets, and to contain some machine guns, artillery pieces, and armored cars as well. But defenders were leaking out of the palace all day Wednesday, October 25, especially very young cadets commanded by older officers, who did not want these children under their command to be killed.

The Kerensky government also "enjoyed" the support of the Mensheviks and the Socialist Revolutionary party; these worthies were willing to condemn the Bolshevik coup, but not to oppose it physically. The middle-class liberals had their own party but no organization and certainly no fighting units. "What kind of a party is it," bitterly demanded one of the defenders of the palace, referring to the liberals, "that can not send us 300 armed men?"[52]

At 9:40 P.M. on Wednesday, October 25, the *Aurora* signaled the assault on the palace by firing blank shells. The troops in the Fortress of Peter and Paul then started to fire live ones. It seems that more than thirty such shots were directed at the palace, but at least twenty-six of them missed.[53] All during that Wednesday, small numbers of Cossacks and cadets had been making their way into the palace, which the Bolsheviks, clearly not very effectively, had surrounded. After the firing from the fortress began, however, the Women's Battalion marched out to surrender. Official reports reveal that at least three of these unfortunate women were subsequently raped and at least one committed suicide. General Knox of the British Legation drove to Smolny Institute (Bolshevik headquarters) to intercede for the women; after some bickering, they were at least spared the fate of being confined for the night in Red Guard barracks.

By 10:00 P.M., the first Bolshevik attack on the palace had been "repulsed." After about an hour, the attack resumed. The attackers this time penetrated the palace itself, which they proceeded to take room by room. The maze of hallways and chambers confused attackers as well as defenders; no one knew the layout of the palace. Most of the cadets surrendered their arms without resistance to the overwhelmingly numerous attackers. By 2:00 A.M. on Thursday, it was all over, and many Red Guards broke into the wine cellars, where they promptly got drunk. "For all the considerable firing, it is not certain that anyone had been killed on the attacking side, and among the defenders there were few if any dead."[54]

In the capture of the Winter Palace, the Bolsheviks had netted all of the members of the cabinet. All except Kerensky.

Where was *he*?

On the morning of October 25, before the real assault had begun, Kerensky at last concluded that no relief troops were coming, and that he would have to go out and bring them. So he left the Winter Palace, driving past groups of Red Guards and garrison soldiers in a car preceded by a borrowed U.S. Embassy vehicle flying American flags.

COUNTERATTACK AND DEFEAT

St. Petersburg was a very large city, and "the feeble Bolshevik coup [there] on October 25" had created relatively little disturbance.[55] Probably very few people in the capital woke up on October 26 with any idea that "the most fundamental social upheaval of modern times had taken place."[56] Some others, quite aware, were determined to reverse this upheaval.

Kerensky had left the Winter Palace at about 11:30 on the morning of October 25; the Bolsheviks had no idea he was gone until they captured the palace. By that time he was in Pskov, 180 miles away at the headquarters of the Northern Front army. Angry at not having been appointed Commander in Chief during the previous summer, the army's leader, General Chermisov, had failed to respond to Kerensky's earlier appeals to send troops to save the provisional government. (It was Kerensky's bad luck that those troops most available from a geographical standpoint for a reconquest of St. Petersburg were either heavily propagandized by Bolsheviks or under the command of conservative opponents of his regime.) Kerensky eventually found a certain General P. N. Krasnov who was willing to obey him, and together they set off toward the capital city, at the head of a force of 700 Cossacks. This was the real beginning of the civil war.

On October 27, they reached Gatchina. Appeals went out to other units to come and help, but few responded to these calls; those that did found their trains sabotaged by pro-Bolshevik railway workers. Thus, from the entire Russian army, Kerensky could muster only his 700 Cossacks. With this little band — smaller than the police force of Omaha, Nebraska — Kerensky went forth to undo the Bolshevik Revolution. Incredibly, he was able to approach very close to the capital. On October 28, his men took Tsarskoe Selo, site of the Summer Palace, where a *garrison of 16,000 troops surrendered to them*.[57] Thus, it is clear that Krasnov could probably have entered St. Petersburg if he had a few reliable regiments; "but the significant fact of the moment was that no such regiments made their appearance."[58] The balance of history swung on Kerensky's inability to gather around himself a mere 3,000 soldiers.

As Kerensky and Krasnov approached ever closer to the capital, anti-Bolshevik elements within the city arose. Cadets seized all the Bolshevik armored cars, the telephone exchange, and even Commissar of War Antonov, he who had led the assault on the Winter Palace. But the St. Petersburg Cossacks, as usual, failed to move. Battered into submission, the cadets had all but given up by the day's end. More people had died fighting on that one day than during the entire Bolshevik coup.

On October 30, Krasnov's forces were on the outskirts of the capital. The attack of that day, the Battle of Pulkovo, failed because the Kerensky troops were too few: to avoid being outflanked, Krasnov had to pull back. In despair, fearing betrayal to the Red Guards, Kerensky left Gatchina disguised in a sailor's uniform. After several months of eluding Lenin's police in St. Petersburg and Moscow, he eventually escaped to the West, via Murmansk, in the summer of 1918, first to Paris and then to the United States.

During this same time bloody fighting raged in Moscow. There were 50,000 armed Bolsheviks in the city, against perhaps only 10,000 anti-Bolsheviks, mainly cadets and members of the Socialist Revolutionary party. When a large group of them stormed the Kremlin and captured it on October 28, many Bolsheviks were slain. Furious combat continued throughout the next day. Then came the news that the Kerensky–Krasnov march on St. Petersburg had failed. Isolated, facing tremendous odds, the defenders of the Kremlin were overwhelmed on November 2. In this battle of Moscow, the Bolsheviks alone had lost 500 men.[59]

RETROSPECT

The February Revolution had been largely unplanned, widely popular, and relatively bloodless; the October Revolution resulted from a conspiracy, with very limited support (no more than 30,000 according to Trotsky's *History of the Russian Revolution*) and cost hundreds of lives immediately, hundreds of thousands in the subsequent civil war (see below) and millions during the Stalinist "peace" that followed.

Nevertheless, the fall of the tsar and the overthrow of the provisional government had many aspects in common. Tsarism was forced to confront its mortal challenge because it had proven itself unwilling even to address the major concerns of key strata of the population. The provisional government found itself politically isolated because it could not solve, or even seem to be solving, the very problems which had overturned its predecessor, problems infinitely aggravated by the disastrous war.

We must grasp two particular weaknesses of the provisional government. First, the liberals in control of that body convinced themselves that they had come to power not because the Russian people were sick of the war but because they were disgusted with the slack and ineffective manner of waging it. Thus, the provisional regime soon became very unpopular. But lack of popularity need not cause the overthrow of a regime. The secret weakness of the liberals is that they had a great distaste for the use of force against their domestic enemies, including those who were committed to using whatever force they could against the government. Most of the members of the provisional government really believed in a government of law and popular consultation. If they were to do away with these things, if they were to adopt coercion against their tormentors, how then would they differ from the bankrupt Tsarist system which they had just cast aside? The war made the provisional government unpopular, but the reluctance to use force at the proper times and places ensured that the government would be overthrown by a disciplined band of resolute fanatics.

St. Petersburg was indeed the cradle of revolution; moreover, its historical role consisted in its ability to resist feeble attacks by disorganized outside forces. In February, the tsar had sent troops under General Ivanov to restore order, but these melted away before they got there. So did the soldiers of Kornilov a few months later; that march was turned back with hardly a shot. Finally, Kerensky's attack on the capital failed in the end for lack of a few battalions.

After the Bolshevik takeover in St. Petersburg and Moscow, the officer corps allowed itself to be dismantled, and many troops left the front lines to go home (after all, the Bolsheviks had shouted, "Peace! Bread! Land!"). The Bolsheviks, having done so much to destroy the Russian army, now paid the price, at Brest-Litovsk, giving up Poland, Finland, the Baltic region, and other large and valuable territories (containing 26 percent of the country's prewar population and 75 percent of her iron industry and coal mines) along with a large war indemnity. Ukrainian nationalists seized Kiev; Georgia fell under the control of the now bitterly anti-Leninist Mensheviks. The economy descended into chaos; real hunger began to stalk the streets of the great cities. Finally, the Cossack territories, those vast stretches between the Ukraine and the Caucasus, rejected the authority of the Bolshevik state; in these regions, the enemies of the Bolsheviks would gather and raise the banner of civil war.

NOTES

1. George F. Kennan, "The Russian Revolution—Fifty Years After: Its Nature and Consequences," *Foreign Affairs*, 46 (October 1967): 10.
2. William Henry Chamberlin, *The Russian Revolution 1917–1921*, vol. 1 (New York: Macmillan, 1935), p. 244.

3. Michael T. Florinsky, *The End of the Russian Empire* (New York: Collier, 1961), p. 146.
4. Hugh Seton-Watson, *Nations and States* (Boulder, CO: Westview, 1977), *passim*.
5. George F. Kennan, "The Breakdown of the Tsarist Autocracy," in Richard Pipes, ed., *Revolutionary Russia* (Cambridge: Harvard, 1968), p. 12.
6. Crane Brinton, *The Anatomy of Revolution* (New York: Vintage, 1960), p. 51.
7. Bertram D. Wolfe, *Three Who Made a Revolution* (New York: Dell, 1964), pp. 360–361.
8. Wolfe, *Three*, p. 362.
9. Florinsky, *End*, p. 247.
10. Katherine Chorley, *Armies and the Art of Revolution* (Boston: Beacon, 1973), pp. 38, 108.
11. Chorley, *Armies*, p. 119; but also see John Bushnell, *Mutiny and Repression: Russian Soldiers in the Revolution of 1905–1906* (Bloomington, IN: University of Indiana Press, 1985).
12. Florinsky, *End, passim*.
13. Leonard Schapiro, *The Russian Revolutions of 1917* (New York: Basic Books, 1984), p. 36; Chamberlin, *Russian Revolution*, vol. 2, p. 74.
14. Schapiro, *The Russian Revolutions of 1917*, p. 53.
15. George Katkov, *Russia 1917: The February Revolution* (New York: Harper and Row, 1967), p. 258.
16. Katkov, *Russia 1917*, p. 274.
17. Schapiro, *The Russian Revolutions of 1917*, p. 43.
18. Schapiro, *The Russian Revolutions of 1917*, p. 45.
19. Chamberlin, *The Russian Revolution*, vol. 1, p. 85.
20. Nicholas V. Riasanovsky, *A History of Russia* (New York: Oxford, 1963), p. 505.
21. See Chorley, *Armies*, pp. 113 ff.
22. Florinsky, *The End of the Russian Empire*, p. 222.
23. Chalmers Johnson, *Revolutionary Change* (Boston: Little, Brown & Company, 1966), p. 99.
24. Chamberlin, *The Russian Revolution*, vol. 1, p. 223.
25. Chamberlin, *The Russian Revolution*, vol. 1, pp. 239–240.
26. Chamberlin, *The Russian Revolution*, vol. 1, pp. 239–240.
27. Chamberlin, *The Russian Revolution*, vol. 1, p. 226.
28. Chamberlin, *The Russian Revolution*, vol. 1, p. 240.
29. Florinsky, *The End of the Russian Empire*, p. 241.
30. Chamberlin, *The Russian Revolution*, vol. 1, p. 232.
31. Chamberlin, *The Russian Revolution*, vol. 1, chap. 7.
32. Chamberlin, *The Russian Revolution*, vol. 1, p. 221.
33. Chamberlin, *The Russian Revolution*, vol. 1, pp. 225, 236.
34. Joel Carmichael, Introduction to N. N. Sukharov, *The Russian Revolution 1917* (New York: Harper, 1962), vol. 1, p. xxvii.
35. Chamberlin, *The Russian Revolution*, vol. 1, p. 257.
36. John Dunn, *Modern Revolutions: An Introduction to the Analysis of a Political Phenomenon* (Cambridge, MA: Cambridge University Press, 1972), p. 47.
37. Chamberlin, *The Russian Revolution*, vol. 1, p. 129.
38. Chamberlin, *The Russian Revolution*, vol. 1, p. 129.
39. See Z. Zeman and W. Scharlau, *The Merchants of Revolution* (New York: Oxford, 1965); G. Katkov, "German Foreign Office Documents on Financial Support to the Bolsheviks in 1917," *International Affairs*, 32 (April, 1956): 181–189.
40. Quotation taken from Geoffrey Fairbairn, *Revolutionary Guerrilla Warfare: The*

Countryside Version (Harmondsworth, England: Penguin, 1974), p. 71.

41. Lucian Pye, *Guerrilla Communism in Malaya* (Princeton, NJ: Princeton University Press, 1956), p. 299.
42. Pye, *Guerrilla Communism*, p. 299.
43. Chamberlin, *The Russian Revolution*, vol. 1, p. 307.
44. Robert V. Daniels, *Red October: The Bolshevik Revolution of 1917* (New York: Scribners, 1967), p. 112.
45. Daniels, *Red October*, p. 108.
46. Leonard Schapiro "The Political Thought of the First Provisional Government," in Richard Pipes, ed., *Revolutionary Russia* (Cambridge: Harvard, 1968), p. 108.
47. Leon Trotsky, "The History of the Russian Revolution to Brest-Litovsk," in *The Essential Trotsky* (London: Unwin, 1963), p. 77.
48. Daniels, *Red October*, p. 123.
49. Chamberlin, *The Russian Revolution*, vol. 1, p. 307.
50. Isaac Deutscher, *Trotsky: The Prophet Armed* (New York: Oxford, 1954), p. 312.
51. Daniels, *Red October*, p. 156.
52. Chamberlin, *The Russian Revolution*, vol. 1, pp. 318–319.
53. Daniels, *Red October*, p. 188.
54. Daniels, *Red October*, p. 195. Chamberlin thinks that six attackers were killed; if this were true, however, these persons surely would have been proclaimed public heroes, either then or later.
55. Stephen F. Cohen, *Bukharin and the Bolshevik Revolution: A Political Biography 1888–1938* (New York: Knopf, 1974), p. 46.
56. Chamberlin, *The Russian Revolution*, vol. 1, p. 323.
57. Daniels, *Red October*, p. 205.
58. Chamberlin, *The Russian Revolution*, vol. 1, p. 330.
59. Daniels, *Red October*, p. 207.

CHAPTER

2

The Civil War

War is the chief promoter of despotism.
—Bertrand Russell

History offers numerous examples of political leaders who might have altered dramatically the course of human events had they been able to avail themselves at the right time of the services of a few thousand, or even a few hundred, reliable soldiers. St. Petersburg, in February and October 1917, comes to mind.

The observation can be made in reverse: How often could the destiny of great segments of mankind have been decisively affected if victorious or near-victorious military commanders had possessed more political sophistication, or at least competent political advisers? Nothing better illustrates this principle than the story of the White commanders and their attempts to reverse the Bolshevik Revolution.

THE BEGINNING

The series of political and military struggles that we will refer to as the Russian Civil War raged over vast areas for several years. To pinpoint this or that event as the beginning of the conflict would invite much fruitless controversy. Excluding Kerensky's near-miss attempt to get back into St. Petersburg, some at least might wish to identify the Ukraine as the place where the civil war started in earnest. Separatist movements, by definition anti-Bolshevik, flourished there from early 1918, especially with the entry of the Germans into the area. Immediately after the Bolsheviks seized power in St. Petersburg, the National Rada (parliament) established itself in the Ukraine. The Treaty of Brest-Litovsk made the territory independent. Then came a brief period of Bolshevik rule, followed by a German occupation and a puppet government, a short-lived nationalist regime, a return of the Bolsheviks, an invasion by White forces (during the civil war most anti-Bolshevik forces were known simply as "Whites," owing to the color of the old Tsarist flag) under

28

General Anton Denikin in the summer of 1919, and another comeback of the Bolsheviks by year's end. In 1920, there was both a Polish invasion and a brief occupation by White forces under Baron Wrangel before the country fell once and for all under Soviet domination.

All during these upheavals, numerous and bloody peasant guerrilla operations, often led by schoolteachers, were complemented by risings in the towns against Soviet authority. In these years of civil war there were also acts of ferocious anti-Semitism, usually fomented by Whites, but sometimes perpetrated by the Ukrainian Red Army. Besides, "the peasant who had been encouraged by Bolshevik agitation to kill the neighboring country squire and loot his property saw no reason why he should deal any differently with the Jewish trader in the nearby town."[1]

DEMOCRATIC ANTIBOLSHEVISM

Apart from upheavals in the Ukraine, the new Bolshevik rulers had to confront the extraordinary activities of the so-called Czech Legion.

The Tsarist government had permitted Czech patriot leader Thomas Masaryk to recruit a corps of more than 30,000 of his countrymen from among its Austrian prisoners of war. This substantial body, along with numerous Russian officers, was supposed to go to the front in France by way of Vladivostok. The journey of the Czech Legion across Siberia was excruciatingly slow, and the legion had not progressed far when it began to run into trouble with the new Bolshevik government. Late in May 1918, Commissar of War Trotsky rashly demanded that the Czechs lay down their arms, threatening immediate executions for disobedience. In response, the Czechs began taking over towns along a 5,000-mile stretch of the Trans-Siberian railway, from Penza to Vladivostok. They often acted in cooperation with local groups of Socialist Revolutionaries (Kerensky's party) and other anti-Bolshevik elements. The Czechs also went into business along the Siberian railroad and, being a practical and talented people, made a lot of money. This revolt of the Czech Legion overthrew Bolshevik authority all the way from the Volga to the Pacific. For a while, it appeared that Lenin's power in Moscow itself would be menaced, but the Czechs eventually lost interest in Russian affairs when it became evident that the anti-Bolsheviks could not resolve their internal discords. Before the revolt of the Czech Legion began, however, the long-awaited Constituent Assembly finally had been elected and convoked. The peasant–populist Socialist Revolutionary party won a clear majority in this assembly, the first and only body in history able to call itself the expression of the free will of the Russian people. The Bolsheviks forcibly dispersed it in January 1918. Later, some Socialist Revolutionary assemblymen, joined by numerous Mensheviks, set up dissident governments at Samara, Omsk, and elsewhere. With the aid of the Czech Legion, the Samara government soon dominated the middle Volga region and captured Simbirsk (Lenin's birthplace) in July and Kazan in August, along with millions in gold rubles rashly sent there by the Bolsheviks for safekeeping. The Menshevik–Socialist Revolutionary regime in Samara called for the repudiation of the Treaty of Brest-Litovsk, the overthrow of the Bolshevik tyranny, and the establishment of a social democracy. The numbers of troops involved in the war between the regime in St. Petersburg and the one in Samara in the crucial summer of 1918 were small: perhaps 65,000 supporting the Reds, against 50,000 Czech and anti-Bolshevik troops.[2] A battle at the obscure town of Sviazhsk, near Kazan, is called by one historian the "Valmy of the Russian Revolution" (after the village in northeastern France where, in September 1792, French revolutionary troops halted the advancing Prussians); if the Red forces there had been beaten, there would have been precious little to stop the Czech and Samara troops from marching on to Moscow. In this battle of Sviazhsk, a mere 2,000 anti-Bolshevik troops had faced perhaps twice that number of Reds. How small a force to affect the course of the world.

The social democratic government at Samara, meanwhile, received little popular backing; it appealed mainly to leftist intellectuals, whereas the workers were often Bolshevik in sympathy and the peasants apathetic.

> It was the tragedy of the Socialist Revolutionaries, who always regarded themselves as a peasant party, that most of the Russian peasants were too ignorant and backward to act consciously on behalf of their own interests. Throughout the civil war one is repeatedly impressed by the fact that the peasants, the great majority of the population, were quite unable to make their influence felt, except in purely negative ways. When the Whites began to bring back the landlords, the peasants organized guerrilla bands and fell upon them. When Red requisitioning bands became too intolerable, the peasants, when they had the opportunity, cut them to pieces. But the idea of creating and actively supporting their own government, which would permit neither the return of the landlords nor the requisitions, was quite beyond the mental capacity of the average peasant. His instinct was that of a primitive anarchist, to pay no taxes and to give no soldiers to any government, whether it called itself Red, White, or democratic.[3]

Thus, a really "democratic" counterrevolution was doomed to failure. The Mensheviks and Socialist Revolutionaries had already shown their ineptitude in St. Petersburg in October 1917 and now could gather no important popular support in the provinces. The indigenous anti-Bolshevik effort would thus have to be mounted by former Tsarist officers, and *therefore would turn authoritarian and reactionary.*

FOREIGN INTERVENTION AGAINST BOLSHEVISM

The Western democracies had at first been exhilarated by the collapse of Tsarism, which they saw as not only politically repressive but militarily inefficient, and its replacement by what everybody expected to be a popular and puissant republican regime. These hopes were dashed, and the Allied governments and peoples outraged, when the antiwar Bolsheviks came to power and immediately repudiated their obligations to their allies and indeed signed the disastrous surrender at Brest-Litovsk, freeing the Germans to turn their full wrath on the faltering Anglo–French front. Nevertheless, most of the Allied troops subsequently sent to Russia were charged only with keeping the forces of the Central Powers out of certain strategic ports and protecting Allied supply dumps behind Russian lines. Some Allied leaders, such as Winston Churchill, wanted a massive Allied intervention to crush the hateful Bolshevik snake in its shell and, during 1918, anti-Bolshevik elements in Russia received much encouragement from the prospects of such large scale Allied aid. The aid never materialized, however.

The Allies could never decide on war or peace with bolshevism. Britain made the largest contribution to the counterrevolutionary effort, landing small numbers of troops in the frozen far north, and giving White forces 250,000 rifles, 200 cannon, much ammunition, and some advisers. This help certainly kept White leaders such as Kolchak and Denikin in the war longer than would otherwise have been the case. Late in 1918, France placed 45,000 troops, including Greeks and Poles, in Odessa, and as many as 70,000 Japanese troops would eventually land in eastern Siberia. (Some very small American units were landed in the far north, but they accomplished little and were soon withdrawn.)

Although the allied governments deeply resented the Bolsheviks' desertion in the war, their refusal to pay Russia's external debts, their confiscation of foreign property, and their domestic outrages, war-weariness kept the Allies from sending sufficient troops to make a decisive difference and, after the armistice with Germany, the whole effort began to seem less than crucial. The Whites "always cherished an exaggerated idea of the willingness of other people to fight their battles for them."[4] But as the French commander in Russia remarked: "No French soldier who saved his life after the Marne and Verdun would want to lose it on the fields of Russia."[5] The Allied interventions were always too little and too late. They never formally recognized the Samara–Omsk regime, and the military disintegration of the Kolchak movement in the summer of 1919 (see below) eventually made such recognition impossible. By October 1919, the British abandoned their last toe-holds at Archangel and Murmansk. Allied intervention had done little other than to allow the Bolsheviks to paint themselves as defenders of the national patrimony against the traitorous Whites, who would sell the country to the British and the Japanese.[6] (We can observe similar metamorphoses: revolutionary movements becoming defenders of the fatherland against foreign intervention in France, Cuba, and Vietnam.)

Having briefly considered the Ukrainian, Czech–Socialist Revolutionary, and Allied components of the anti-Bolshevik effort, it is time to turn to the civil war (properly so-called): the major attempts of indigenous counterrevolutionary forces (the Whites) to remove the Bolsheviks from power by military conquest. We will consider the activities of Admiral Kolchak first. Table 2.1 is a chart of events that may be of some assistance to the reader in following the narrative in the remainder of this chapter.

THE KOLCHAK EPISODE

The first of the major counterrevolutionary drives crystallized around the unlikely figure of Admiral Aleksandr Valisyevich Kolchak. Born in St. Petersburg in 1873, the son of an engineering officer, Kolchak worked his way up through the naval ranks on merit. He served gallantly against the Japanese at Port Arthur and acquired a national reputation as an Arctic explorer. Of unblemished personal integrity, he enjoyed during his period of civil war leadership the support of the British representative at Omsk. "Kolchak was in some ways the embodiment of the simple faith of the old-fashioned officer. He believed that a crisis could be overcome by loyalty, decency, meticulous devotion to duty, and good sense."[7]

But Kolchak's career had been narrow and highly specialized. He had had no experience whatsoever in commanding land forces. Worse, Kolchak's base consisted of vast and sparsely settled Siberia, with a population of no more than 12 million and hardly any industry. The Bolsheviks, in contrast, usually held territories with a population of more than 60 million people and almost all of Russia's industry. Any possibility of a Kolchak victory, therefore, or even of his survival, depended on his ability to win popular support for his cause, first in Siberia and then in the Bolshevik-controlled areas. To this crucial and difficult task he was inadequate both by training and disposition, possessing neither the skills of a popular leader nor the vision of a political thinker.

This unlikely commander of a doomed cause came to his destiny in a roundabout manner. Disgusted by the insubordination that the February Revolution had unleashed within the Black Sea fleet, Kolchak resigned his command in the fleet in July 1917. He traveled via Britain to the United States, where he stayed for at least two months. Returning to Russia, he was in Vladivostok when the Bolshevik coup occurred. Determined now to serve with the British forces, Kolchak had made his way to Singapore when he received a message from the Russian ambassador in Peking urging him to return and fight for the counterrevolution. He reached Peking in April 1918, and by September he had arrived in Omsk, temporary capital of what was left of the Menshevik–Socialist Revolutionary regime. The executive committee of that government was badly split and ineffective, the Constitutional Democratic (liberal) party had come out in favor of an emergency dictatorship, and the garrison at Omsk was composed largely of Siberian Cossacks, a group not noted for

Table 2.1. The Russian Civil War: 1918–1920

	Eastern Front	Southern Front	St. Petersburg Front	Foreign Aspects
1918				
May	Czech Revolt			
June	Omsk Government			
August				Allies in Murmansk
November	Kolchak in power			
December				French in Odessa
1919				
February		Denikin in command		
March	Kolchak offensive			Kun Regime in Budapest
May		Denikin offensive		
June	Kolchak defeated	Denikin victories: Tsaritsyn, Kharkov; Denikin in Kiev		
September			Yudenich offensive	
October		Denikin in Orel; Denikin defeated; loses Kharkov, Kiev		
November			Yudenich beaten	
1920				
January	Kolchak resigns			
February	Kolchak killed			
April		Wrangel in command		Polish War begins
May				Poles in Kiev
June		Offensive by Wrangel in Kuban		Reds take Kiev
July				Reds take Vilna
August				Battle for Warsaw
October		Red offensive against Wrangel		Polish armistice
November		Wrangel evacuates Crimea		

33

liberal ideas. On November 17, 1918, a coup disposed of the executive committee, and the cabinet elected Admiral Kolchak supreme ruler and commander-in-chief of all Russian land and naval forces. Kolchak then declared for "victory over Bolshevism" so that "the people may choose the form of government it desires without obstruction."[8]

Why didn't the Kolchak regime come out in favor of a Tsarist restoration? Some of its leaders feared alienating public opinion in America and Europe by such a reactionary stance; others remembered the damage done to the monarchical image by the recent Rasputin scandals. But most of all, a Tsarist restoration was not plausible because there was no imperial figure to rally around. Tsar Nicholas and his entire family had been held captive by the Bolsheviks in Ekaterinburg. When the Czech Legion approached, the prisoners, women and children included, were taken into the cellar on July 18, 1918, and there they were murdered, every one. Only Grand Duke Nicholas was still alive, but he was far from being a striking personality, and he was about to leave Russia. The best program Kolchak could conceive of in the fall of 1918, therefore, was a new constituent assembly.

Kolchak did not get along with the Czechs, who were no longer much involved in fighting and who disapproved of the coup by which the admiral had come to power. He also was constantly plagued by the operations of Red partisan bands. The pro-Bolshevik guerrillas flourished for several reasons. The Bolsheviks had been overthrown in Siberia before they had really begun to alienate people, whereas Kolchak had to demand taxes and recruits; thus, many Siberians soon came to detest the Whites more than the Reds. And when the Bolsheviks had been chased from the area in the early summer of 1918, they had left behind many nuclei to organize a guerrilla effort. Kolchak underestimated the strength of these partisan bands, and against them often used undisciplined units whose cruelties to the civil population cost the regime much popular sympathy. Finally, the tsars had used Siberia as a dumping ground for criminals, and this element played a big role in the anti-Kolchak guerrilla effort.

Despite all of these daunting difficulties, Kolchak launched the first great White offensive in March 1919. He menaced Kazan and Samara, advancing as far as Glazov in early June. But he had a hard time obtaining enough recruits and lacked both instructors and arms for the ones he had. On July 14, the Reds came back through the Ural mountains, capturing Ekaterinburg, capital of Ural territory and scene of the massacre of the imperial family. Some of Kolchak's commanders wanted to retreat far into Siberia and regroup for a last stand, but the admiral decided in favor of a complicated maneuver to envelop the Red Army. After bitter fighting, the White plan failed, and by early August Kolchak's forces were in full retreat, losing 15,000 men as prisoners to the Reds.

By the end of the summer Kolchak still commanded a formidable army of about 50,000 men, but the much larger Red forces continued to advance east, having tranquilized the peasantry of European Russia with the mendacious slogan of "Land to the peasants," a slogan that the Whites were not able to match.

With inferior numbers and inadequate equipment, Kolchak launched another offensive at the end of September 1919. This too soon failed. Kolchak was finished. His capital of Omsk fell to the Reds on November 14. Retreating through Siberia, Kolchak gave his personal bodyguard the option to leave him and seek their own safety; almost to a man, they abandoned him. On January 4, 1920, Kolchak abdicated his office in favor of General Anton Denikin and took a train to Irkutsk under Allied protection. But when the admiral arrived there, the French commander of Allied forces in the city, General Maurice Janin, handed him over to pro-Soviet elements. Lenin telegraphed to Irkutsk that the admiral must be sent to Moscow for a show trial.[9] The approach of White forces near the town, however, sealed Kolchak's fate. On February 7, 1920, he was shot by a Chekist firing squad, and his body was thrown into an ice hole in the Angara river.

"The strongest proof both of the depth and the fierceness of the Bolshevik Revolution was the number of people who were willing to endure every deprivation, to risk death itself, rather than remain under Soviet rule."[10] So it was in Siberia with the fall of Kolchak. "Trains of death" carried hundreds in desperate flight east, where without food and medicine, they starved or died of typhus. And the Orenburg Cossacks, men, women, and children, seeking to escape bolshevism, marched over the wastes of Central Asia seeking refuge in Sinkiang. Of the 150,000 who began the journey, only 30,000 survived.

Kolchak failed for many reasons. He controlled the wrong part of Russia. He could not compete with the Soviets' "Land to the peasants" deception. He had no land warfare experience. And he lacked the political skills that might have made such warfare worthwhile: after all, as Clausewitz insists, "war is merely the continuation of politics by other means."[11] Kolchak had no policy except to attack the overwhelmingly superior Reds.

Nonetheless, even in all these conditions, the Bolsheviks had been able to defeat Kolchak only with much difficulty. And there were far more serious challenges to come.

THE "GALLANT KNIGHT"

The next and the most serious effort to overthrow the Bolshevik dictatorship originated in southern Russia. The commander of this series of campaigns was General Anton Ivanovich Denikin. As Trotsky correctly observed: "Denikin is incomparably more serious an enemy than Kolchak."

The backbone of the forces Denikin commanded was called the Volunteer

Army, which rose up in the regions inhabited by the Don Cossacks. General Kornilov, who had escaped from Petersburg immediately after the Bolshevik coup, had been the original leader of the army. He was killed in action in April 1918. Leadership of the southern White forces devolved on Denikin, his 46-year-old second in command. The son of a serf, a man of great personal integrity and honor, called by many the "gallant knight," Denikin had risen through the ranks. Unlike Kolchak, he was an experienced commander of land forces. He was in control of a much better base of operations than Kolchak ever had: the Cossack territory of southeast Russia has been compared to the counterrevolutionary French Vendée; marauding bands of undisciplined Red guerrillas did nothing to make Soviet policies more attractive to the free-living and comparatively prosperous Cossacks, and supplies were easily available through a good network of railways from the Black Sea. The southern theater had also attracted far more Tsarist officers than had Siberia; all told, of the 500,000 who had held commissions in the Tsarist army at the time of the February Revolution, perhaps 200,000 would do service at some time with one or another White army.

Unfortunately for Denikin, and for the cause of antibolshevism in general, Cossack leaders, especially in the Don area, were willing enough to kill Bolsheviks who trespassed into their territory but were too shortsighted to grasp the idea that the only true security for Cossack liberties was to be found in the extirpation of bolshevism at the center. Eventually this provincialism of the Cossacks was to cost Denikin and his army (and the Cossacks) very dearly.

In the early months of 1919, however, Denikin was sweeping all before him. During May and June he won great victories over the 13th, 8th, 9th, and 10th Red armies; the commander of the 9th Red Army came over to the White side, and the North Caucasian Red Army lost 50,000 prisoners to a numerically weaker force. The victorious Whites entered Kharkov on June 25; five days later, Tsaritsyn (Stalingrad), called the "Red Verdun," fell to Denikin's troops under the command of General Wrangel. (This onslaught prevented the Bolsheviks from going to the aid of Bela Kun's Communist dictatorship in Hungary, which was soon overthrown.)

Flushed with these successes, and feeling that he had no alternative other than to maintain his momentum, Denikin made the fateful decision to advance rather than consolidate his gains and pacify the rear areas. At the time, the decision seemed plausible, and early events justified it. By mid-July the Whites were mustering 151,000 men against only 172,000 Bolshevik troops, very favorable odds for the Whites in comparison to most of their other campaigns. And the White tide surged on: Poltava was taken on July 31, 1919, and Kiev fell to them a month later.

On October 13, Denikin's forces captured the city of Orel; the last remaining stronghold between the Whites and Moscow was now the town of Tula.

Denikin was only 250 miles away from the Kremlin, a distance shorter than that between Philadephia and Pittsburgh or Kansas City and St. Louis. Orel proved, however, to be the highwater mark of the Denikin drive. The Reds had been preparing a massive counterattack and threw 186,000 men against Denikin's 113,000. When the decisive Red attacks came, Denikin's men were spread over a very wide territory, hundreds of miles between the Volga and the Dniester rivers. Under these circumstances, the Whites could not hold Orel and evacuated the city on October 20, 1919; this was the turning point of the entire campaign on the southern front. After this, the White tide receded even more rapidly than it had advanced. To understand the defeat of Denikin in purely military terms is not difficult: he was heavily outnumbered and far from his base. But Denikin found it impossible to make a stand and to hold onto at least the bulk of the territory he had conquered because of deplorable *political* conditions in his rear areas. In the rural districts under White control "anarchy was the rule rather than the exception"[12] (see below). Moreover, some of Denikin's units could hardly travel, owing to their enormous booty. Because of this, the Reds easily and rapidly reconquered the Ukraine, taking Kiev on December 16. Rostov fell in January 1920. Even then, Denikin's position was not hopeless; he was behind the Don and Manitch rivers and still commanded 50,000 men, a force not greatly inferior to the number of his immediate Red foes. The Whites even succeeded in retaking Rostov and holding it for a few days late in February. But the Bolshevik pressure proved irresistible. Denikin decided to evacuate his whole force, along with thousands of civilian followers, into the Crimea (which was available to him because the Reds, having failed to envision it as a future White base, did not block the routes into it). The evacuation of the Denikin forces took place from the port of Novorossik on March 26, 1920. It was a scene of indescribable chaos and tragedy: there were not enough ships even for the soldiers, much less the multitudes of civilian refugees desperately anxious not to be left behind to face the Red vengeance. Some British ships in the area helped with the evacuation, but more than 20,000 soldiers and civilians had to be abandoned to the Bolsheviks. Having established his new headquarters in the Crimea with 35,000 troops in early April, Denikin resigned his command to his assistant, General Wrangel. (Denikin eventually made his way to France and later to the United States, where he died in Ann Arbor, Michigan, in 1947.)

The White forces had always been severely handicapped by the extreme localism of most of their draftees and Cossack allies, something not really under Denikin's control. But Denikin failed, as Kolchak had failed before him, to attract popular support with a realistic and powerful program or even to provide for those behind the lines a government that offered justice, decency, or simply minimal physical safety. It is political factors such as these that account at least in part for the ultimate failure of Denikin and all he sought to represent.

It is true that in April 1919, on the insistence of his British advisers, Denikin issued a statement of aims that included land reform, labor legislation, and a national assembly to be elected by universal suffrage. But those in charge of carrying out White policy on the scene gave scant reason for anybody to take these promises seriously. Millions of Russians who had no love at all for the Bolsheviks were not prepared to risk their lives just to see everything restored as it had been in the bad old days. Denikin's expressed aims were vague, and his protestations of commitment to social justice were mocked by the actions of many of his subordinates. The White-occupied areas were too often the scene of vicious pogroms, grisly class vengeance, and shameful rapine. Corruption, speculation, greed, and waste characterized the White administrative apparatus. Admiral Kolchak himself had been moved to send Denikin a letter warning him against favoring landlords too obviously over the peasants, but "Denikin's forces came to be looked on more and more as a landlord's army."[13] None of Denikin's counselors could claim to speak for the peasants or the workers. There was no move to form an alliance with the numerous and now bitterly anti-Red Mensheviks, and trade-union organizers, even anti-Communist ones, led a precarious existence.

Furthermore, Denikin's policy toward Russia's national minorities was grotesquely inadequate to the demands of the hour. As Chamberlin, a much-admired student of these events, observed:

> In carrying the revolution to success and in the subsequent civil war [Lenin] recognized and took full advantage of two outstanding features of Russian life: the thirst of the peasants for land and the dissatisfaction of the non-Russian peoples of the former Tsarist empire with Russian overlordship.[14]

Denikin completely lost any chance he may have had of turning the desires of the peasants to own land against the Bolsheviks; and to the oppressed nationalities, hungry for the bread of equality, he offered the stone of Russian chauvinism. His slogan "Russia shall be great, united, undivided" had little meaning for most peasants and workers; it was absolute poison to Ukrainian nationalists and the Georgian and Caucasian tribesmen whom he sought to rule and mobilize. Wherever White power reached in the Ukraine, even the teaching of the native language in the state schools was forbidden. Neither did the Whites hide their opposition to secession and independence for any groups formerly within the tsar's empire (the Reds, of course, had no intention of permitting anyone to exercise the oft-proclaimed right of secession and national determination, but they kept their real plans well hidden until they had won).

Even more disastrous, Denikin's conservative nationalism alienated Marshal Joseph Pilsudski, whose Polish army stood idly by in the western Ukraine while the recovering Reds pushed Denikin farther and farther back (an error of judgment on Pilsudski's part for which Poland pays the price today). True, it is hardly realistic to expect that a lifelong officer in the Tsarist army such as Denikin would easily adjust himself to the spectacle of an independent Poland, much less ask its leaders for military assistance against his own countrymen. Furthermore, Denikin could not escape from the fact that his principal support came from groups both socially conservative and militantly nationalistic. Therefore, although the judgment of one historian may seem too harsh— "indeed it was the tragedy of the genuine patriots in Denikin's ranks that the old Russia which they were consciously or unconsciously fighting to restore proved itself in practice both incapable and unworthy of restoration,"[15] it is beyond argument that "the Whites sacrificed political consolidation for the lure of immediate military gains, and then proceeded to throw away the advantages won in the field."[16]

THE MARCH ON ST. PETERSBURG

Between the time Denikin took Kiev and his entry into Orel (August through October, 1919), 57-year-old General Nicolai Nicolayevich Yudenich made a spectacular attempt to capture the very "cradle of the revolution." His base was Estonia, a tough little republic that had successfully resisted the Soviet onslaught that buried neighboring Latvia by January 1919. Yudenich had a little army of 17,000 that would have benefited immeasurably from the assistance of a German force of 15,000 in the area; however, the latter force stupidly turned away from an assault on St. Petersburg to invade Latvia. Hence, the Yudenich army was much inferior in numbers to its Red opponents.

The help of the newly independent and militarily capable Finns would also have been of incalculable help to Yudenich, but the stubborn refusal of most White leaders to recognize the statehood of Finland closed off any possiblity of aid from that quarter. (The victory of the anti-Bolshevik Finns under Mannerheim has been called "the first White victory of international significance,"[17] but the Finnish experience seems to belong under the heading of national independence struggles rather than to that of Russian civil war, so let us congratulate the Finns on their achievement and pass quickly back to Yudenich's doomed drive on St. Petersburg.)

In October 1919, with Denikin in possession of Orel and only 250 miles from Moscow, Yudenich launched his offensive against St. Petersburg. It was a desperate gamble: he commanded fewer than 18,000 against a Red army of 25,000 backed by a city of 1 million (although Yudenich did have the benefit of a very high proportion of former officers in his army). Yudenich's order to cut the St. Petersburg–Moscow railroad link somehow failed to be obeyed, a fatal mishap, for supplies and reinforcements could thus come into the beleaguered city. Yudenich's progress nevertheless so alarmed Lenin that he spoke in favor of abandoning the city; Trotsky vigorously and successfully dissented and laid plans for street fighting. On October 20, the White troops had reached Pulkovo heights, the last line of defense for the Reds. By October 23, however, while Denikin was being whipped in the Ukraine, it became clear that the Whites simply were without the necessary mass to take the city. Oh, for 10,000 Finnish soldiers! The attack had failed, and Yudenich lacked the resources for a long siege. Falling back into Estonia in the second half of November, the White army was disarmed and eventually disbanded.

THE POLISH WAR

In April 1920, the long-anticipated Russo–Polish war broke out. If it had occurred one year earlier, when Kolchak was still on the offensive around the Urals and Denikin was about to take Tsaritsyn, or six months earlier, when Denikin was in Orel, the Bolshevik regime would probably not have survived. That the Poles held back until both of the major White commanders had been repulsed was in part the price the Whites paid for their Great Russian chauvinism.

The war between Poland and Russia was perhaps inevitable. For the Bolsheviks, the spread of their revolution to the West was necessary both for its ideological justification and its physical survival. The aims of Poland's leader, Pilsudski, were equally clear-cut and quite menacing for Russia. He aimed at nothing less than the creation of a broad belt of independent states from former Russian territory: not just Poland and Finland, but Estonia, Latvia, Lithuania, the Caucasus, as well as the liberation (or the Polish conquest) of the Ukraine. The achievement of Pilsudski's program would have pushed Russia's frontiers away from Poland and set her well along the path to the status of a second-class power.

The Russo–Polish conflict, and the Russian civil war to which it was intimately related, were characterized by great offensives that swept all before them and then, because of mounting casualties, exhaustion, enemy reinforcements, and lack of supply, ran out of steam and in turn were assaulted by equally expansive counteroffensives that soon suffered a similar deflation.

On May 6, 1920, less then two weeks after the war began, the highest point of Polish military fortunes was attained with the occupation of Kiev. This victorious invasion of sacred Russian soil by the detested Poles called forth a new wave of enlistments in the Red Army by former Tsarist officers who had previously held aloof or lived underground. Thanks in part to their ability to don the ill-fitting coat of nationalism, the Bolsheviks launched a counteroffensive that swept into Minsk (July 11) and Vilna (July 14), forcing Lithuania into the war on the Russian side. The fall of Brest-Litovsk seemed to herald the birth of a Red Poland that would be an invasion bridge to Germany itself. Proclaimed Lenin: "We shall break the crust of the Polish bourgeois resistance with the bayonets of the Red Army." While Lenin boasted of an imminent Red conquest of Poland, real starvation stalked the streets of St. Petersburg and Moscow, which were choked with uncollected refuse.

Red Poland never materialized: the Polish peasantry vigorously rejected the Reds, hardly any of them joining the ranks of the advancing Bolshevik army, and the Russians never reached the main Polish industrial regions, where their propaganda might have had more success.

The culmination of the brief but intense war was the battle before the gates of Warsaw. The Red forces were under the command of Mihail Tukhachevsky, a 27-year-old former Tsarist officer. Talented but inexperienced, Tukhachevsky made some bad troop dispositions, whereas Pilsudski and his French military adviser, General Weygand, formerly chief of staff to General Foch, executed some good counterstrokes. Budenny's vaunted Red cavalry failed to come up to Tukhachevsky in time; at the height of the battle, the Reds found themselves with no more than 60,000 troops against 90,000 Polish troops. On paper, the Red Army in 1920 had five million officers and men; yet against both Poland and the Wrangel Whites they could mobilize only 200,000. When the issue of a Red Poland, and perhaps a Red Germany, was being decided in front of Warsaw, *only about one of every eighty Red Army soldiers was there.*

The turning point came on August 16, 1920, with Pilsudski's counteroffensive. The Red Fourth Army was forced to cross into German East Prussia, where it was interned. Polish troops were back in Brest-Litovsk by August 19, and Budenny was defeated on August 27. Once it was obvious that Poland would not be Red, the Moscow government was anxious to make peace in order to turn full attention to Denikin's successor, General Wrangel. The two governments signed an armistice at Riga on October 12, 1920, with terms that were rather favorable to the Poles.

The Red offensive against Wrangel began five days later, the last great episode of the Russian civil war.

BARON WRANGEL AND THE FINAL ACT

Early in 1920, it must have seemed to many that the Russian civil war was over. Kolchak was dead, the Red Army occupied the Don and Kuban areas, the remnants of Denikin's army, 35,000 demoralized soldiers, had been chased into the Crimea. It was at this nadir of its fortunes, however, that the counter-revolution found what it had so sorely lacked since the days of the Kornilov coup: a leader militarily competent *and* politically sagacious.

Baron Piotr Nichlayevich Wrangel was born in 1878 and saw service as a cavalryman in both the Russo–Japanese war and World War I. Much more politically adept than Denikin, Wrangel's slogans summed up his policies and his flexibility: "Even with the Devil, but against the Reds" and "To Make a Left Policy with Right Hands." Wrangel knew that the political key to White victory, or at least White survival, lay in coming to grips with the land question. His policy was based on a sensible recognition that a revolution had indeed taken place in Russia and that pure restorationism was a sterile and suicidal stance. Wrangel determined to relaunch Stolypin's plan to create a landholding peasantry as a bulwark against bolshevism. The peasants in those areas controlled by Wrangel were to be allowed to retain most of the lands they had seized, paying to the state one-fifth of their harvest over a 25-year period, to be used to compensate the former owners. As he said in a press interview in April, 1920:

> Russia cannot be freed by a triumphant march on Moscow but by the creation even on a small bit of Russian soil of such order and such living conditions as would attract the people who are suffering under the Red yoke.[18]

(In 1920, almost any living conditions would have contrasted favorably with those that existed in Bolshevik Russia.) As his foreign minister, Wrangel appointed none other than P. B. Struve, a founder of Russian Marxism, the man who in 1897 had composed the first manifesto of the Russian Social Democratic party (which soon split into Bolsheviks and Mensheviks). This appointment illustrated the alienation from the Bolsheviks of so many progressives and also how desperately Wrangel was reaching out for support to elements that had previously been anathema to the Whites.

On the military side, Wrangel transformed his troops, in danger of becoming a demoralized rabble, into a good army. Remarked one Red observer, "[q]ualitatively, it was the best fighting force of which the Russian and international counterrevolution ever disposed in armed struggle against the Soviet republics."[19] So impressed was the French government with Wrangel's combination of military competence and political realism that it recognized him as de facto ruler of all South Russia on August 10, 1920 (when the Red drive against Warsaw was at its peak).

But all of this came too late. Wrangel followed an intelligent strategy, and his troops fought well; nevertheless, by the end of 1920, after nearly three years of effort, the counterrevolution was physically and spiritually exhausted, and Wrangel's forces were simply too small.

Wisely avoiding the inhospitable Ukraine, Wrangel decided to invade the territory of the Kuban Cossacks to establish contact with a large guerrilla group calling itself the Army of the Regeneration of Russia. Commanded by General Ulagai, an upright officer who acted sternly to prevent the kind of pillaging that had so undermined Denikin's operations, 7,000 Whites landed on the Kuban coast of the Sea of Azov on August 13. But the Reds mobilized 30,000 troops against Ulagai, and most of the local Cossacks refused to rise up in his support.

After the Kuban failure, Wrangel sought to link up with the Poles, who were advancing again after the Battle of Warsaw. Wrangel's inadequate numbers could not force a crossing of the Dnieper river, however, and on October 12 came the thunderbolt of the Polish armistice. Now the whole crushing weight of Trotsky's military machine came down upon Wrangel. His stand in the North Tauride pitted 35,000 Whites against four times that number of Reds. The battle began on October 28, and culminated in the Bolshevik drive of November 7, the third anniversary of the St. Petersburg coup. Wrangel's men fought bravely, but so did the Reds who outnumbered them. Even in the last hours of defeat, however, Wrangel showed his merit, successfully evacuating into Turkey almost 150,000 soldiers and civilians from his crumbling Crimean stronghold. And so, for all practical purposes, the Russian civil war came to an end.

Although it ended in failure, the White struggle had not been without major consequences. Denikin's offensive in the spring of 1919 had fatally deprived the Kun regime in Budapest of Bolshevik assistance; Wrangel's offensive in the summer of 1920 helped to save Warsaw, whose fall would have had incalculable effects in Europe. Although the Poles showed scant gratitude to Wrangel (he was, after all, a Russian nationalist and therefore an enemy) they permitted many Denikin troops who had fled into Polish territory to go to Wrangel's assistance.

TROTSKY BUILDS THE RED ARMY

A principal condition for the Bolshevik coup of October 1917 had been the steady disintegration of the Russian army. This process continued after the Bolsheviks came to power, exposing St. Petersburg to the threat of an easy German occupation. In early 1918, the Bolshevik regime was almost totally dependent on a force of 17,000 tough Latvian riflemen. Posted at strategic points, these troops bore the brunt of early fighting in the Ukraine, but they were too few and could not be everywhere. Meanwhile, ominous signs of approaching civil war emphasized the low military value of the Red Guard battalions. Clearly, the Bolsheviks were going to have to create a new army, and it would have to be a *real* army, based on military orthodoxy and not on revolutionary rhetoric, a force prepared to deal with something more formidable than teenage cadets and untrained women's battalions. While the Bolsheviks planned and debated this new army, what was left of the old army was losing 500 men a day on the northern front alone.[20] In these desperate circumstances, Leon Trotsky was made commissar of war in March 1918. He was 38 years old.

Trotsky's problems were gigantic, staggering. In the early days, "everything was missing, or to be more exact, no one knew where to find anything." One had to start literally from scratch: "we must teach our soldiers personal cleanliness and see that they exterminate vermin." By mid-1918, the Bolshevik regime still had no real army in the field, and a White offensive at that time might have meant the end of everything. As a few thousand reliable troops would have averted the February Revolution or carried Kerensky back into St. Petersburg, so a few thousand good soldiers could have rousted Lenin out of the Kremlin. But the Whites were also disorganized, and the forces involved in the early days of civil war fighting were very small. Even in 1919, however, according to one authority,[21] if Kolchak, Yudenich, and Denikin had been able to coordinate their efforts, the Bolsheviks almost surely would have been defeated. But the Whites were operating on exterior lines, separated from each other by thousands of miles, with each army independently recruited and supplied and each commander anxious to win glorious prizes for himself.

Meanwhile, Trotsky set to work building the new Red Army according to principles derived largely from his reading: First, there must be rigid discipline, including reprisals against the families of deserters; second, Red military units must consist, as far as possible, of *politically reliable* persons; third, the new army would be worthless if it did not obtain an infusion of thousands of former Tsarist officers to get it started.

On the subject of discipline Trotsky was absolutely ferocious, going far beyond anything the Tsarist regime would have considered: "Officers must make soldiers choose between possible death at the front and inevitable death in the rear!" He demanded that officers be equipped with revolvers and extolled the value of exemplary shootings of troublesome recruits. Trotsky wanted a regular army on regular military principles: the old chain of command, with no committees, no election of officers, no endless philosophical debates. When Trotsky denounced the soldiers' committees and proclaimed the day of centralization and discipline, he seemed to many Bolsheviks to be contradicting the very essence of the revolution. Trotsky nevertheless plunged ahead. The elective principle was finally abolished on April 29, 1918, while Trotsky roared out threats:

> I issue this warning: if any detachment retreats without orders, the first to be shot will be the [Bolshevik] commissar, the next the commander . . . cowards, scoundrels, and traitors will not escape the bullet—for this I vouch before the whole Red Army![22]

To ensure political reliability, the Bolsheviks would have preferred an army composed entirely of proletarian volunteers. But enlistments from this source were disappointing in quality and quantity. The Central Executive Committee of Soviets therefore decreed compulsory military service in May 1918; by the end of the summer, there were almost half a million men in the Red Army. Trotsky saw to it that the proletariat—for whom all this was theoretically being done anyway—was drafted first, then the "poor peasants," followed by the "middle" peasants.[23]

Nothing Trotsky ever did aroused so much controversy within the ranks of the Bolshevik party as his acceptance into the new Red Army of former

Tsarist officers, about 49,000 of them between June 1918 and August 1920. How, many people demanded, could you protect the Red revolution with an army led by reactionary officers? It seemed to be madness. But the Soviet military schools were not producing enough officers, and Trotsky won for this project the backing of Lenin himself, who declared that the revolution could only be saved by expertise, not by "party ignoramuses."[24] The first ex-Tsarist military man of stature to join Trotsky was M. D. Bonch-Bruevich, former commander of the northern front, who organized the Red general staff. From the former Tsarist ranks came Mikhail Tukhachevsky (who would fail at the gates of Warsaw) and many others destined to be prominent in Soviet affairs for decades. And when the Polish war broke out, thousands of hitherto reluctant Tsarists served the Red Army with authentic nationalist zeal.

The problem that Trotsky faced was nevertheless a real one: how to ensure that the new army with its antirevolutionary officers would not be turned against the Bolsheviks. As with all other matters, Trotsky's first idea was to threaten bloodcurdling reprisals: officers who expressed politically imprudent thoughts, who went over to Kolchak or Denikin, or who merely performed poorly in the field, knew that their families would suffer for it severely. Trotsky also set up concentration camps for Tsarist officers who fell into his hands but refused to join the Red ranks (of about 500,000 Tsarist officers, only 50,000 at most served with the Reds, whereas four times that many joined the White forces).

In addition to taking family members as hostages, Trotsky used political controls to guard against officer disloyalty. Wherever possible, smaller units composed of reliable Bolsheviks were placed within larger units of draftees and were thus in a position to provide a good example to the fainthearted and to guarantee armed resistance to any officers who sought to participate in a coup. As another control measure, Trotsky used political commissars. Their main role was not ideological indoctrination of troops but surveillance of officers to ensure the subordination of the army to the party. Kerensky had used political commissars in the army, but only at the highest levels; Trotsky placed them everywhere, and no commander's writ was valid unless countersigned by one of the commissars. Thus, the Red Army grew to 800,000 men by December 1918, and to 3 million by January 1920. Most of these soldiers never saw front-line combat; shortages of arms and equipment impeded efficient use of this great host, and large numbers were needed behind the lines to fight peasant uprisings and guerrillas. Despite Trotsky's most vigorous efforts, incredibly high desertion rates caused constant difficulties for military operations: even official Soviet figures put the number of deserters from the Red Army in 1919 and 1920 at an astounding 2,846,000.[25]

The other side of Trotsky's insistence on orthodox military methods was his rejection of guerrilla warfare as a principal weapon of the Bolshevik regime. The Bolsheviks, after all, were in control of the state, including the great population centers and industrial regions; they could hardly abandon the defense of these areas and retain credibility. But there were more ideological reasons for rejection of guerrilla warfare (except in the most extreme circumstances behind White lines). Guerrilla warfare in the conditions of Russia in 1919–1920 would have had to have been based on small peasant bands recruited from a narrow area and loyal to a local chief; successful liberation of White areas by victorious peasant guerrillas would end all hope of establishing Bolshevik authority in the countryside. Trotsky blasted this kind of war as "elemental petit-bourgeois anarchy"; for him, to abandon reliance on his professional Red Army tactics and embrace a strategy of guerrilla warfare would be equivalent to "switching from heavy industry to the artisan's shop."[26]

Trotsky is an arresting example of an authentic intellectual who built a victorious army. He was both a lover of books and a political realist—hence his drafting of Tsarist officers. Dashing around in the armored train that he boarded in August 1918, bracing the faltering Red troops with his fiery oratory, he inspired confidence, he seemed to be everywhere. He thoroughly appreciated the less romantic side of warfare: soldiers needed bread, and "meals must be properly cooked." A member of the military revolutionary council of the western front once sent Lenin a telegram exemplifying Trotsky's thinking: "it is a thousand times better to have no more than one million men in the Red Army, but all well-fed, well-clothed, well-shod ones."[27] (What would the world be like today if the Tsarist military had operated under such a principle?)

Nowhere does Trotsky's towering role in the revolutionary epic command our attention as much as in the siege of St. Petersburg. In October 1919, Lenin and the Politburo were so afraid of the threat from Yudenich that they were ready to abandon the city and retreat to Moscow, even to the Urals. But Trotsky refused to hand over the "cradle" to the vengeance of the Whites. He took command of the city defenses himself, and even his critics concede that his inspirational energy saved St. Petersburg.[28]

In spite of—or more precisely, because of—his undeniable and conspicuous successes, Trotsky was getting himself into deep trouble. He stimulated the traditional Socialist distaste for military matters and distrust for military heroes. All of the Bolshevik leaders had studied the French Revolution, they all feared the appearance of a "Red Napoleon." The ever-present factor of envy did its corrosive work as well; Stalin and Zinoviev plotted against Trotsky, undermining him and slandering him: he was the protector of Tsarist officers, preferring them to good Bolsheviks whom he persecuted, he had caused Communist commissars to be shot without sufficient reason, etc. These charges surfaced at the height of the civil war, but remained in circulation for years, playing no small part in Trotsky's final political defeat and exile. (Eventually, even Trotsky's name would be expunged from Soviet history books. The architect of the Red Army and the savior of St. Petersburg is now an "unperson.")

A BRIEF LOOK BACKWARD

Not only the outcome but the often near-run aspect of the Russian civil war left an indelible mark on the Soviet state and all Europe. "For the Soviet leaders it was a devastating and a formative experience."[29] The conflict "had a profound influence on the regime and on its driving force, the Bolshevik party; and thus may be said to have played a substantial part in the shaping of the Party-dominated Russia of today."[30]

George F. Kennan, whose judgments are always to be taken with great seriousness however much one may wish to qualify them, attributes the victory of the Reds in the contest to two main factors: (a) the divisions among and ineptness of the Whites, and (b) the "extraordinary discipline, compactness, and conspiratorial tightness of the Communist party" under the "magnificent political leadership—bold, ruthless, determined, and imaginative—" of Lenin. "The Bolsheviki came out ahead very largely because they were, in this maelstrom of poorly organized political forces, the only political force that had hardness, sharpness, disciplined drive and clearly defined purpose."[31] This discipline, hardness, and sharpness were supremely valuable in allowing the Reds to create armed forces that were and remained subordinate to the party leadership.

We need not join in the mythologizing of the Red Army of the civil war. It was obviously good enough to fulfill its principal task, that of beating back the Whites, but it accomplished this only with great difficulty, although it enjoyed great numerical superiority on every front almost all the time. Against the army of newly independent and half-organized Poland, the Red Army failed. No great military leader arose from this army, whose most dominating figure by far is the civilian Trotsky. Neither Whites nor Reds ever had enough men; both suffered from all the problems associated with conscription. (Despite the great advances made during World War I, neither side was able to use air power to advantage.)

The Red Army suffered desertion on a truly mammoth scale; whole regiments (such as the Semyonov Guards) passed over to the Whites at critical moments, and mutiny was an ever-present danger (as at the fort at Krasnaya Gorka on the Gulf of Finland). These distressing symptoms of profound weakness in the Red Army were, however, uncoordinated events occurring in a void, and hence failed to have the major effects that they might have had under other circumstances.

One reads of the counterrevolution's failure to generate "popular support, the absence of which was the fundamental cause of the defeat of the Whites."[32] There is much merit in this view; nevertheless, certain qualifications are called for. Both Red and White forces were led by men of middle- and lower-class origin; the bulk of the troops on both sides consisted of reluctant peasants commanded by former Tsarist officers. Neither side was very successful in energizing the vast peasant stratum of the population.

> A powerful strain of peasant anarchism runs through the whole course of the Russian Revolution. The Bolsheviki, in their effort to create a new social and economic order, and the Whites, in their desire to restore one [this is not entirely fair to Wrangel] both found their active supporters mainly in the cities. Neither had real roots in the peasant villages.[33]

Above all, we must always remember that the Bolsheviks were able to obtain the peasant troops they had because, beyond naked coercion, at which they excelled, they propagated a colossal, calculated lie: that they wanted to give the land to the peasant to do with as he pleased. If the peasants of 1920 had been able to catch but a glimpse of what Bolshevik land policy would be after 1928, few would have fought for the Bolsheviks and many would have fought against them, especially under Wrangel. But who could possibly have imagined in 1920 that within a few years the Communist state would declare a war of extermination on the peasantry? The Communists, moreover, promised the national minorities that once the civil war was over they would have a free choice on secession. These groups would discover soon enough, but too late, that the Bolsheviks' definition of "free choice" was quite different from that of most other people.

At the same time, much — perhaps a very great deal — of the support that the Bolshevik government was able to generate derived from its being quite unexpectedly cast, by the Allied landings and the unsuccessful Polish war, in the incongruous role of defender of the motherland.

Clearly, the Whites suffered grave and probably fatal political handicaps. But the general strategic situation played no less decisive a role in their undoing. The beginnings of the civil war found the Reds in possession of the most populous provinces and the centers of industry. The Reds fought mostly on interior lines, under one overall command, and could thus shift troops relatively easily from one front to another as the dangers of the hour dictated. This central position, and the fact that they were often on the defensive, helped enhance that unity of purpose, that "compactness" and "hardness" so admired by Kennan. The White armies, in contrast, always operated on the periphery. They were rarely in effective communication with one another, and could not shift troops from one front to another. This lack of physical coordination mirrored and encouraged an absence of clearly articulated and commonly held political aims. Finally, the Whites felt, with good reason, that they could not simply remain passively in possession of outlying regions; if they were going to win the war or even survive in the long term, they had to be always on the offensive, always pressing toward Moscow. The savage

Russian winter, however, is almost always on the side of the defense, and that meant, most of the time, on the side of the Bolsheviks.

SUMMARY

The Whites faced daunting obstacles of a purely military/strategic nature. They disastrously lessened their chances of overcoming these obstacles through two key political mistakes. First, being unable to show the same cold-eyed appreciation of political realities displayed by the Bolsheviks at Brest-Litovsk, the Whites refused to recognize the aspirations of Poles, Finns, and Ukrainians; thus, they earned their suspicion and forfeited their help. Second, they failed to offer the peasantry, which constituted most of the population, a serious land program until it was too late.

Thus, the civil war ended in a complete victory for the Bolsheviks. They paid a very high price for it, however. The conflict deprived Russia, through battle death, police liquidation, starvation, or exile, of almost all of her middle and upper classes, the most catastrophic "brain drain" in history. Above all, owing to the Bolshevik preoccupation with the White threat, Bela Kun's Red Hungary was smothered, and Red Poland was not born until 1945. Hence, Communism was confined to one country, with Stalin in the wings getting ready to make a virtue of necessity.

NOTES

1. William Henry Chamberlin, *The Russian Revolution 1917–1921* (New York: Macmillan, 1935), vol. 2, p. 231.
2. Chamberlin, *The Russian Revolution*, p. 16.
3. Chamberlin, *The Russian Revolution*, p. 19.
4. Chamberlin, *The Russian Revolution*, p. 166.
5. Chamberlin, *The Russian Revolution*, p. 166.
6. See George F. Kennan, *Russia and the West under Lenin and Stalin* (Boston: Little, Brown & Company, 1960), chap. 2; David Footman, *Civil War in Russia* (New York: Praeger, 1962), chap. 4.
7. Footman, *Civil War*, p. 212.
8. Chamberlin, *The Russian Revolution*, p. 178.
9. Footman, *Civil War*, p. 242.
10. Chamberlin, *The Russian Revolution*, p. 204.
11. Carl von Clausewitz, *On War* (Princeton, NJ: Princeton University Press, 1976), p. 87.
12. Chamberlin, *The Russian Revolution*, p. 261.
13. Chamberlin, *The Russian Revolution*, p. 256.
14. Chamberlin, *The Russian Revolution*, p. 137.
15. Chamberlin, *The Russian Revolution*, p. 252.
16. Richard Luckett, *The White Generals* (New York: Viking, 1971), p. 388.
17. Luckett, *The White Generals*, p. 150.
18. Chamberlin, *The Russian Revolution*, p. 322.

19. Chamberlin, *The Russian Revolution*, p. 320.
20. John Erickson, "The Origins of the Red Army," in Richard Pipes, ed., *Revolutionary Russia* (Cambridge, MA: Harvard, 1968), p. 237.
21. Isaac Deutscher, *Trotsky: The Prophet Armed* (New York: Oxford University Press, 1954), p. 433.
22. Deutscher, *Prophet Armed*, p. 421.
23. Deutscher, *Prophet Armed*, p. 409.
24. John Ellis, *Armies in Revolution* (New York: Oxford University Press, 1974), p. 192.
25. Chamberlin, *The Russian Revolution*, p. 30; Katherine Chorley, *Armies and the Art of Revolution* (Boston: Beacon, 1973), p. 201.
26. Ellis, *Armies*, pp. 180–181.
27. Ellis, *Armies*, p. 193.
28. Deutscher, *Prophet Armed*, p. 445.
29. Luckett, *The White Generals*, p. xvii.
30. Footman, *Civil War*, p. 15.
31. George F. Kennan, "The Russian Revolution Fifty Years After: Its Nature and Consequences," *Foreign Affairs*, 46 (October, 1967): 7.
32. Chamberlin, *The Russian Revolution*, p. 283.
33. Chamberlin, *The Russian Revolution*, p. 221.

PART

2

Armies Versus Civilians

From Budapest in the 1950s to Tehran in the 1970s, heavily armed regimes that appeared impregnable even to knowledgeable observers were swept away by crowds of unarmed civilians.

Both the Hungarian Communists and the shah of Iran confronted serious problems regarding their legitimacy. In the Hungarian case, Communist legitimacy was weak because many Hungarians remembered well the country's disastrous experience with a previous Communist dictatorship, and because the current Communist masters of the country had been crudely placed in office and were visibly maintained there by the power of the Soviet Union, to which they were embarrassingly subservient.

The legitimacy problem of the shah of Iran was comparable to some degree with that of the Budapest Communist regime. The shah was closely and openly identified with the United States; indeed, the Central Intelligence Agency played a controversial role in keeping the shah on his throne during a crisis in the early 1950s. More important, the shah ruled over a largely Shiite Muslim population, whose religious leaders traditionally were reluctant to recognize the authority of any secular government, and who viewed many of the shah's key reforms, especially the emancipation of women, as fundamental attacks on religion.

In Hungary, what might have been merely a demonstration in the capital city turned into spontaneous revolution through miscalculation on the part of the authorities. The much-indoctrinated Hungarian army refused to fire on crowds of civilian demonstrators and actually joined with them in some instances. The vaunted power of the party–police state collapsed in a matter of hours.

In contrast, the triumph of the Iranian revolutionaries required many agonizing months of confrontation and bloodshed. The shah, undergoing treatment for the cancer that would eventually kill him, slowly demoralized his

51

troops by having them fire on mobs of religiously intoxicated civilians while refusing to use the levels of force necessary to restore order.

Hungarian communism was restored to power by a massive and effective Soviet military intervention; the U.S. government allowed its long-time ally in Tehran to be toppled from power and chased from the country.

The Hungarian uprising of 1956 raises questions about the necessity of leadership in revolution and the ability of armed civilian volunteers to confront regular military forces. The tactical errors of the shah, reminiscent of St. Petersburg in February 1917, underline the dangerous incalculability of deploying conscript troops against their fellow nationals.

3

The Hungarian Revolution

In time of fair weather, prepare for storms.

— Machiavelli

The revolution that exploded in Hungary in October 1956 has many arresting aspects, some of which it shares with other upheavals, others of which (unfortunately for the Hungarians) were unique to it.

First, "the Hungarian Revolution was never planned or organized."[1] In its spontaneity, it reminds one of the February Revolution in Tsarist Russia, except that, like a fire breaking out in a long-parched forest, one might have expected an upheaval in the Russia of those days, beset by the hardships involved with being on the verge of defeat in a world war. The Hungarian events, on the other hand, were more like an earthquake that unleashes its devastating power with few warning signs that contemporary observers could have been reasonably expected to discern. Second, the Hungarian Revolution provides an opportunity to view the devastating effects of dissension and division within the ruling elite, in this instance the Communist party, on the stability of a regime, especially one based on repression. Third, and more particular to the Hungarian case, the revolution of October 1956 brushed aside, *in only a few days*, a regime that before the cataclysm struck must have appeared to an outside observer as absolutely secure, with all the techniques and panoply of modern dictatorship: a Leninist-model party, quite large and well disciplined, a tightly controlled press and communications system, an army totally indoctrinated by the party and undefeated in a war, an omnipresent and terror-inspiring political police, even large concentrations of foreign troops stationed in the country for the very purpose of guaranteeing the stability of the incumbent regime. All this—and much more—was swept away in a manner so complete and in a time so short as to require one to reexamine many easy generalizations about the ability of Leninist dictatorships to mold and manipulate those who live under them. Fourth, the fate of the Hungarian

Revolution provides unmistakable confirmation of the widely accepted dictum that volunteer civilian forces, no matter how highly motivated, no matter how enthusiastically supported by the population, are no match whatsoever for well-equipped regular forces wielded by a government determined to restore its physical control of the country whatever the cost. The events in Hungary are in total contrast to the events in Cuba and Iran, where the ruling regime either failed to mobilize its forces in a serious manner or vacillated fatally between repression and concession. One must note, however, that the troops that carried out the thorough, bloody, and swift extirpation of the Hungarian Revolution were foreigners—Russians (and this was not the first time that Russian troops had entered Hungary in order to suppress a revolution). Without the physical availability of the Russian army, and the last-minute decision of its masters to use it to the hilt, the Hungarian Revolution would no doubt have gone into the textbooks as a classic case of the ability of a populace, driven too far, to pull down the mighty from their seats and demolish the bastille.

COMMUNIST HUNGARY: THE FIRST EXPERIENCE

Hungary's experience with communism has been unique in that it is (so far) the only European country whose people overthrew a Communist regime by force only to have it bloodily reimposed upon them by an invasion of the Soviet army. But this is not the Hungarians' only unique experience with communism. Hungary rid itself of a Communist dictatorship *twice*, and *twice* got it back: Hungary was alone among European nations outside Russia in having a Communist dictatorship installed as a result of the *First* World War and that dictatorship was, in its turn, unique in the circumstances in which it came to power, the incompetence which characterized its brief rule, and the manner in which power fell from its hands.

In 1918, with the military collapse of Austria–Hungary imminent, a republic was proclaimed in Budapest, eventually headed by Count Karolyi as provisional president. The Hungarian Republican government soon discovered to its dismay that the victorious Allies intended to hold it responsible for all the alleged sins of the Habsburg monarchy, which it had just overthrown. The Allies were determined to permit Hungary's hostile neighbors and subject minorities, especially the Czechs and the Romanians, to satisfy their nationalist aspirations at Hungary's expense to an apparently unlimited degree. Indeed, the Allies dealt more harshly with Hungary than with any of the other defeated Central Powers, Germany included. Incredulous and outraged at Allied demands on Hungary, the bourgeoisie who had created the provisional republic decided to take vengeance on the Allies by turning the Communist tide against them; they handed power in Budapest over to the Reds. The latter, having received rather than having taken power (Trotsky later maintained that the main cause of the defeat of the Hungarian Communists was the absence of armed struggle preceding the takeover of power), found that their immediate task was the physical defense of the Communist regime, and therefore of Hungarian territorial integrity, against the Allies. The Revolutionary Governing Council proclaimed itself on March 21, 1919, under the leadership of Communist party head Bela Kun, who went to government headquarters from the prison in which he had been confined for revolutionary agitation.

Bela Kun was born in a Transylvanian village in 1886. At the age of 16, he joined the Social Democratic party, and a few years later became editor of the penny tabloid *Forward*. He joined the army in 1915, apparently to escape charges of embezzlement. Taken prisoner by the Russians in 1916, he was sent to the prison camp at Tomsk, where he promptly became a Bolshevik agitator. The Bolshevik revolution freed Kun from the camp; he went to Petrograd, where he met Lenin, became friends with Bukharin, wrote for *Pravda*, and opposed the Treaty of Brest-Litovsk.

The Tsarist armies had taken thousands of Hungarian prisoners. When the Bolsheviks came to power, they offered the prisoners their freedom if they joined the Red Army; nearly 100,000 Hungarian officers and men took advantage of the offer. From these ranks, the men who were to carry the torch of Red revolution into Hungary would be recruited. Typically, the Hungarian Communist party was founded (and not for the last time) on Russian soil, at the Hotel Dresden in Moscow, on November 4, 1918.

In his book, *Peasant War in Germany*, Friedrich Engels had written:

> The worst thing that can befall the leader of an extreme party is to be compelled to take over a government in an epoch when the moment is not yet ripe for the domination of the class he represents and for the realization of the measures which that domination implies.

These words might have seemed prophetically addressed to Kun and his small, made-in-Russia Communist party in 1919, especially in view of the fact that the bourgeoisie had *handed power over* to them. But in the heady atmosphere of post-Petrograd Europe, Engels and his fuddy-duddy cautions seemed out of style. Had not Lenin proved that a small band of determined men could make the proletarian revolution anywhere?

In his desperate gamble, Kun seemed to have some big cards to play. Many people besides the Communists expected the proletarian revolution to break out all over central Europe any day; the Budapest regime could also expect large numbers of Red Army troops to arrive from Petrograd. Both of these expectations proved illusory. In May 1919, Red Army units were indeed on their way to aid Kun, but mutiny and lack of discipline delayed their progress; then Denikin launched his White offensive from the south (see chapter 2), and that was the end of any effective help from Red Russia.

As might have been expected from the circumstances of its birth, the Kun regime sought to exploit the embittered nationalism of the middle class. Kun used to give a popular lecture entitled "Wilson and Lenin," in which he castigated the former's principle of self-determination in the name of which Hungary had been stripped of many of her historic provinces. But in the end, his efforts to woo the bourgeoisie through anti-Allied nationalism foundered on the rocks of corruption, extortion, and anti-Semitism. Corruption in the Kun administration was a real problem, referred to frequently even in the party press and official pronouncements.[2] Nor did it do the regime any good to have most Communist officals residing at Soviet House, "a luxury hotel on the Danube,"[3] while Budapest was a scene of economic distress. Meanwhile, groups of thugs calling themselves "Lenin's Boys" indulged in extortion and general brutality with the apparent tolerance of the authorities. Finally, Jews were disproportionately represented in the leadership of the Communist party (and of their Socialist allies as well)[4]; this would have been a grave political liability even if the times had been peaceful and prosperous.

The Kun regime created only disasters for itself. Agricultural policy will serve as an example. The Communist rulers of Hungary were totally urban, completely ignorant of peasant ways and problems, and profoundly unsympathetic to peasants as a class. Kun actually seems to have believed, on the basis of a conversation he once had with a rural day-laborer, that the Hungarian peasantry would welcome agricultural collectivization. Thus, unlike Lenin, who lied to the Russian peasants about what was going to become of the land, Kun made it perfectly clear right from the beginning that all landholdings were going to be taken over by the state. This naive candor (to give it no other name) destroyed any chance the regime might have had to garner significant support in the countryside, where most of the population of the country lived.

The peasantry was further alienated (along with other segments of the population) by the regime's vigorously anti-religious policies. Prayers were forbidden in Budapest schools, crucifixes were torn from the walls of all school buildings, and the country was filled with reports of outrages against religious objects and places (all these things occurring amid widespread popular perception that the regime was, in effect, Jewish).[5] Plans were afoot to deport all priests and nuns to Austria; in fact, Kun was working on plans to force everybody in Budapest who was not engaged in industrial production or vital services to leave the city.[6] And, in case anyone still believed in the bright future of a Communist Hungary, Kun decreed the prohibition of alcoholic beverages.

Having begun by ignoring the warning of Engels about revolutionaries coming to power prematurely, and having failed to follow Lenin's example in winning at least temporary support among the peasantry by lying to them about land policy, Kun finished by flagrantly violating Lenin's perhaps most often repeated dictum that *the Party must always remain separate and distinct* from all allied or front organizations. Kun instead engineered the merger of his Communists with the Hungarian Socialists. This tactic was to become familiar in post-World War II Eastern Europe, where it took the form of the forcible swallowing-up of a smaller social democratic party by a larger and more disciplined Communist party.[7] In the Hungary of 1919, however, all was different. The Hungarian Socialists not only were far more numerous than the Communists, they had behind them decades of organizational experience, whereas the Communist party which had had power thrust upon it in March 1919 was only four months old. The Hungarian Socialists were far stronger than the Russian Mensheviks had ever been; the Hungarian proletariat was far weaker than even the weak Russian proletariat. The Hungarian Communists had not seized power for themselves in a St. Petersburg-style night-time putsch, but rather had been bundled from the jail cell to the cabinet room because nobody else would accept the responsibility for dealing with the voracious Allies. It was thus Kun's Communists who were in fact swallowed up.

The whole program of the Kun regime was remarkable: in a peasant country, *collectivization*; in a Catholic country, *anti-Catholicism*; in a pleasure-loving country, *prohibition*. Finally, the Leninist cadre itself (such as it was) was merged, or submerged, in a gelatinous mass of semirevolutionary, semicompetent Budapest Socialists.

That only the merest puff of wind (or gunsmoke) was required to blow down this tragi-comic regime is proven by the fact that in the rescue of the Hungarian people from their first experience with Communist rule, the role of the rescuer was filled by none other than the Romanian Army.

In an effort to hold the support of Hungarian nationalists, and also to facilitate the spread of the inevitable Communist revolution to Romania (objectives typically contradictory), Kun sent the Hungarian Red army on an offensive into Romania on July 21, 1919. The attack ran into difficulties, then turned into a rout, spelling the end of the nineteen-week-old regime in Budapest. On August 1, the Revolutionary Governing Council held its last meeting, to be advised by Kun that "the dictatorship of the proletariat has been defeated economically, militarily, and politically." It was all the fault of the Hungarian proletariat, which clearly needed "the most inhumane and cruel dictatorship of the bourgeoisie to become revolutionary."[8] Then, according to a prearranged plan, Bela Kun and some of his favored ones boarded a train to escape to the West, with many Communists and almost all the Socialist collaborators left behind to face the Romanian and counterrevolutionary music.[9]

The godfathers of the Comintern were so embarrassed by the grotesque ineptitude and resounding failure of the Kun regime that they dissolved the Hungarian Communist party in 1921. Years later, Stalin's Great Purge scooped up at least 19 former Hungarian People's Commissars, and scores of lesser

Communist fry, in its gory tentacles.[10] During those same years, Kun himself was subjected to extensive torture but refused to admit that he was a member of the Grand Trotskyite Conspiracy. He reportedly went insane in his Russian jail and was executed in the cellar of Butyrka Prison on November 30, 1939.

SETTING UP THE SECOND COMMUNIST REGIME

The inoculation that the Hungarian people received under Kun would undoubtedly have protected them from any resurgence of Communism for generations, if the choice had been in their hands. But in 1944, Germany's armies were in full retreat all across eastern Europe, with the Red Army pressing close upon them. The fighting swept into Hungary; "Behind the Soviet combat troops came the political experts of the NKVD [Stalin's political police] accompanied by a number of Hungarian Communists who had been living in exile in the USSR."[11] At the war's end, the Communists and Socialists agreed to a coalition ticket for the Budapest municipal elections. So confident were they of victory that the Communists permitted the balloting to be free; as a result, the conservative Small Farmer's party polled 51 percent of the vote.[12] After this humiliating outcome, the commander of the Soviet army in Hungary, Marshall Voroshilov, consented to holding national parliamentary elections in November 1945 only on condition that after the elections, no matter what their result, a coalition cabinet would be formed that would include the Communists, with the key ministry of the interior (which controlled the police) reserved specifically for them.[13] Despite the open support of the Soviet occupation forces, the Communists polled only 17 percent of the vote in the relatively free parliamentary elections, while the Small Farmers received an overwhelming 59 percent.[14] In light of these unmistakable proofs of Communist debility, the ministry of the interior was at first handed over not to them, but to one Ferenc Erdei, technically a member of the Peasant party but actually a Communist sympathizer; under him, that all-important ministry "soon became a Communist preserve."[15] In early 1946, however, the Communist party finally demanded this post and, because the Russian authorities insisted on a coalition cabinet including the Communists and because the Communists would not join a coalition cabinet unless they had the interior ministry, they got it, installing the veteran Communist Imre Nagy.

Soon thereafter, because the Communist-controlled printers' union refused to print the "reactionary calumnies" of the Small Farmers' party, their newspapers were effectively silenced.[16] Scenting blood, the Communists began to demand a purge of "nondemocratic" elements within the Small Farmers party, and the leader of this unfortunate party, one Zoltan Tildy, urged his followers to accept all of the demands of the Communists, including the purge of key leaders. (The Communists controlled Tildy because they possessed information about secret scandals in his family.)[17] When the national assembly nevertheless refused to remove the parliamentary immunity of Bela Kovacs, a Small Farmers' party leader, the Soviet military command arrested him anyway (February 25, 1947) on charges of conspiracy against the occupation forces. The Communists now wanted new national elections, determined this time to see that the results were the right ones. Opposition leaders found themselves not only deprived of the ability to communicate with their voters through the press, but also unable to hold campaign rallies due to disruption by organized gangs of thugs. When opposition leaders requested police protection for their public meetings, they were informed that the authorities could not be expected to control "the just anger of the people against the enemies of democracy."[18]

Even in the atmosphere of intimidation and outright fraud, in the elections of August 1947 the Communists were able to garner only 22 percent of the vote. The Communists had now had enough of this inexplicable intransigence; within six months they dissolved the major opposition parties and sent their leaders into exile, and the Social Democrats were forced to merge with the Communists (things had changed greatly since 1919) into the Hungarian Worker's party. By the end of 1948, Communist domination of Hungary was complete. Early the next year, parliament was again dissolved, new elections were held, and the Communists — surprise of surprises — polled more than 90 percent of the vote.

Now firmly in power, the Communists carried out the policies that became a pattern throughout the Eastern bloc: mass purges in the party and without, an all-out drive for industrialization at any cost, rapid collectivization of agriculture (and the vast economic dislocations resulting from this program).

Those who were of bourgeois origins were branded collectively as the class enemy. They endured many deprivations under the new order, not least of which was exclusion from access to higher education. The regime vigorously propagandized the working class about the duty to be class-conscious and politically concerned; at the same time, by taking over and gutting the unions, the party-state deprived the workers of the means to press for such traditional worker goals as shorter hours and higher pay. Indeed, in Communist Hungary, the unions usually operated as instruments by which the government sought to extract greater and greater efforts from the workers. With regard to the peasantry, the familiar tale was reenacted. Learning from Kun's expensive error, the Hungarian Communists after the end of World War II encouraged the peasantry to take over the holdings of the landlords, and indignantly denied that they had secret plans for collectivization. Once the Communists were firmly in control, however, collectivization became exactly the policy the party decreed, to the utter outrage of most of the rural population and to the detriment of the standard of living; the collectivized sector of Hungarian agriculture was much less productive than the private sector, and the country was rapidly losing the ability to feed itself.

Presiding over this melange of repression, guilt by association, and ideologically-induced economic scarcity was party boss and prime minister Matyas Rakosi, the "Little Stalin of Hungary." This "miniature imitation of the Soviet autocrat" was "one of those top Communist leaders who, having arrived at a stage of cynicism in matters of ideology, knows only one ideology, that of power."[19] Distaste for Rakosi and his unbounded cult of personality had been increasing in Moscow before Stalin's death; the Russian embassy in Budapest had kept Moscow well informed of great and growing popular restlessness both with his policies and his style. When Stalin finally died and was succeeded by the combination of Malenkov and Beria, Rakosi's game was up. Summoned to Moscow, Rakosi was criticized to his face for filling too many top jobs in Hungary with his fellow Jews.[20] Besides, the day of tin-god dictators was over; collective leadership was now the fashion, and Rakosi, if he wished to retain the chairmanship of the Hungarian party, had to divest himself of the premiership, which went to Imre Nagy, the only non-Jew in the top leadership of the Hungarian party. Rakosi returned to Budapest, biding his time.

Premier Nagy (born in 1895) introduced what came to be called the *New Course*: less police terror, more consumer goods and, especially, some concessions to the peasants. The collectivization drive was stopped; the so-called Kulak lists, inclusion on which could keep a peasant from getting credit and fertilizer and expose him to harassment by thugs, were abolished. Hungarians were grateful for the breathing space afforded by the New Course. Nevertheless, the regime does not seem to have benefited significantly from these changes, because the authors of the previous Stalinist repression, notably Rakosi, were still quite visibly entrenched in key positions.[21]

The New Course also allowed many victims of previous purges to leave prison and resume, as well as they were able, their previous lives. Perhaps nothing else undermined the credibility of the party, especially in the view of intellectuals, as much as this tacit admission that it had made gross mistakes through which innocent and valuable persons had suffered grievously.

But the New Course, introduced to reflect changing circumstances in Moscow, came to a sudden halt when these circumstances changed once more. The dumping of Malenkov by Nikita Khrushchev and his regime in 1955 meant, among other things, that the Nagy government was doomed. In April 1955, Nagy not only lost the premiership but was stripped of all party offices as well. Rakosi had his sweet revenge, and his clear intent to reimpose Stalinist measures appalled many who had rallied to the New Course. His Moscow masters had not given Rakosi a completely blank check, however; above all, he was not permitted to reintroduce police terror against his opponents within the Hungarian party. The men in power in the Kremlin, having suffered for years from the politicization of the police and having recently killed the arch-police terrorist himself, Lavrentii Beria, laid down the rule that the secret police could not be used in intraparty rivalries. The Hungarian police approved fully; they had been amazed and offended when during the New Course all blame for past misdeeds had been pinned on them. The subsequent purges within police ranks had shown how dangerous it could be for policemen to take sides, or even appear to take sides, in kaleidoscopic party disputes.[22] (These attitudes partly explain the failure of the police to act vigorously at the beginning of the revolution in 1956.)

In early 1956, the Hungarian regime was beset with many severe problems. Splits within the Communist leadership were serious, bitter, and open; the intelligentsia (especially writers, a particularly influential class in Hungary) were alienated and often hostile; the contrast between what the regime promised and what it delivered was blatant to a dangerous degree. Factionalism was not the only ailment afflicting the party organization. After World War II, it had sought to grow too rapidly and took in many ideologically unprepared persons, including former Fascists as well as large numbers of Jews.[23] Ten years later, the party had grown ideologically rigid and socially closed. It provided many of its members with a life-style well above that of ordinary Hungarians and isolated them from what the general population thought and felt. Thus, the party allowed itself to fall into the perilous habit of thinking that Communist rule was "irreversible."[24] Finally, the deeply nationalistic Hungarians, not necessarily excluding many Communists, were constantly irritated by the all-too-visible presence of Russian occupation troops.

Underneath the calm, drab surface of Communist Hungary, powerful and turbulent forces were awaiting an opportunity to burst forth.

THE HUNGARIAN UPHEAVAL

In February 1956, Russian party boss Nikita Khrushchev delivered to the assembled leaders of Soviet Communism a ferocious attack on the crimes, personal and political, of Joseph Stalin, formerly known officially as the "Genius of Mankind." This so-called "Secret Speech" of Khrushchev's was soon published all over the world. Because the indictment of Stalin was really an indictment of the whole Soviet system, it caused a cataclysm throughout the Communist world. In Hungary, the speech profoundly upset the intellectuals, many of whom were still sincere, if alienated, Communists. It was also widely discussed well beyond party circles. So great was the confusion and turmoil in the aftermath of Khrushchev's exposé and denunciation of the crimes of the Stalin era (which had ended only three years before) that in the summer of 1956 the political examinations in the Hungarian military schools had to be cancelled: no one knew any more what the right answers were.[25] At the very height of the turmoil produced by the events in Russia, party boss Rakosi admitted (confession was now in style) his complicity in the judicial murder of Laszlo Rajk. A former minister of the interior and of foreign affairs, Rajk had been framed by Rakosi with antiparty crimes and was hanged in October 1949. (Soon thereafter, another of Rakosi's prey, Interior Minister Sandor Zold, had killed his family and himself rather than be arrested.) Rajk's widow had kept up a ceaseless campaign to clear her husband's name and, when the truth was known, "Hungary had the distinction of being the only country in Eastern Europe with a self-confessed murderer of Communists at the head of the ruling party."[26] Rakosi tried to pin his Stalinist misdeeds against party comrades on the police; as a result, when he tried to address a meeting of high secret police officials in April 1956 he was openly hooted.[27] Rakosi now became a target of public vilification, and hence a great liability to the regime. Soviet party chieftain Anastas Mikoyan accordingly flew to Budapest in July. He informed the Hungarian central committee that Rakosi had to go. Go he did. Here now was an opportunity for the regime to preclude any serious trouble by throwing the detested Rakosi to the wolves and putting in a cleaned-up "reform" Communist administration. Instead, Rakosi's successor as party head was his long-time partner and alter ego Erno Gero, a very unfortunate choice, as time would demonstrate.

The searing indictments of once-infallible party leaders, public confessions of guilt by once-all-powerful bosses, reinstatements and rehabilitations of once-condemned figures, the more and more open criticisms and demands for change from the lower levels of the party, the articles in establishment intellectual organs openly ridiculing the high living of party bureaucrats[28] — all these things signaled to the population at large that change was possible, perhaps inevitable, and in a totalitarian regime such thoughts are in themselves revolutionary. As the summer gave way to autumn, the tumultuous events in Poland taught Hungarians that a Communist regime could be openly and massively challenged and that great changes in leadership and concessions in policy could be extracted, even in the teeth of threats of massive military intervention by the neighboring Russians. Along with Khrushchev's Secret Speech, the upheavals of that autumn in Poland shook the Communist world to its foundations.

In the midst of all this ferment, the public reinterment of the former criminal-traitor Laszlo Rajk took place on October 6. The funeral procession turned into a silent but unmistakable demonstration against the regime. Everyone now saw that the populace could turn out into the streets without necessarily being savaged by the police.[29]

All was now in readiness.

The key date, the physical beginning of what became the Hungarian Revolution, is October 23, 1956. On that day a student demonstration was to take place in Budapest at the statue of the Polish patriot, General Bem (a hero of the Polish Revolution of 1830 and of the Hungarian Revolution of 1848 that had been suppressed by Russian intervention). In light of events in Poland, the political implications of this planned demonstration were obvious; in addition, a nationwide assembly of university students at the Budapest Technological University had just passed a series of resolutions demanding withdrawal of Russian troops from Hungarian soil, honest elections by secret ballot, freedom of speech and of the press, and the reappointment of Imre Nagy as premier. Consequently, at about one o'clock in the afternoon, the ministry of the interior withdrew permission to hold the demonstration, but about an hour and a half later voided the prohibition, perhaps to avoid a public flouting of its authority. Thousands of students converged on the Bem statue, joined by large numbers of workers and off-duty soldiers. This student–worker–soldier demonstration marked the turning point of protest in Hungary from an essentially intraparty fight to a mass struggle. Most of the students were of proletarian or peasant origin. Heavily politicized by the party, they had constantly been promised a bright, just, abundant society, and they had been shatteringly disappointed and offended by the dull, mendacious, and pinched reality of Communist Hungary.[30] The crowds grew larger by the hour. Then they began to move from the Bem statue across the river Danube to the square in front of the Parliament building. After repeated urging, Nagy consented to address the vast throng. His speech was a dud; he really had nothing to say to these demonstrators. Fundamentally, Nagy was a Communist and was made deeply uneasy by this outpouring of popular dissatisfaction with communism. After his disappointing speech (he had called the demonstrators comrades and they had shouted back, "No more comrades!"), he disappeared from public view and was not to be seen during the next decisive hours or even the next decisive days.

Nothing really irreversible had yet occurred, but everyone was reluctant to let the day end. It was announced that party boss Gero would make a radio address at 8 P.M. Tens of thousands of people began to gather in front of the State Radio Building, several blocks distant from Parliament. Gero then gave his radio talk, a speech so maladroit and insulting that commentators later speculated that it was intended to provoke the crowd to violence. Gero called the orderly demonstrators a mob and the students a gang. He constantly invoked Hungarian friendship and admiration for the Soviet Union, used all the stale, canned phrases of Marxist ideology instead of addressing the problems and questions that were on the minds of all, told what everyone knew to be outright lies about conditions in Hungary, and delivered the entire ill-advised speech in a tone of voice that reminded all who heard it of his totally irritating personality.

After the speech, some students demanded that their resolutions be read over the state radio. Then, at about 9 P.M., according to the U.N. Special Committee on the Problem of Hungary, the first shots were fired: members of the security police began firing into the crowd from upper windows of the State Radio Building.[31] No one is sure how many persons were killed or wounded, but the Hungarian Revolution had begun.

THE COLLAPSE OF THE REGIME

The Rakosi–Gero satrapy rested on an impressive panoply of force: the security police, the regular police, the army, and the Soviet occupation troops. All these elements were in place on October 23, 1956, and on paper they provided the regime with an apparently unassailable series of bulwarks. In fact, the system of repression on which Rakosi and his henchmen depended collapsed in a few days.

The security police, known at different times as the AVO and the AVH, were the first line of defense for the regime. With special weapons and uniforms, and with unlimited license to terrorize the population, the AVO was almost universally detested by the Hungarian people for its viciousness and brutality. AVO elements had opened fire on the unarmed demonstrators on the night of October 23. Fearless when the arrest and torture of single suspects or even a whole family was involved, AVO men tended to be much more discreet when confronted by crowds of civilians. Soon after the shootings at the State Radio Building they disappeared into their various holes. It was thus necessary to rush reinforcements to the building; they arrived in the form of regular army units and elements of the Frontier Guard Command, a branch of the army believed to be especially reliable. But when these troops reached the scene of the demonstration, soldiers and officers who were in the crowd called out to them not to open fire. Accounts of what happened next vary, but the regular troops refused to fire on the demonstrators and the Frontier Guards actually began handing over their weapons to members of the crowd.

With this refusal of army units to protect the security police from the wrath of the people, the Hungarian Communist regime, for all practical purposes, was finished.

All through the night of October 23 and into the following days, the demonstrators and those who joined them received arms, from individual soldiers, from depots, and from workers' militia centers. Many of the students knew how to handle these guns because they had undergone compulsory military training in their universities.

During those same days, AVO units continued their mass firing into civilian crowds. On October 25, in Parliament Square, more than 100 unarmed men and women were massacred in this way.[32] And in the city of Magyarovar, the AVO killed another 80 civilians.[33] For these reasons, it was not uncommon in those late October days to see in various parts of the country the bodies of AVO men hanging from lampposts or other hastily selected instruments of popular justice. (A later Communist administration would state that 234 AVO men had been victims of this "white terror."[34]) In many places, however, the AVO completely disappeared, or, as in the towns of Pecs and Gyor, actually went over to the revolution.

If the AVO had proven itself totally inadequate to deal with popular chal-

lenges to the regime, the regular police force, especially in Budapest, actually aided the revolution. The regular police were subject to a selection process less stringent and an ideological indoctrination less thorough than that
experienced by the AVO, nor were they carefully isolated, like the security
police, from the civil population. Supervision of the regulars was in the hands
of AVO men, who carried out their task with typical harshness and haughti-
ness. The AVO also received higher pay and wore snappier uniforms than
the regular police. Thus, the sympathy of the latter for the demonstrators and
their evident satisfaction at seeing the AVO put so quickly to rout is not sur-
prising. In the first hours of the revolution, Budapest Police Chief Sandor
Kopacsi told his men not to fire on the crowds, and the next day ordered that
weapons be provided to the demonstrators; in fact this had already occurred
at several police stations.[35]

Individual members of the Hungarian army, officers and men, had participated in the demonstrations in front of the State Radio Building on the
evening of October 23. Throughout all the days of upheaval that followed,
the regime found to its consternation that the army was useless as an instrument for restoring order. Attempts by the high command to get the army to
assist Soviet troops were ignored, met by wholesale desertion, or openly
disobeyed. In the provinces, where most of the Hungarian army was located,
units either remained aloof from the fighting between armed civilians on one
side and AVO men and Soviet troops on the other, or distributed weapons
to their compatriots and even joined individually in the revolution.

It is true that relatively few regular Hungarian army officers and enlisted
men took an active part in the struggle against the Russian occupation troops
that began to rage after October 23 (although, on October 28, the ministry
of defense felt compelled to issue the telltale assurance that all regular army
men who had "become separated from their units" would be permitted to return unmolested[36]). The high command, with very few exceptions, remained
loyal to the regime. In general, however, the regular army completely failed
to defend the regime, and in some places, as in Magyarovar, it assisted the
insurgents in destroying the security police.[37]

As in France in 1789, in Russia in 1917, and in Iran in 1978, the events
in Hungary in 1956 demonstrate the profound instability of regular army
troops when deployed against civilians of their own nationality.

If the general stance of the regular Hungarian army toward the revolution
can be described as one of aloofness (that is, most soldiers stood by com-
placently while the exasperated citizenry dismantled the party-state), the attitude of the military cadets must have shaken every single assumption the
Hungarian Communist regime ever held. These young cadets, the flower and
hope of the regime, carefully selected to ensure the proper class background,
heavily indoctrinated with Marxist–Leninist truth, either placed their skills
at the service of the insurgents or maintained order in their local districts while

the insurgents went to fight in other areas. (The behavior of the military cadets in Hungary supports the contention of many students of the Latin American military that the class origins of the officer corps do not explain its political position: "the army is its own class." Or perhaps the carefully selected young proletarians at the military academies did not perceive the Rakosi–Gero duo as truly representative of the proletariat.)

How is one to account for the total failure of the Hungarian Communists, after a decade of apparently permanent power, to build a politically reliable or even controllable military force? Certainly, the desertion of the regime by the army cannot be explained in terms of any gross oversights or obvious mistakes on the part of the government. All the tried and true methods that had worked well enough in the Soviet armed forces were used in Hungary. The Hungarian army employed the familiar technique of using commissars ("political officers") to guard against treachery and to weed out the unconvinced. The AVO maintained agencies at many levels of the army, and no army commander had any jurisdiction over Russian officers attached to them, providing (presumably) a super-efficient variation of the commissar technique. But none of this was effective. What went wrong?

One reason why the well-trained and well-watched Hungarian army collapsed so easily must surely be that many officers and men had long heard nothing but bitter complaints about the regime from their worker or peasant families. Everyone in Hungary knew that the top leadership of the country was badly split, everyone hated Rakosi and Gero, everyone deplored the absence of everything from the stores, everyone detested the continued Russian occupation. The officers and men of the regular army must also have resented the omnipresence of the arrogant and deadly AVO, the heavy price that the army had to pay for Russian World War II surplus equipment,[38] and the fact that the Rakosi regime had in its time hanged a number of very high army officers.

Most of all, perhaps, the Hungarian army was simply disinclined to turn its guns on students, workers, and fellow soldiers in order to protect murderous AVO men. But the simple decision not to fire on the people was in itself a revolutionary act, a decision to let the regime suffer what it must, a decision from which there could be no turning back.

However complex or simple the motives of the Hungarian soldiers, the resounding, radical collapse of Hungary's Leninist masters had indeed been awesome, like a phenomenon of nature.

> They had the People's Army, the police, the security police, and the workers' militia. Now within a few hours all they had built seemed to crumble away in their hands; the army refused to fight and turned over its weapons to the rebels, the police disobeyed and disappeared from the streets, the workers' militia joined the rebellion, and the Security Police changed from hunter to hunted.[39]

What a picture.

Thus, the Hungarian Communists, confronted everywhere and at once with a massive popular revolt, were forced to the humiliating but quickly grasped expedient of calling upon the Russian army to save them from their own people.

SOVIET INTERVENTION: FIRST PHASE

Soviet intervention against the revolution of the Hungarian people took place in two phases, the first of which extended from October 24 to October 29.

Since the eruption of massive violence in Poland during the summer, Soviet troops had been active in Hungary; between October 20 and October 23, they had been placed on the alert.[40] At the time of the killings at the State Radio Building, two Soviet mechanized divisions were in the country, along with some additional army and air-force elements. Soviet military units, normally kept 30 miles outside the city, began appearing in the streets of Budapest at about 2 A.M. on October 24, a few hours after the AVO had fired on the demonstrators in front of the State Radio Building. On the same day, two more mechanized Soviet divisions entered the country from Romania. Soviet Foreign Minister Shepilov later informed the U.N. General Assembly that Soviet troops went to Budapest in response to a request from the prime minister, raising the question of how troops could have been mobilized and moved by 2 A.M. in response to a request received in Moscow that same day.[41] (Further insight into the true nature of the Hungarian Communist regime may be developed by reflection upon the fact that Hungary's permanent representative to the United Nations, known as Peter Kos, was actually a Soviet subject named Leo Konduktorov.[42]) Russian troops in Budapest and elsewhere had no clear instructions from the Kremlin about whom they were supposed to fight; apparently in Moscow they were still trying to figure out exactly what was happening and what the least damaging course might be. Russian troops who had long been stationed in Hungary also displayed a reluctance to fight in defense of the AVO against students and workers. Nevertheless, after October 24, combat between the insurgents (becoming known all over the world as Freedom Fighters) and Soviet military units and AVO men became widespread, if intermittent.

The Communist regime had taught guerrilla tactics to large numbers of civilians after World War II (in case of another German invasion). University students had to take military training, and thousands of other civilians had been compelled to make a close study of the events of February and October 1917 in St. Petersburg. All this was now turned against the regime and its Soviet protectors.[43] Soviet tanks, sent into operation in Budapest without the necessary infantry support, suffered severe losses. All told, perhaps 200 Russian tanks were destroyed or damaged, half of all the Soviet armor in Hungary.[44] The morale of Soviet troops plummeted.[45] Soviet military action in this first phase ended on October 28 with the announcement that all Russian forces would be withdrawn from Budapest. Russian officers attached to Hungarian units relinquished their posts on the same day or the next, and eventually most of them returned to Russia.

The initial Soviet intervention against the Hungarian Revolution had been a complete fiasco. Politically, it had transformed a mass uprising against a detested native clique into a national movement of a whole people against a foreign occupation and its quisling servants, a development that increased the aversion to the regime of many once-loyal Communists.[46] Militarily, the intervention was equally disastrous: not only had it failed to protect the crumbling dictatorship, but the Freedom Fighters and their supporters were ecstatic at having been able to inflict so much damage on Soviet armor and having thus "won" the battle with the Red Army. Clearly, if the Hungarian Revolution were ever to be suppressed, much larger numbers of Soviet troops and far more ruthless tactics would be necessary.

REVOLUTIONARY HUNGARY

Who directed the Hungarian Revolution once it got rolling? One might expect the answer to be the middle class, especially the intelligentsia. After all, that element directed the French, Russian, Chinese, Cuban, and other revolutions. But in Hungary, things (so many things) were different. The middle classes were thoroughly frightened and cowed after a decade of Communist threats and repression.[47] Students, relatively few of whom came from the middle class, were very active in the early fighting, especially against the Soviet tanks, but in fact "it was the industrial workers whose revolutionary activity lasted longest and was the best organized."[48] In the provincial mining centers, the workers went on strike, vowing that they would return to their factories when Soviet troops returned to their barracks.[49] Provisional revolutionary councils of workers and students sprang up in Budapest and other places, with nationwide links established between them, until free elections could be held for a new parliament. Other than free elections, these councils demanded the restoration of the secret ballot, freedom to organize political parties, worker participation in nationalized industries, the decollectivization of agriculture (with limits on the size of individual holdings), and religious liberty.[50]

The sudden appearance of these orderly and democratic provisional councils was one of the most impressive aspects of Hungary's brief days of freedom. Equally impressive, on the other side of the coin, was the complete collapse of Communist party morale once it became evident that the AVO could not, and the regular army would not, protect it. Members of the party, especially of the middle and upper ranks, so heavily indoctrinated with what is called scientific socialism, believed that everyone else was also. Least of all could they imagine that the workers and the students, the very groups in whose interest Hungary was supposed to be run, could turn against them, against the party, against "History."[51] Nor, probably, could any of them have imagined, until they were confronted with the dread reality, that the mighty panoply of repression that they had erected so carefully could be swept away so casually. Yet within seventy-two hours of the shootings in Parliament Square, the country witnessed "the almost complete disappearance of the Communist Party," the once-feared and vaunted organization of fully 800,000 members, more than one Hungarian in every ten.[52] One of the very first responses of the party to the crisis was to appoint a new boss: 44-year-old Janos Kadar became party first secretary on October 25. The next day, the party central committee declared that a reorganized Hungarian government would have "the mission of making good without fail the *mistakes* and *crimes* of the past."[53] And a few days later came the final admission of moral and political bankruptcy: Kadar, in a radio address to the nation, announced the dissolution of the old party and the formation of a new one, to be called the Hungarian Socialist Workers party. Once again the promise was explicitly made to "break away from the crimes of the past once and for all."[54]

While the party leaders were disappearing from the scene, or trying to salvage something from the wreckage by appointing new faces and adopting a new name and a new program, the government itself announced major concessions to its rebellious people. Hungary's relationship with the USSR was viewed by most Hungarians, even Communists, as exploitative; new negotiations with Russia would begin. Most significantly, a full amnesty was promised to all who would lay down their arms by 10 P.M. on October 26. But no one took advantage of this amnesty. On the contrary, three days after its proclamation, Freedom Fighters occupied the building of the ministry of the interior, the very citadel and symbol of government power. (The insurgents found the place defended by two janitors.) The jails were opened, and political prisoners and common criminals alike were released.[55] The government announced the dissolution of the AVO on October 29, and the next day "granted recognition" to the political parties that had been reconstituting themselves: Smallholders, Social Democrats, and Christian Democrats. On that same day, some insurgents liberated Cardinal Mindszenty from the close confinement in which he had been held after having been let out of prison in 1955.

One of the consequences to be expected from such a rapid and complete breakdown of state authority is a sudden increase in private violence and other criminal acts. AVO men were indeed often lynched on sight, some events with anti-Semitic aspects occurred, and without doubt some private acts took place that could only be described as criminal. But on the whole, the fall of the Communist state was accompanied by remarkably little criminality; in the words of Ferenc Vali, a student of these events, there was "no looting, no storming of shops, no general breakdown of discipline. The crowds did not even start an indiscriminate persecution of Communists. Even in small towns, where party members were highly conspicuous, "decent" Communists were left unharmed."[56]

SOVIET INTERVENTION: SECOND PHASE

Whatever the nature of the debates that had been going on inside the Kremlin since October 24, by the end of the month the die was cast: on November 1, Premier Nagy received word that 3,000 Soviet tanks had entered the country. At 2 P.M., Nagy informed the Soviet ambassador (none other than Yuri Andropov) that if the Soviet troops were not immediately withdrawn, Hungary would renounce membership in the Warsaw Pact. Ambassador Andropov then told the Nagy government that Soviet units were pouring into Hungary and taking over all the airports only to facilitate the quick departure of Russian civilians from the country.[57] At 5 P.M., Nagy and his cabinet declared that Hungary no longer adhered to the Warsaw Pact.

The noted Yugoslavian Communist dissident Milovan Djilas, among others, has expressed the belief that if Hungary had successfully withdrawn from the Warsaw Pact, the effects on Russia and its empire would have been incalculable.[58] Nagy seems to have believed, with astounding naivete, that the USSR would actually tolerate a "free but friendly" Hungary on its borders. Nevertheless, several authorities on the Hungarian Revolution[59] insist that Nagy's attempt to take Hungary out of the defense organization was a *consequence*, not a *cause*, of the Soviet invasion. Whatever the truth of that disputed question, there is no doubt that the Russian leaders had plenty of reason to decide finally to crush the Hungarian Revolution. They knew well that the disturbances in Poland had directly contributed to the upheavals in Hungary: what would Hungary's uprising lead to? The very survival of the Soviet satellite system was at stake. Military action against little Hungary would also entail much less risk than intervention against Poland, a nation of 30 million. Finally, the Western Allies were totally preoccupied and bitterly divided by the Suez invasion by Israel. Therefore, the Red Army began its massive movements.

By November 3, 1956, Soviet military units had surrounded Budapest and had cut off all the main roads leading to the west. (Those of the AVO who were left also reappeared and rendered what assistance they could in destroying the revolution.) The Hungarian army did not offer effective resistance to this Russian invasion; the events of the previous week had left it scattered and confused, and pro-Soviet officers sabotaged anti-Russian plans where they were able.

November 3, 1956, is as important a date as October 23 in the history of the Hungarian Revolution. Not only was the Soviet army by that date in a position to begin the strangulation of Hungary, but a new Hungarian government was being formed—in the Soviet city of Uzgorod!—with Janos Kadar as premier; several members of the Soviet Politburo were in attendance at the birth of this new cabinet. And in those same hours, delegates of the Nagy cabinet, including Defense Minister Pal Maleter (a regular officer who had joined the revolution), were negotiating with the Soviet military command in Hungary under a flag of truce. Against all international law, and to the everlasting dishonor of the Soviet army, the Hungarian negotiators were suddenly seized and thrown into prison, thus almost decapitating the Hungarian Revolution with one shameful blow.

At dawn on November 4, Nagy announced from a radio station in the Parliament building that Soviet troops had invaded Hungary in order to crush the lawful government. "Our troops are fighting back; the government is doing its duty." The Freedom Fighters were putting up a furious resistance, but the end was clearly at hand. Later that day, Nagy found refuge in the Yugoslavian embassy. About two weeks later, he left the protection of the embassy for his home, under a guarantee of safe-conduct from Premier Kadar; he was immediately arrested by Soviet military police and carried to an unknown destination. In 1958, the Kadar regime announced that Nagy, after a secret trial, had been executed. Thus, Imre Nagy, who tried to be a good Communist *and* a good Hungarian, met a martyrdom as ineffective as his life had been.

In one of Nagy's last statements before he sought refuge among the Yugoslavs, he had said: "Today it is Hungary's turn and tomorrow or the day after tomorrow it will be the turn of other countries."[60] The Hungarian government for days begged the outside world to come to its aid, not with speeches but with soldiers. Having believed Communist propaganda, which for years had proclaimed that the West, and especially the Germans, were poised to move rapidly against Hungary, the revolutionaries were surprised and alarmed when Western intervention did not take place.

Why indeed did the West stand by and watch as the Soviet army drowned the Hungarian Revolution in blood?

For all practical purposes, Western intervention meant intervention by the United States, and the American government under President Dwight Eisenhower felt itself prevented from doing anything more than sending food shipments to the beleaguered Hungarians. The United States was then nearing the culmination of its quadrenniel presidential campaign. On the day that General Maleter was treacherously seized by his Russian interlocutors, Secretary of State John Foster Dulles was undergoing surgery. On October 29, Israel, soon to be joined by Britain and France, invaded Nasser's Egypt; the Suez invasion greatly distracted and divided America and its allies, and provoked a wild clamor from Third World regimes (which had very little to say about the events in Hungary). But above all, President Eisenhower believed that the geopolitical situation rendered any effective U.S. aid to the Hungarians — short of unleashing a world war — impossible:

I still wonder what my recommendation to the Congress and the American people would have been had Hungary been accessible by sea or through the territory of allies who might have agreed to react positively to the tragic fate of the Hungarian people. At it was, however, Britain and France could not possibly have moved with us into Hungary. An expedition combining West German and Italian forces with our own, and moving across neutral Austria, Titoist Yugoslavia, or Communist Czechoslovakia, was out of the question. The fact was that Hungary could not be reached. . . . Sending U.S. troops alone into Hungary through hostile or neutral territory would have involved us in a general [world] war.[61]

Resistance raged in Budapest and surrounding areas for several days after November 4, and then subsided into guerrilla war. Most of the fighting came to an end by November 14; the insurgents, heavily outnumbered and surrounded, had run out of ammunition. India's Prime Minister Nehru said that the Hungarian Revolution had cost 25,000 Hungarian and 7,000 Russian lives. Between October 24 and November 14, 1956, approximately 200,000 Hungarians had fled into Austria or Czechoslovakia. Then the Russian fist closed completely, and Hungary was silent.

NOTES

1. Ferenc A. Vali, *Rift and Revolution in Hungary* (Cambridge, MA: Harvard University Press, 1961), p. 271.
2. Frank Eckelt, "The Internal Policies of the Hungarian Soviet Republic," in Ivan Volgyes, ed., *Hungary in Revolution, 1918–1919* (Lincoln: University of Nebraska Press, 1971), p. 87.
3. Rudolph Tokes, *Bela Kun and the Hungarian Soviet Republic* (New York: Praeger, 1967), p. 194.
4. Gabor Vermes, "The October Revolution in Hungary: From Karolyi to Kun," in Ivan Volgyes, ed., *Hungary*, p. 48; Tokes, *Bela Kun*, p. 193.
5. Eckelt, "Internal Policies," p. 69; Tokes, *Bela Kun*, p. 193.
6. Tokes, *Bela Kun*, pp. 195–196.
7. Hugh Seton-Watson, *The East European Revolutions* (New York: Praeger, 1956).
8. Tokes, *Bela Kun*, p. 203.
9. Tokes, *Bela Kun*, p. 199.
10. Tokes, *Bela Kun*, p. 218.
11. Seton-Watson, *East European Revolutions*, p. 190.
12. Seton-Watson, *East European Revolutions*, p. 193.
13. Vali, *Rift*, p. 31fn.
14. Vali, *Rift*, p. 29.
15. Seton-Watson, *East European Revolutions*, p. 192.
16. Seton-Watson, *East European Revolutions*, pp. 194–195.
17. Seton-Watson, *East European Revolutions*, p. 198.
18. Seton-Watson, *East European Revolutions*, p. 200.
19. Vali, *Rift*, pp. 44–45.
20. Paul Kecskemeti, *The Unexpected Revolution: Social Forces in the Hungarian Uprising* (Stanford, CA: Stanford University Press, 1961), p. 43; Paul E. Zinner, *Revolution in Hungary* (Freeport, NY: Books for Libraries Press, 1962), p. 163.

21. Kecskemeti, *Unexpected Revolution*, pp. 4–5; this excellent little book is must reading for all students of the Hungarian revolution.
22. Kecskemeti, *Unexpected Revolution*, pp. 73–74.
23. Zinner, *Revolution in Hungary*, p. 74.
24. Zinner, *Revolution in Hungary*, pp. 156–157.
25. General Bela Kiraly, "Hungary's Army: Its Part in the Revolt," *East Europe*, vol. 7 (June 1958), p. 6.
26. Zinner, *Revolution in Hungary*, p. 213.
27. Kecskemeti, *Unexpected Revolution*, p. 75.
28. Kecskemeti, *Unexpected Revolution*, p. 77.
29. Zinner, *Revolution in Hungary*, p. 227.
30. Kecskemeti, *Unexpected Revolution*, p. 84.
31. Vali, *Rift*, p. 269.
32. Vali, *Rift*, p. 274.
33. Vali, *Rift*, p. 292.
34. Vali, *Rift*, p. 310.
35. Vali, *Rift*, p. 307.
36. Vali, *Rift*, p. 314.
37. Vali, *Rift*, p. 315.
38. Vali, *Rift*, p. 72fn.
39. Vali, *Rift*, p. 275.
40. Vali, *Rift*, p. 277.
41. Vali, *Rift*, p. 276.
42. Vali, *Rift*, p. 329.
43. Kiraly, "Hungary's Army," pp. 7–8.
44. Vali, *Rift*, pp. 278–279.
45. Vali, *Rift*, pp. 278–279; for the struggle against the Russians, see James Michener, *The Bridge at Andau* (New York: Fawcett, 1978); Melvin J. Lasky, *The Hungarian Revolution: A White Book* (New York: Arno, 1957), and many others.
46. Vali, *Rift*, p. 277.
47. See especially Zinner, *Revolution in Hungary*.
48. Kecskemeti, *Unexpected Revolution*, p. 114.
49. Vali, *Rift*, p. 293.
50. Vali, *Rift*, p. 335.
51. Vali, *Rift*, p. 283.
52. Vali, *Rift*, p. 287.
53. Vali, *Rift*, p. 288. [My italics.]
54. Vali, *Rift*, p. 303.
55. Zinner, *Revolution in Hungary*, p. 288.
56. Kecskemeti, *Unexpected Revolution*, p. 112.
57. Vali, *Rift*, p. 365.
58. *The New Leader*, November 19, 1956.
59. For example, Vali, *Rift*, p. 365.
60. Vali, *Rift*, p. 376.
61. Dwight D. Eisenhower, *The White House Years: Waging Peace* (Garden City, NY: Doubleday, 1965), pp. 88–89.

4

The Fall of the Shah: Iran 1978

Nothing is more dangerous than to introduce a new order of things.
— Machiavelli

In January 1978, the shah of Iran appeared to be one of the most powerful rulers in the world. One year later, his regime had disappeared. Both in terms of its consequences for world politics, and of the valuable lessons it offers to students of revolution, the fall of the shah is one of the major events of the last fifty years.

The Iranian revolution, which brought to an end one of the very last of the globe's real monarchies, took place in circumstances that would normally seem unpropitious. "According to the political laws of the twentieth century, an authoritarian system was not supposed to succumb to civilian revolution short of a lost war with foreign powers."[1] Further, Iran offers another telling example, to anyone who still needs one, of the primacy of politics over economics. In the eyes of critics of the United States in Iran, American economic penetration of that country, above all in the key areas of oil and arms, amounted to what was often described as a "stranglehold." How easily that stranglehold was cast off by a political upheaval! Many observers interpreted the Iranian upheaval as the result of an Islamic resurgence, a harbinger of an international revolt of religious fundamentalists against modernization and Westernization that would shake the entire system of world political and economic relations. Finally, the Iranian revolution was to have a major impact on the prestige of the United States. America's allies all over the world — Morocco, Saudi Arabia, Israel, even the West Germans who had long feared an American "disengagement" — watched attentively as the United States let its primary ally in the Middle East (after Israel) slip into chaos. What kind of assistance could these allies count on if and when they found themselves in crisis? The overthrow of the shah was perhaps on a par with the debacle in Vietnam in suggesting to American allies and enemies throughout the world that the United States was a power in decline.

The accumulating problems of the shah of Iran, which eventually caused the crisis of his regime, included the question of his legitimacy, economic difficulties, the attitude of the U.S. government, and the hostility of key religious leaders. These factors interpenetrated and aggravated each until the ultimate cause of the fall of the regime could become operative: the failure to identify and pursue a coherent and appropriate strategy of physical defense of the government against its overt enemies.

THE PROBLEM OF LEGITIMACY

Political legitimacy means that those who live under the authority of a given government view that government's authority as rightful. Illegitimate governments extract obedience by force; legitimate governments receive obedience by choice. It is much cheaper, and much safer, from the government's point of view, to rule over subjects who consider it legitimate. Governments are normally so considered when the leaders have come to power through processes widely held to be correct. These processes vary from society to society and from era to era, and include inheritance, divine appointment, election, and other forms. Governments may also be seen as legitimate if their policies and style of ruling are congruent with the value systems of their subjects. Another important source of legitimacy for a government is the fact or belief that it has been in existence for a very long time.

Contemporary Iran, like almost all countries in the Third World (and not only those) was very inhospitable terrain for the growth of political legitimacy. Iran has large linguistic and ethnic minorities, jealous of their rights and suspicious of any central government. The country's numerous tribal nomads have for centuries looked upon the government, any government, as an alien and hostile force interested only in imposing conscription and taxation. And unlike most Muslim countries, Iran adheres overwhelmingly to the Sh'ia tradition, which through the centuries "has given only a grudging recognition to the legitimacy of any secular king."[2]

These structural–historical aspects of Iranian society boded ill for any government. The regime of the shah suffered additionally from being new. The Pahlavi dynasty, in fact, had produced by the time of the revolution only two rulers: both had been born commoners, and both died in exile. The founder of the dynasty had been Reza Pahlavi, an army officer and former prime minister and minister of war. After crushing a Bolshevik-inspired revolt in the north, Reza marched with his victorious army into Tehran; Parliament elected him shah in December 1925. Believed to be pro-German, Reza Shah Pahlavi was removed from his throne by an Anglo–Soviet invasion in 1941; he died in South Africa three years later.

He was succeeded by his son Mohammed Reza, born in 1919. While still a young man, the new shah confronted a major crisis in the person of Mohammed Mossadegh. Born in 1881, educated in Switzerland, Mossadegh was the son of a wealthy landlord and a relative of the Qajar dynasty that had been deposed by Reza Pahlavi. Politically prominent in the 1920s, Mossadegh retired to private life in protest against the coronation of Reza. When the British and the Russians removed Reza in 1941, Mossadegh returned to active politics and soon acquired a reputation as a nationalist. Wily, with a certain charisma, Mossadegh began to challenge the young shah over the alleged exploitation of Iran by British oil interests. This was a sensitive and popular issue at the time, and the shah felt compelled to appoint Mossadegh his prime minister. Mossadegh soon plunged the country into a protracted confrontation with the Anglo–Iranian Oil Company (and with the British government behind it). He did not foresee the difficulty his government would have in selling its nationalized oil on the world market; government revenues began to decline, and so did Mossadegh's popularity. Seeking new supporters, Mossadegh turned more and more to the Tudeh Party (the Iranian Communists); this caused a further erosion of his image among conservative and moderate nationalists. In August 1953, Mossadegh prepared rigged elections as a proximate step to a coup. The shah attempted to relieve him of his position, but mobs in Tehran forced the young monarch to flee the country. Before the month was out, however, huge counterdemonstrations forced Mossadegh's resignation, the shah returned, and Mossadegh went to jail.

It was no secret that the Eisenhower administration had become alarmed by Mossadegh's increasing reliance on the Tudeh and his plans to establish a dictatorship. The Central Intelligence Agency was active in August 1953, working with Mossadegh's enemies and the shah's friends, both in the army officer corps and in the streets of the capital. Thus the seed was planted for the myth that grew up later, a myth very damaging to the legitimacy of the shah, that he had been put back upon his throne through the efforts of the CIA and against the will of the Iranian people. Scholars have long discounted the real importance of CIA intervention in the events of 1953: "it would be misleading to conclude that the United States helped oust a popular nationalist government and replaced it with an unpopular and antinationalist one." Instead, "the CIA merely provided minimal financial and logistical aid" so that Iranians themselves could get rid of Mossadegh.[3] No matter what kind of foreign participation there may have been in Mossadegh's overthrow, he would certainly not have fallen "if significant elements of the population had not lost faith in his leadership."[4] Nevertheless, the connection between the shah and American interference would come to dominate many Iranian minds as Iran's dependence upon American technology and arms became ever greater. Iranian sensitivity increased with the number of Americans living and working in the country; by 1978, there were 47,000 Americans in Iran and 53,000 other foreigners. All these streams of discontent would one day come together in a flood of xenophobic nationalism, inundating the monarchy and sweeping over the entire strategic Middle East landscape.

THE ECONOMY

Many students of revolution have identified rapid economic change, including economic development, as a long-term cause of revolution. All major economic changes, including the kind that economists consider positive, are destabilizing: real economic growth and technological innovation are always damaging or threatening to at least some groups in a society. Iran was no exception. The decade between 1963 and 1973 was characterized by great economic growth and relatively low inflation (along with progress in education, health, women's rights, and land reform). But the *Bazaaris*, the socially influential merchants of Tehran and other cities, resented many of the changes that economic advance entailed; for instance, the shah's modern banking system charged a much lower rate of interest than did the Bazaaris, and for this and similar reasons their opposition to the shah took root and grew. After 1973, great quantities of money poured into Iran because of the enormous increase in oil prices, convincing the shah to embark upon a crash program of industrialization. He also greatly increased the purchase of sophisticated U.S. military hardware. Partly as a result of these policies and partly because of a neglect of the agricultural sector, food and housing prices began to rise. Soon Iranian society was afflicted with a serious and increasing rate of inflation, always a politically destabilizing factor. By the end of the 1970s, many Iranians, especially of the urban middle class, had become deeply disillusioned with the shah; great expectations aroused by the oil bonanza had become in actuality a higher and higher cost of living, with real shortages of housing, especially in the capital city. Because the shah had concentrated power increasingly in his own hands and had taken all the credit when things were going well, there was no way for him to avoid being left holding the bag when the slump and its consequent frustrations occurred. Nor were things improved by sensational revelations of financial peculation even within the shah's own family.

THE UNITED STATES AND THE SHAH

Throughout the latter half of the nineteenth century and up to World War I, Iran had been a bone of contention between the Russian and British empires. During World War II, Iran began to look to the United States to protect it from British and Russian imperialism; the Roosevelt administration had come to view Iran as a testing ground for the possibility of East–West cooperation after the war and the gradual implementation of democratic government in what today would be called Third World countries. After the end of the war, the country became the focus of Soviet ambitions; through secessionist movements backed by Russian occupation forces and fueled by the activities of the Tudeh party, Stalin clearly intended to detach Iran's northern provinces and set them up as an Iranian Soviet Republic, possibly as a prelude to the communization of the entire country. When Harry Truman succeeded to the presidency, he vigorously resisted Stalin's plans for Iran, taking the case to the United Nations. That body insisted that Soviet troops evacuate Iran (it was a different United Nations in those days). "Thus it was that Iran became the first battlefield of the Cold War."[5]

Eisenhower's intervention in Iran has already been mentioned, and more and more the Kennedy and Johnson administrations looked upon Iran as a major factor in their foreign policy calculations. The nation's growing oil wealth, the successes of the shah's reform programs (the "White Revolution"), and the shah's ability to maintain power despite internal and external challenges, all convinced Washington that Iran could play the role of a stabilizing anchor in the tempestuous Middle East, especially in the strategic Persian Gulf area. Finally, Iran became the centerpiece of the Nixon administration's strategy to contain Soviet expansionism around the periphery of the USSR by American allies rather than by American troops. The Peking government, for generally similar reasons, became a supporter of the shah during the 1970s.

By 1977, the shah of Iran had achieved the status, in the words of Henry Kissinger, of "a leader whom eight presidents of both parties proclaimed — rightly — a friend of our country and a pillar of stability in a turbulent and vital region."[6] Under the Pahlavis, Iran had resisted Soviet threats and had carried out significant programs in landholding, women's rights, and profit-sharing for workers; it had also effectively aided U.S. interests at the time of the 1973 Arab oil embargo. Thus, "Iran under the shah was, in short, one of America's best, most important, and most loyal friends in the world."[7]

Then Jimmy Carter became president. Things began to change. Carter proclaimed a whole new approach to global realities and American interests, a foreign policy whose keynote would be human rights. At first this was rather naively understood to mean that Washington was going to pressure the Soviet Union to see that it complied at least minimally with the Helsinki Accords. Instead, Carter's human rights campaign meant that the United States would unilaterally reexamine its relationship with many of its oldest allies and, if their records on human rights did not measure up to its standard, discard them. The shah of Iran was soon found wanting in this area, and his long history of friendship toward and support of the United States, as well as his undeniable reform record, did not serve to protect him from human rights zealots in Washington. Some in the Carter administration did not like the shah, and did not want to help him even when his regime was in crisis, no matter what the consequences might be for the Iranian people or the U.S. position in the Middle East and in the world in general. These advisers looked upon aid to the shah as a betrayal of human rights, a consideration for which somehow overrode any and every other question. This viewpoint on foreign policy was unique in the history of the United States and probably of any other country.

Principally, the shah failed to measure up to the new standards proclaimed by the Carter administration in his treatment of internal opposition forces, specifically in the activities of the Iranian secret police, Savak. Certainly Savak engaged in some morally deplorable and politically stupid practices, but the organization apparently never exceeded 3,000 full-time employees in a nation of more than 28 million people. Scholars agree that the number of victims of Savak has been greatly exaggerated, both before and after the revolution,[8] and that the brutality of the secret police was much overplayed by the U.S. media and the shah's domestic enemies.[9] The government of the shah would not have received very high grades from the authors of the *Federalist* papers, but neither would those of most members of the United Nations. The Iran of the shah had its shortcomings, some of which could have and should have been cleaned up rather easily by an alert and politically astute regime. But overall, "while this was an authoritarian state, it was not totalitarian,"[10] and its human rights record could have stood in comparison with that of a great majority of Third World or Eastern Bloc states and *especially with that of the regime that came after it.* During 1976 and 1977, to refurbish his image in this area, the shah invited representatives of the International Red Cross, Amnesty International, and the International Commission of Jurists to visit his country and report to the world what they saw.[11] Nevertheless, the image of the shah's regime as one totally dependent on a savagely cruel secret police persisted and increased in importance. Everything now began to go wrong for the government. For instance, Muslim fundamentalists had begun setting fire to movie houses that showed "sinful" films; on August 20, 1978, such a theater fire killed 377 persons in Tehran. The shah's enemies in Iran and Washington maintained, without evidence, that this outrage was actually the work of Savak, and the accusation was widely publicized and widely believed.

In fact, the shah had numerous enemies, unfortunately for him, they were not of the stripe that could be placated with human rights reforms, no matter how extensive.

Among the shah's opponents were armed guerrillas. Elements among them had been given training in Cuba as early as 1965.[12] The failure of the different guerrilla movements to take hold was registered by their turning to "urban" guerrilla warfare in the 1970s. In 1975 and 1976, they managed to murder two U.S. Air Force colonels, three American civilians working for Rockwell on a communications project, and many others.[13] Some observers insist that there was, in addition, a well-organized international terrorist movement in the country dedicated to the shah's overthrow, and that these terrorists received support from Libya, Cuba, Syria, and the PLO.[14]

Besides guerrillas and terrorists, much of the country's student population was opposed to the shah. This was both ironic and unfortunate, because owing to economic development and educational reforms under the shah, the

Iranian student population had increased eightfold between 1963 and 1978.[15]

Student opposition to the shah was nothing that should have surprised or even particularly disturbed sophisticated American observers. In underdeveloped countries, student opposition has little to do with the kind of government the society has and the kind of policies it pursues. Student criticism of the regime, any regime, is abstract, utopian, diffuse, and often inconsistent; hence, *"student opposition can only marginally be influenced by reforms or ameliorative government action."* [italics added][16] The causes of this interesting phenomenon are not entirely clear, nor need the search for them detain us here; what is of interest is one distinguished scholar's tart conclusion that, given the implacable nature of this kind of opposition, "the appropriate response to middle-class [student] radicalism is repression, not reform."[17]

Such prescriptions were, of course, utterly alien, even incomprehensible, in the atmosphere of the Carter White House. The administration wanted the shah to inaugurate human rights reforms, and a confused shah uneasily attempted to comply.

Keen observers of politics, such as Machiavelli and de Tocqueville, have observed that the most dangerous time for the stability of any authoritarian regime is when it embarks on a period of liberalization. It was into just such a phase that, in response to Carter's human rights campaign, the shah's government entered. It introduced profound changes, including relaxation of press censorship, permission for exiles to return, and a move toward free elections. Eventually Savak and police officials, and even high army officers, would be put on trial by the shah's regime on charges of corruption and/or brutality. It was all to no avail. Not only did the shah's reforms fail to quiet or even temporarily appease his middle-class opponents, they gravely worsened the political situation. Freedom of the press allowed the reporting of exaggerated instances of death and destruction and the hurling of every conceivable accusation against the regime; tales of torture filled the pages of almost every newspaper and seriously discredited the shah. Among the returning exiles were many who had been or would become guerrillas and who would soon join or even organize massive demonstrations against the government.[18] The shah's promise of free elections in the near future merely convinced his enemies that they had him on the run.[19] The entire effort to pacify the middle-class critics of the regime failed; the shah's radical enemies were not only not appeased, they were aroused to more and more vociferous demands, including finally the demand that the shah abdicate. Of course, the increased turmoil resulting from the shah's efforts to liberalize his regime provided more grist for the mill of his Washington critics, who ascribed all the troubles in Iran to the shah's massive and incorrigible violations of human rights.

But the supreme irony of the situation lies in this, that even if the shah's gestures and concessions to the middle class had borne fruit, it probably could not have saved his throne, for in fact, "the growing middle class at the centre of modern Iranian society was least involved in the revolutionary movement and the last to join the rush to topple the shah."[20] It was not the shah's violation of human rights that provoked the vast popular demonstrations that finally brought his downfall; rather, it was the rapid pace of forced modernization, which ignored or even contemptuously attacked traditional society and thus challenged the values by which millions of humble Iranians lived, that brought on the crisis of the regime. The truly dangerous and implacable foes of the shah and his system could not have been less concerned with such things as freedom of speech, of the press, of religion; on the contrary, such ideas were to them symbols of degeneration, the perversion of traditional Muslim Iranian society by the encroaching, relativist, disintegrative values of the licentious West. The true generators, the true victors, of the Iranian revolution were the *ulema* — Muslim teachers learned in the Qu'ran and the Shari'a. These religious leaders constituted a clergy powerful among the people and opposed to the shah.

THE CLERGY AGAINST THE KING

The Islamic clergy had many reasons for their deep and increasing hostility toward the shah. He was committed to the modernization of Iran, and to him this included freedom of religion and the consequent duty of the state to protect law-abiding religious minorities from persecution by the majority. In practice, this meant that the shah was seen as the protector of Jews (despised by the clergy) and the Bahai sect (an heretical offshoot of Islam and even more despised). What the Islamic clergy wanted to do to the Bahais would become all too evident after the shah's fall; until that time they seethed with resentment at his toleration of the religious groups they detested.

Many of the clergy hated the shah because of his land reform program, which often meant transferring to peasants lands that had once supported clerical societies and the works of religion. As early as the fall of 1962, clergymen, including the soon-to-be-famous Ayatollah Khomeini, led bloody demonstrations against the "impious" policy of land reform, demonstrations that resulted in the deaths of several religious scholars in the holy city of Qom.

Even more important as an offense to the clergy was the shah's policy of emancipation of women. In a traditional Muslim society, females occupy a social position that is difficult to distinguish from that of indentured servants. The shah extended elementary education to girls, and women were encouraged to attend universities, enter the professions, and appear in public with their faces uncovered. In the eyes of the clergy, this uprooting of women from their protected and proper place in Muslim society, and the promiscuous intermingling of the sexes with the volcanic consequences that had to follow, spelled the total demoralization of society and the destruction of Iranian civilization.

The shah was not unaware of the growing antagonism of the religious leaders to his policies and his person, a problem of no minor dimensions, because there were 180,000 *mullahs* (clerics) in the country, one for every 200 Iranians. He might well have sought to placate the clergy or at least segments of it. Indeed, a step was taken in this direction, in the form of government stipends to clerics, but this alone was not enough to counterbalance all the other irritants. He might have tried to set up a monarchist faction within the clergy, or even to encourage a major schism; he might have sought to take total control of the clergy by making them completely dependent on the state for their income and by concentrating in government hands the selection of key religious leaders. Or he might have undertaken to cow the mullahs completely by giving them dramatic proofs of the high and certain costs of opposition to the regime. In fact, the shah adopted none of these policies, choosing instead the worst of all possible courses: continuing to offer provocations to the religious leaders without depriving them of the ability to attack and undermine his regime. Machiavelli writes that enemies are either to be caressed or annihilated, but, in this instance as in others, the shah neglected the study of Machiavelli, to his great loss and that of many of his countrymen. In 1976, the shah further antagonized the clergy when he decreed the replacement of the Islamic calendar with the monarchical (pre-Islamic) calendar. In 1977 came the unkindest cut of all: the government discontinued subsidies to the clergy. The long-smoldering malevolence of the clerics was close to the flame point.

True enough, in neighboring Turkey during the 1920s and 1930s, the reforming dictator Kemal Ataturk had taken on the Islamic establishment, deliberately provoking in every conceivable way (including policies later enacted in Iran) a religious reaction. Indeed, unlike the shah, who was a devout Muslim, Ataturk made no secret of his detestation of Islam, which he viewed as the principal cause of ignorance, poverty, and weakness in his country. In the end, Kemal crushed by force of arms all religiously inspired attempts to overthrow him. But Ataturk's situation was different from the shah's in crucial ways. Kemal was an authentic national hero, the victor of Gallipoli and the only Turkish commander to emerge victorious from the calamity of World War I. The shah, in contrast, far from being a national hero, exuded for many the faint but unmistakable aroma of dependence on infidel foreigners. Ataturk ruled over a country in which the hold of religion on great strata of the masses had grown weak. In the shah's Iran, however, Islam was not only still deeply imbedded in the popular conscience, it was growing stronger, especially in the capital city (for reasons presented in the following paragraphs). Moreover, the Islam of Turkey was of the mainstream, or Sunni variety, whereas Iranian Muslims are mostly Shiites. If mainstream Islam may be described as generally displaying a relatively tolerant catholicity, Shiite Islam is distinguished by a remarkable intolerance and is especially inclined to be judgmental and rebellious toward unjust political authority (and this usually has meant *any* political authority). Shiite extremism was more than theoretical: Iranian zealots had assassinated Prime Minister General Razmara in 1951 and Prime Minister Hassan Ali Mansur in 1965 (out of Shiite Islam had evolved the order of the *Assassins*, from the Arabic for "under the influence of hashish") and had carried out at least two attempts on the life of the shah himself.[21]

Relations between the shah's government and the clergy reached a crisis in early January 1978, when a major newspaper printed a slanderous attack on the prominent cleric, Ayatollah Khomeini. Resentment in devout circles knew no bounds, especially in Qom, a holy city, completely isolated from the flood of modernization sweeping across Iran, a city without theaters, bars, alcohol stores, or luxury shops, a city of veiled women and intense young seminarians.[22] In this heated atmosphere, a violent demonstration against the government, stirred by the press attack, resulted in the deaths of 70 people, including several apprentice clergy.

No one knew it at the time, but the events at Qom signaled the end for the shah.

Who was this Ayatollah Khomeini, around whom the final, mortal struggle between government and clergy was to rage? Born in central Iran in 1902, Khomeini was the product of a long line of Shiite religious leaders. As early as 1941, he had written a book attacking Reza Shah for his land reforms and views on women's rights. Khomeini had since then written many other works, most of them bitterly attacking the monarchy and expressing his hatred for Jews, Bahais, Christians, and Americans, proclaiming "We want a ruler who would cut off the hands of his son if he steals, and would flog and stone his near relative if he fornicates."[23] Such were the delicate sentiments of the man whom Andrew Young, President Carter's ambassador to the United Nations, called "a saint." So extreme indeed was Khomeini that many of his fellow clergymen viewed him with distaste, but the crude newspaper attack (permitted if not instigated by the government) rallied all the mullahs to his defense and turned him almost overnight into *the* symbol of religious resistance to all the hateful Westernizing and secularizing trends embodied by the shah.

From exile, Khomeini sent into Iran tapes of volatile sermons that were played by his devoted and increasingly numerous followers at mosques and other public places. The Khomeini tapes were supposed to be religious sermons, but were actually incitations to rebellion against the shah, the enemy of true religion, and his infidel American backers. If the shah's government had made a big mistake in permitting Khomeini to be the object of an inflammatory press assault, it made another even more important one in October 1978: Khomeini sought the permission of the French government to go to

Paris and establish a headquarters, and the Iranian government failed to object. This was a key error, because the excellent Parisian communications system provided direct links to Tehran, and now hundreds of thousands of people could actually see with their own eyes the austere visage of the man who previously had been only a disembodied voice on a radio or cassette player.

The greatly augmented ability of Khomeini to communicate his ideas to the Iranians could hardly have come at a worse time for the shah's regime. Economic development had caused the population of the capital city to swell enormously: Tehran's 1956 population of 1.5 million had soared twenty years later to 4.5 million. Most of this increase was due to an influx of rural people, drawn by the lights and promises of the glittering and exciting capital. Like many such rural immigrants in other societies, tens of thousands of these disoriented newcomers turned for solace and direction to their clergymen, and by 1978 many of the mullahs were prepared to participate in a drastic anti-shah mobilization. A second development from which the clergy were able to profit was the too-rapid pace of change in Iran; the increasing numbers of high-living "foreign infidels," especially Americans, helped produce a "resurgence of traditional Iranian chauvinism towards foreign influence, which the Shah and his reform came to symbolize."[24] Khomeini, with his Islamic fundamentalism, xenophobia, and populism, had a proto-ideology perfectly suited to attract the lower classes of teeming Tehran, who were both uprooted from their familiar if austere way of life and confronted daily by foreign and secular influences that scandalized and frightened them.

Early in 1978, it became apparent that Khomeini was able to mobilize by the tens of thousands Iranians who would not only demonstrate on the streets for him and against the shah, but who were in many instances quite willing to risk their lives for the cause—the abdication of the shah—of which Khomeini was fast becoming the embodiment. Khomeini's ability to call out larger and larger demonstrations was decisive to the Iranian revolution, because it eventually triggered a decision:

> the calculated decision by the key sectors of the Iranian labor force (government employees and oil industry workers) that he was the likely winner of a power struggle; therefore attaching themselves to his Islamic banner. Opportunism played no small part in the overthrow of the shah.[25]

But an essential piece of the puzzle is still missing. If "key sectors of the Iranian labor force" went over to Khomeini's side because they thought he was going to be the winner, why did the government permit Khomeini to appear in this guise? Why, that is, did the government of the shah fail to repress the demonstrations of Khomeini's followers (Khomeini himself of course remained in Paris until the fighting was over), preferably before they had gotten too big, but in any event before they resulted in the collapse of the regime?

Where, in other words, was the repressive apparatus of this regime that existed, so it was endlessly repeated in some quarters, solely by repression?

THE ARMY AGAINST THE REVOLUTION

The rioting by student clerics at Qom triggered massive demonstrations in other cities. At Tabriz, for example, on February 18 and 19, hundreds were killed or wounded. The size and violence of these outpourings rendered them completely beyond the control of the police; therefore, Iranian army troops quickly became involved in the crescendo of confrontation. Tanks appeared in the streets of Tehran on May 11.

What of this army, on which so much money had been lavished, whose high cost had become one of the issues with which the shah's critics belabored him, and on which now depended the fate of the government?

In 1977, the army consisted of 220,000 officers and men, with another 130,000 in the other services. The officer corps was, for the most part, quite loyal to the shah, and enjoyed a high standard of living with good salaries and many perquisites. But in the ranks below the well-paid officers, things were not good.

In the first place, this army had never fought a war. True, in the mid-1970s some elite units had seen action in Oman, but this episode served mainly to expose disturbing deficiencies: a poor system of communication, a rigid bureaucratic mentality throughout the command structure, and most of all, a wide gulf of misunderstanding between officers and men. And most of the troops had not had the benefit of even this limited and ominous experience.

Now, any type of army would have been hard-pressed to contain the religiously intoxicated rioters swarming through the streets under the direction of their holy men. The type of forces best suited to that kind of responsibility would have been relatively small and homogeneous, professional and cohesive, long-enlisted and well-paid, recruited heavily from among Iran's ethnic and religious minorities, and above all, carefully isolated from civilian, especially urban, society. The army of the shah was not anything like this. Between 1972 and 1977, the army had expanded by more than half, a much too rapid growth rate in light of the kind of challenge it now had to confront. Far too many of the troops were short-termers, peasants and poor urban workers, from the very civilian elements that were becoming restless under the shah's enforced modernization and that were most subject to manipulation by the mullahs. Draftees from village and campus made up 20 percent of the entire army; in the infantry, however the branch most likely to confront demonstrators, *conscripts amounted to 40 and 50 percent*.[26] The holy men skillfully exploited the religious susceptibilities of the draftees, constantly urging them to desert the shah and join the side of God.[27] These appeals could not, especially over the long run, fail to have an effect; hence, the regime's increasing reliance upon the army was bound to become more and more perilous and self-defeating.

The situation in Tehran was especially desperate, owing to the great numbers of peasant immigrants easily aroused to religious frenzy by the clerics. This urban *lumpenproletariat* of young males without families (often, in the early riots, paid by the Bazaaris, who had their own reasons for wanting to see the shah destroyed) provided the cannon fodder for the campaign of the holy men against the government.[28] Foreign observers often recorded that these mullah-led mobs faced the shah's troops fearlessly, almost as if inviting death[29]; the *Economist* noted a peculiar insouciance, even "gaiety," in the face of violent death, an attitude that severely limited the army's effectiveness.[30]

The soldiers were on the streets for months, listening to the chanting and praying and cursing of the mob, the Friday sermons blaring from mosque loudspeakers, and the inescapable voice of Khomeini on radio and cassette tape. There was no let-up in the furious clerical campaign to topple the regime. If these soldiers had possessed proper riot-control equipment, effective but nonlethal, the loss of life during the last months of 1978 would have been greatly reduced and the draftees would have felt much better about having to confront civilians. But, partly as a result of the Carter administration's emphasis on human rights, such equipment was denied to countries like Iran, and the troops consequently had to rely almost exclusively on lethal firepower to contain the mobs and protect themselves. On September 8, 1978, "Black Friday" as it was later called, a particularly horrendous riot shook Tehran and took the lives of perhaps 700 persons. Khomeini and his associates proclaimed that the soldiers who had done the firing were Israelis and Iranian Jews.[31] After Black Friday, the number of incidents in which junior officers disobeyed orders or in which soldiers joined the crowds or even shot their own officers, increased at an alarming rate. On December 11, at the height of a particularly passionate celebration of a holy day, mutinous troops of the Imperial Guard, widely believed to be the most politically reliable unit in the entire country, killed 12 of their own officers.

Only a miracle could save the tottering regime now.

VACILLATION AND DESTRUCTION

The structural weaknesses of the Iranian army notwithstanding, it was undoubtedly powerful enough to crush the civil disturbances in the first half of 1978.[32] Possibly even as late as October of that year, vigorous and skillful repression would have restored stability and given the regime a breathing space to plan some serious moves. But the shah used his army with neither vigor nor skill. What Iranians witnessed instead was "an ineffectual response from the throne" to the activities of its sworn enemies that merely helped "to create contempt for the shah's authority."[33] According to one study of the revolution:

> sometime during the summer or fall of 1978, Mohammed Reza disengaged from the conflict—resolved that he would not permit mass bloodshed; that, whatever happened, he would not go down in history as the perpetrator of a conflict that might well become a civil war—and awaited the inevitable outcome.[34]

Some have ascribed the shah's unwillingness to fight a prolonged civil war with his enemies for the security of his throne and the destiny of his nation to the fact that he was taking anti-cancer drugs that sapped his physical and moral vitality. There is undoubtedly truth in this: the shah was, in the fall of 1978, a dying man. But it would be overly cynical to emphasize this aspect and to discount completely the shah's reluctance to hold onto his power by means of a vast blood bath.

> The shah was no bloodthirsty villain. He genuinely felt responsibility as a symbol of the national identity and, in his own words, as head of the Iranian family. His reign had been based on a nationalistic goal of building Iran into a mighty and respected nation. Such sentiments forbade him from setting off a public bloodbath in his own country, among his own people; he did not want to be regarded in the world's eyes as another Idi Amin.[35]

Or, in the shah's words, "A sovereign cannot save his throne by spilling the blood of his own countrymen.[36] Thus, the army was forced to assume a defensive stance, and slowly crumbled.

Apart from the illness that consumed him and the scruples that inhibited him, the shah's inability to choose finally between repression and surrender reflected his difficulty in making sense out of the signals sent from the Carter administration. Would Washington help its stricken ally or not? As late as December 1978, when questioned about the prospects of the shah's survival, President Carter responded with "I don't know." Later during that month, the lack of clear policy was symbolized by the affair of the U.S.S. *Constellation*, which the White House first ordered from Subic Bay to the Persian Gulf and then ordered back again.

Carter administration actions, and lack of action, all during the year 1978, which so confused and troubled the shah (and many other American allies) resulted in part from lack of good American intelligence on the real seriousness of the challenge faced by the shah and the true nature of his enemies. The U.S. intelligence apparatus, still reeling from the domestic political attacks on it of the mid-1970s, understood neither the strength and anti-Americanism of the shah's enemies nor the seriousness of his illness until very nearly the end. Both French and Israeli intelligence had a much better appreciation of the shah's weaknesses, political and physical, and passed this on to Washington, but the Americans at the top level dismissed it.

The failure of the administration to heed foreign warnings about the nature of the Iranian crisis stemmed in part from the crowded agenda it had been facing: Israeli–Egyptian peace plans, Salt II, the Panama Canal, relations with Peking, and other problems. But the inability of the Carter White House to make or stick to a definite policy toward the shah's government also flowed out of the deep differences between Secretary of State Cyrus Vance and National Security Advisor Zbigniew Brzezinski. The latter had a simple and clear analysis of the Iranian situation: the shah was America's ally, and must therefore be supported by word and deed. Even if America could not save his regime, even if the shah was really going to go down, it would be much better from the point of view of the effect on her other allies for America to be seen going down with him rather than abandoning him. Secretary of State Vance took an entirely different approach. He had never cared for the shah and believed that the United States could make a deal with the revolutionaries who would succeed him. Thus, on November 19, when Leonid Brezhnev issued a menacing order to the United States to stay out of Iranian troubles, Vance replied with a lawyer's platitudes. "Foreign observers were entitled to conclude that the United States had left the shah to his fate."[37]

The State Department also encouraged Iranian military commanders to establish or keep open contacts with the mullahs.[38] But the army had sworn its oath to the person of the shah; for many years he had exercised effective control over it, and numerous officers, especially in higher ranks, felt a real personal loyalty to and personal dependence on the monarch. Any settlement between the Americans and the mullahs that did away with the shah would mean the disintegration of the army, for there would be no one with enough prestige to hold it together. Officers who foresaw this denouement tried to accommodate themselves to it — another reason why the attempts of the shah to maintain order through the army failed.

Whatever the reasons for the shah's lack of vigorous leadership — his deteriorating health, his concern for the lives of his countrymen and his own historical image, his dismay at America's failure to stand by him — this absence of firm guidance severely disoriented the army. The shah made it clear enough to his military commanders that he wanted them to restore order, but they very quickly perceived that he considered large-scale shedding of blood out of the question. Under these circumstances, the unit commanders never knew exactly what to do; this was "martial law without martial law." They therefore permitted the riots and demonstrations to come to them — rather, to the soldiers under their command. So far from leading to a minimization of conflict, the army's passivity and restraint emboldened the mullahs and their more exalted followers to push the soldiers harder and harder.

However the blame ought to be apportioned, there is no doubt that the government's failure to produce an energetic and sustained response to escalating mob violence fatally undermined it. The long months of confrontation with clergy-led demonstrations thoroughly destroyed the morale of many enlisted men and not a few officers. The continuing and much-dramatized reports of bloody confrontations between urban mobs and royal troops played directly into the hands of the shah's enemies at home and in Washington. Finally, only after they had become convinced that the government was not going to use its repressive power to the full did the moderate oppositionists join with Khomeini in his extreme demands: the abdication of the shah and the establishment of an Islamic theocracy.

One might recall the words of Crane Brinton about a somewhat similar situation:

> The Russian ruling classes, in spite of their celebrated Asiatic background, were by the late nineteenth century more than half ashamed to use force, and therefore used it badly, so that on the whole those on whom force was inflicted were stimulated rather than repressed.[39]

As his last card, the shah appointed a military cabinet on November 6, 1978. Some observers maintain that if a vigorous military government had come to power in September, all might yet have been saved.[40] The anti-shah forces had all been fairly well unified under Khomeini by mid-October, however, and now the riots were really too big for the army to handle effectively. Neither could the army deal with the strikes, which had become massive; the military did not have the capacity to run the country's power, transport, and communications systems, nor the oil industry, which had been largely shut down by strikes organized by the Tudeh Party (the Tudeh had been active in the oil fields of the south for many years). In addition, the cabinet appointed under General Gholam Reza Azhari conducted itself in the most bureaucratic manner imaginable, merely carrying out the vague directives of the now-despairing shah. Very little was done to quell or even contain the riots.

It quickly became obvious to everyone that the military solution was no solution at all, and there was nothing left for the shah to do but appoint an opposition cabinet. This was finally done on December 29, 1978, with the nomination as prime minister of a long-time opposition politico, Shahpour Bakhtiar. It was supposed to be Bakhtiar's role to effect a last-hour compromise between the monarchy and the rioters, but it was too late for compromise. Bakhtiar had come into office with no support whatever from either the Khomeini forces or the army and was able to build none. He was the Iranian Kerensky, with an administration even briefer and more ineffective than the original Russian model.

A few days after the Bakhtiar appointment, the deputy commander of NATO, U.S. Air Force General Robert Huyser, arrived in Tehran. Huyser, without informing the shah, told the Iranian army generals that Washington did not want them to stage a coup but rather to support Bakhtiar. Everyone in Tehran knew that the Bakhtiar government had absolutely no chance of doing anything and assumed that Washington must know it too. The generals therefore interpreted Huyser's words as meaning: let the disintegration of the country continue.[41] They began to be truly afraid, not for the monarchy, which was obviously doomed, but for the army, the existence of the officer corps, and indeed for their very lives. Like almost all of the Carter administration policy toward Iran, the Huyser mission was to have gravely negative consequences for the shah and for the United States, because

> it pushed the United States into a position in which it had no support from any segment of Iranian society. General Huyser helped to weaken the shah while not capitalizing on his abandonment to improve ties with the opposition. Thus, when the opposition [Khomeini] took power, it was not widely recognized that American policy had both hastened the fall of the shah and prevented the bloodshed which would have accompanied a military coup.[42]

The end now came quickly. On January 9, 1979, President Carter announced that the shah ought to leave Iran; a week later, the shah arrived in Cairo. Khomeini returned to Iran on February 1; the day before, the U.S. Embassy ordered all American dependents to leave Iran. A few days later, Bakhtiar resigned as prime minister, and the army withdrew from Tehran. In time, all of Iran's generals but five (one who went over to Khomeini and four who managed to escape to the West) were killed, along with many other officers and civil servants.

Therefore, the Iranian authoritarian tradition, from the Pahlavis to Mossadegh to Khomeini, lives on. None of those who made the revolution, and few who followed them, were the least interested in establishing democracy or concerned with human rights, as these terms were understood in Jimmy Carter's Washington. But those Americans who helped undermine the shah because they did not find him sensitive enough to human rights must assume at least some responsibility for the policies toward human rights of those who came after him.

NOTES

1. George Lenczowski, "The Arc of Crisis: Its Central Sector," *Foreign Affairs* 57 (Spring 1979): 802.
2. Lenczowski, "Arc of Crisis," 802.
3. Barry Rubin, *Paved with Good Intentions: The American Experience and Iran* (Harmondsworth: Penguin, 1980), p. 88.
4. Richard Cottam, *Nationalism in Iran* (Pittsburgh, PA: University of Pittsburgh Press, 1964), p. 229.
5. Rubin, *Paved with Good Intentions*, p. 29.
6. Henry Kissinger, *White House Years* (Boston: Little, Brown & Company 1979), p. 1258.
7. Kissinger, *White House Years*, p. 1262.
8. Rubin, *Paved with Good Intentions*, p. 176.
9. Lenczowski, "Arc of Crisis," 807; James A. Bill, "Iran and the Crisis of '78," *Foreign Affairs* 57 (Winter 1978–1979): 324.

10. Lenczowski, "Arc of Crisis," 803.
11. Rubin, *Paved with Good Intentions*, pp. 192–193.
12. Robert Graham, *Iran: The Illusion of Power* (New York: St. Martin's, 1980), p. 216.
13. Graham, *Iran: The Illusion*, p. 217.
14. Michael Ledeen and William Lewis, *Debacle: The American Failure in Iran* (New York: Knopf, 1981), p. 105ff. This book is indispensable for an understanding of the American role in the fall of the shah.
15. Graham, *Iran: The Illusion*, p. 214.
16. Samuel P. Huntington, *Political Order in Changing Societies* (New Haven, CT: Yale University Press, 1968), p. 369.
17. Huntington, *Political Order*, p. 373.
18. Graham, *Iran: The Illusion*, p. 237.
19. Graham, *Iran: The Illusion*, p. 250.
20. V. Petrossian, "Dilemmas of the Iranian Revolution," *World Today* 35 (January, 1980): 23.
21. Graham, *Iran: The Illusion*, p. 230.
22. Graham, *Iran: The Illusion*, p. 223.
23. Ledeen and Lewis, *Debacle*, pp. 106–107.
24. Graham, *Iran: The Illusion*, p. 251.
25. Graham, *Iran: The Illusion*, p. 250.
26. Rubin, *Paved with Good Intentions*, p. 226.
27. Jerrold D. Green, *Revolution in Iran: The Politics of Countermobilization* (New York: Praeger, 1982), pp. 119–120, 125–126.
28. Graham, *Iran: The Illusion*, pp. 226–227.
29. Graham, *Iran: The Illusion*, pp. 226–227.
30. *The Economist*, February 3, 1979, p. 36.
31. Green, *Revolution in Iran*, p. 98.
32. Roger Cooper, "Crisis in Iran," *World Today* 35 (February, 1979): 42.
33. Rubin, *Paved with Good Intentions*, p. 205.
34. Ledeen and Lewis, *Debacle*, p. 140.
35. Rubin, *Paved with Good Intentions*, p. 219.
36. *Now*, December 7–13, 1979, p. 33.
37. Ledeen and Lewis, *Debacle*, p. 164.
38. Ledeen and Lewis, *Debacle*, p. 167.
39. Crane Brinton, *Anatomy of Revolution* (New York: Vintage, 1965), p. 53.
40. Ledeen and Lewis, *Debacle*, chapter 5.
41. Green, *Revolution in Iran*, p. 136.
42. Green, *Revolution in Iran*, pp. 136–137.

PART

3

Armies Versus Professional Rebels

The Chinese, Cuban, and Nicaraguan civil wars are all examples of Samuel P. Huntington's "Eastern Model" of revolution: the government's regular armed forces confront territorially based guerrilla movements that slowly expand their activities into large-scale military operations. All of the defeated governments were long-time allies of the United States. All were opposed by revolutionary groups that played down their plans for social transformation and emphasized broad appeals to nationalism (China, Nicaragua) and constitutional restoration (Nicaragua, Cuba). Foreign intervention—Japanese in the case of China, American in Cuba and Nicaragua—played a vital role in the outcome. Above all, the defeated governments committed egregious errors both with regard to the disposition of their forces and to the relations between those forces and the civil population.

Despite these similarities, each of these examples of the Eastern Model displays an arresting peculiarity, quite aside from the obvious (but no less notable for that) differences in the magnitude of the societies in which these struggles took place.

It was out of China (and to a lesser degree Cuba) that the myth of the invincible guerrilla developed. Mao, indeed, perfected his theories of revolutionary guerrilla warfare during the 1930s and 1940s. Yet the Communists achieved their final victory only after years of hard fighting by large conventional armies against a government that was never fully in control of its own armed forces and whose prestige and power had been shattered by a calamitous Japanese invasion and occupation.

The triumph of the Cuban revolution, on the other hand, resulted not from the defeat of the Batista regime but rather from its collapse. Batista's army had neither the training nor the equipment for counterguerrilla operations, and its officers displayed a distaste for battle and a tendency to treachery. The conquering Castro commanded remarkably small forces, whom he led to victory after desultory fighting with few casualties.

The combat in Nicaragua, though bitter, was smale-scale. The Somoza regime had come to power before most of its subjects were born and commanded the best fighting force in Central America. The struggle might have gone on indefinitely to an unforeseeable conclusion if it had not been for a double intervention in favor of the rebels by the Carter White House.

5

Protracted Conflict in China

"In no country in the world have soldiers dominated politics so extensively and for so long as in China."[1] And in the first half of this century, no Chinese soldier-politician was more powerful than Chiang Kai-Shek. Supported by a large nationalist party and possessed of considerable military forces, Chiang was, in the 1930s, slowly but successfully pursuing the unification and modernization of his country. Japan then launched a full-scale invasion of China that smashed what Chiang had built and drove many into the arms of Mao's Communists, guaranteeing that the departure of the Japanese would unleash a civil war of massive proportions. Thereafter, Mao's military brilliance and Chiang's military blunders hurled China into a new era.

Contemporary Chinese politics begins with the Revolution of 1911. A major catalyst of this upheaval was the rapid and total defeat of Chinese forces in the Sino–Japanese War (1894 to 1895). The contrast between Japan, with her booming industries and modern armed forces, and China, economically backward and militarily feeble, astounded and humiliated a whole generation of young Chinese. They concluded that national salvation required new institutions and strong measures. Mounting discontent and confusion led to the unexpectedly easy overthrow of the decadent Manchu dynasty in 1911. Conservative elements predominated in this cautious revolution, and the presidency of the revolutionary republic passed into the hands of Yuan Shih-Kai, a distinguished conservative statesman and military reformer. Believing that centralized government was essential if China were ever to be able to defend herself against Japan and other foreign predators, Yuan sought to make himself emperor. History has proven Yuan's assumptions correct: republicanism failed resoundingly in China, opening the way to Communist dictatorship. But Yuan's imperial aspirations offended many and provoked a new rebellion, under the leadership of the remarkable Dr. Sun Yat-Sen. Born in 1866, educated at an Anglican college in Honolulu, and awarded a medical degree by a Hong Kong hospital, Dr. Sun devoted all his energies to revolutionary politics. He took a prominent role in the Revolution of 1911 and then opposed

Yuan's monarchism. Seeking a formula for republican stability, Sun developed his three principles of nationalism, socialism, and democracy, and in 1912 founded a party, the Kuomintang, to be a vehicle for the realization of these principles. Sun sought to establish a new republican regime, but its authority did not extend much beyond the area of Canton. The death of Yuan in 1916 inaugurated the era of warlord politics, in which provincial military governors exercised semisovereign powers in alliance with or in defiance of the central Peking government. A full decade after the overthrow of the old imperial dynasty, China had achieved neither unity nor order.

THE DEVELOPMENT OF THE KUOMINTANG

Sun Yat-Sen had been impressed with the courage and loyalty displayed by a young Japanese-trained officer named Chiang Kai-Shek and appointed him his military adviser. This was a major reason for Chiang's rise to prominence in the leadership of the Kuomintang. Another was his willingness and ability to be the principal liaison between the Sun regime and the Soviet government.[2] In August 1923, Chiang went to Moscow on a political–military mission that resulted in the Russians sending Michael Borodin to be a personal adviser to Sun and political consultant to the Kuomintang.

Russian policy toward China in those days was based on orthodox Marxist analysis: What China needed was unification and independence under the leadership of her bourgeoisie, not a proletarian revolution. To promote these ends (which were seen as serving the Russian interests against Japanese expansion) the Russians sent military advisers and equipment along with Borodin. The Kuomintang (KMT), for its part, had from earliest days adopted certain Bolshevik methods, including party cell organization, the political commissar system in the armed forces, and heavy political indoctrination of troops. After 1924, the KMT adopted the Leninist practice of democratic centralism (complete subordination of lower party organs to higher) and the doctrine of party dictatorship over the Chinese nation. The first KMT party congress, held at Canton in January 1924, also called for alliance with the Soviets, collaboration with the Chinese Communist party, and creation of a KMT base among peasants and workers.[3]

The KMT program of the early 1920s was both simple and gargantuan: to eliminate the warlords, to abolish the unequal treaties that foreign governments had long imposed on backward and divided China, and to modernize the country under the leadership of the educated and propertied classes.[4] To achieve these goals, the party from the beginning had sought to build its own armed forces. It established a military academy at Whampoa in June 1924. Sun Yat-Sen himself officially inaugurated the school, with Chiang Kai-Shek as director, Soviet General Vasily Blücher as chief of staff and a young man named Chou En-Lai as political commissar. The principal Chinese members of the faculty, including Chiang, were graduates of the Japanese military academy, Shikan Gakko. The initial corps of students consisted of 499 chosen from among 3,000 applicants. The original course of instruction consisted of six months' training, based on Leninist principles and stressing political indoctrination above all.[5] After his break with the Soviets, Chiang would turn to the German army for assistance and training, and the name of the Whampoa Academy would be changed to Central Military Academy. Nevertheless, the early graduates of the school were ever after known as the "Whampoa Clique," whose existence was greatly to complicate Chiang's post-1945 campaign against the Chinese Communists.

Highest KMT priority was elimination of warlord control over northern China. Warlord activities interfered with trade, undermined agriculture, and invited meddling by both the Japanese and the Russians. Hence, the long-planned Northern Expedition from the KMT base in Canton began in July 1926 under the leadership of Chiang himself (Sun had died in 1925). First Shanghai, then Nanking, and finally, in June 1928, Peking fell to Chiang's forces. In the midst of the anti-warlord expedition, Chiang chose to end his collaboration with the Communists and turned violently upon them. Hampered by orders from the Comintern in Moscow, orders that had more to do with the rivalry between Stalin and Trotsky than with conditions in China, the Chinese Communist party (CCP) was decimated by Chiang, its small but growing urban base completely uprooted.

The Northern Expedition and the suppression of the CCP resulted in what appeared to be the unification of China, but appearances were deceptive. Some warlords had been destroyed by the KMT, but others had been allowed to join it, with their adherents and armed followers. This expansion of the KMT through absorption of warlords, who usually had views and aims very different from that party, seriously diluted its cohesiveness and energy. Chiang was never to transcend the costs of his too-early and too-easy success. Choosing quick victory rather than slow but genuine consolidation, Chiang allowed the KMT and its armies to become too large and heterogeneous. Later events made it impossible for him to undertake a thorough housecleaning of the KMT, the serious weaknesses of which would become painfully clear years later when Chiang's forces came to grips with the smaller but compact and cohesive armies of Mao Tse-Tung.

CHIANG, THE COMMUNISTS, AND THE JAPANESE

Chiang had stopped short of the total elimination of the warlords because he wanted to marshal all of his available strength against the Chinese Communists. A protracted conflict between Chiang, with his capital at Nanking, and the northern warlords might also have provided too much of a temptation to the Japanese to intervene in strength. Chiang's determination to concentrate on the CCP as the most dangerous long-term enemy brought him success: In September 1931, KMT forces, with German military advisers and under Chiang's personal command, were on the verge of capturing the city of Jui-chin, capital of the "Chinese Soviet Republic." But the 1931 Japanese invasion of Manchuria totally upset Chiang's strategy.[6] After much hesitation, Chiang decided not to offer major resistance to the Japanese (who set up a remote and at that time lightly populated Manchuria as the puppet state of Man-chukuo) so that he would have time to modernize his armies and complete the elimination of the Communists. This decision to concentrate on building up internal cohesion before seriously challenging the Japanese — "the Japanese are sores on the Chinese body, but the Communists are germs within it" — was sound from the strategic and historical points of view. Its unpatriotic overtones, however, cost Chiang much support among intellectuals and younger KMT officers.

The KMT officially based itself upon the ideology of Sun Yat-Sen, whose ideas were to a large degree amorphous and unsophisticated. Neo-Confucian and fascistic concepts also contended for attention within the party. Chiang himself came more and more to identify foreigners as the root cause of almost all of China's ills, and eventually espoused the aim of a restoration of tradi-tional Chinese society based on Confucian social ethics. Thus, the very top leadership of the party lacked a vigorous and realistic analysis of China's condition; therefore, they could not create a plausible program for recon-struction and modernization. The KMT's gradual adoption of Confucian thought, along with its cavalier attitude toward democratic liberties, further alienated many intellectuals. (Even these intellectuals might have blinked at such faults if they had believed that the KMT was actually capable of resolv-ing China's desperate problems; but more and more they came to doubt any such capability.)

Neither did the KMT tackle the peasant problem in any systematic way. "The Kuomintang was the party of the bourgeoisie."[7] As such, it was only halfheartedly interested in addressing the rural question, and any tendencies toward radical experimentation ran headlong into the resolute opposition of the local gentry. But if the KMT's passive attitude toward rural reform is not hard to understand, it was nevertheless to prove extremely costly. To the skepticism of the intellectuals toward the KMT was added the apathy of the peasants, incalculable handicaps for a party committed to modernizing the country.

Nevertheless, in spite of all these serious problems and shortcomings, the KMT during this so-called Nanking Decade (1928–1937) was making meas-urable progress on several fronts. Its economic accomplishments were far from negligible, and included a centralized system of tax collections, an improved road network, efforts to increase grain production and control insects, and a rate of industrial expansion averaging more than 6 percent annually.[8] The

KMT strove to make education standardized, more extensive, and based on a single form of the language. There were real strides in the field of women's rights: the KMT outlawed concubinage, introduced divorce, and sought to protect the right of free choice in marriage. In summary:

> although today Nationalist China has become a synonym for corruption and ineptitude, to foreign observers at the time it was a truism that the provinces ruled by Nanking [the KMT] were the heart of an emerging, modern state which was attracting the loyalty of more and more Chinese.[9]

The policies of the KMT, with all their imperfections of conceptualization and application, would undoubtedly have borne impressive fruit if, after 1931, China had been able to enjoy a generation or even a decade of peace. But the Japanese invasion of 1937, aimed at the subjugation of China proper, swept all away.

The new Japanese war involved catastrophe for the KMT on several fronts. First, it drove the KMT government away from its home base in the coastal cities, thus accentuating within the party the influence of reactionary rural landlords. Second, it decimated the new army that Chiang had been painfully constructing. Third, it weakened the control of the central authorities over provincial military commanders, because the latter now had the option of allying with the Japanese or their puppets (remember that some of these provincial leaders were former warlords, only nominal converts to the KMT; for these reasons, in promoting officers, Chiang had to give great consideration not to their professional competence or even simple honesty but to their loyalty to him. This practice would have severe consequences for the KMT in their civil war with the Communists after the defeat of the Japanese). Finally, and most important, the Japanese invasion saved the beleaguered Communist party from almost certain extinction as a military force and provided it with an opportunity for expansion, which the party did not fail to grasp. When the Japanese war began, the CCP controlled 35,000 square miles (only 1 percent of the territory of China) with about 1.5 million persons. When the Japanese surrendered eight years later, Communist territory extended to 225,000 square miles and included 65 million subjects.[10]

THE CHINESE COMMUNISTS: A NEW MODEL OF REVOLUTION

In the early 1920s, the Chinese Communist party followed an impeccably orthodox Marxist line: the next stage of China's evolution was that of bourgeois national development, and thus the CCP must support the leadership of the KMT. After 1925, however, KMT rebuffs to the Communists, including assaults and arrests in several places, caused the CCP to reconsider this strategy. The irresistible attraction of the Leninist coup in St. Petersburg, the doubling of the Chinese proletariat between 1916 and 1922 (to 2 million) the impressive growth of the CCP itself (from 400 members in 1923 to 93,000 in 1927), the belief in the "hegemony of the proletariat" and a corresponding tendency to view the peasantry as cannon fodder — all these combined to turn the CCP to a Leninist strategy of urban insurrection. The disastrous failure of that strategy in 1927, followed by a similar catastrophe in 1930, discredited the Leninist line. Meanwhile, population increases in the countryside, combined with a decrease in the total area under cultivation, enormously stimulated peasant indebtedness and discontent. These factors united to bring to the fore in the CCP new leaders, principally Mao Tse-Tung, with an orientation toward a strategy of rural revolution. Ultimately, this new leadership would appeal successfully to growing numbers of peasants by offering them what they wanted: improvement in their material and social condition. In essence, the CCP would learn to offer to the peasant the KMT program, which the KMT had failed to put effectively into practice. Not only would Mao shift the locus of struggle in Chinese revolutionary politics from the city to the countryside; he would also redefine the importance of that struggle. In the strict Leninist view, the battle against imperialism in the colonialized periphery of the world (including China) was merely a stimulus to the "real" revolution in Europe. Mao elevated the fight of the Chinese Communists against the Japanese and the KMT to central historical importance, however, in effect proclaiming it the dress rehearsal for the global uprising of the world's backward societies.[11] Herein lay one of the principal roots of the Sino–Soviet rift that was to alter the shape of world politics in the 1960s and later.

Mao developed his countryside strategy because he had to. The classic Leninist model of the urban coup was no good for vast and overwhelmingly rural China. Moreover, the Communists had proven too weak to confront the armed power of Chiang and his KMT directly. The superiority of the weapons of any modern army and the long period of training necessary to master their effective use have often led rebels to guerrilla warfare. In China, that meant turning to the peasantry.

Mao soon came to believe that Chinese conditions were ideal for guerrilla action. The peasant was intensely concerned with his immediate environment. He could thus be convinced to fight to protect or to seize control of it. Guerrilla bands could also allow their peasant members to go home for sowing and harvesting without disrupting everything, as would have happened in a regular army. The vastness of the country, with poor communication over much of it, greatly hampered KMT counterguerrilla efforts; it also stimulated Mao to develop the concept of the *secure regional base*: a remote and sparsely populated area away from the fighting, useful both for development of a regular army and as a laboratory for political and social experimentation. Mao was creating what Samuel P. Huntington called the Eastern Model of revolution; in this scenario, revolutionary forces do not attempt to seize power at the center (as in the Leninist model) but instead establish themselves in a place relatively safe from government interference and then seek to spread out gradually from this base area, taking over one new province after another, until at last they isolate the government in its capital city.[12] This erection of an independent, self-sufficient, peasant-based "Soviet Republic" within and against the larger Chinese state represented a major deviation from earlier CCP strategy, not to speak of traditional Marxist teaching. Its viability depended in no small measure on *the government's incapacity to deploy massive air power against it.*

Of necessity, then, Mao came to associate Communist revolution with protracted military struggle. "Every Communist," he declared, "must grasp the truth that 'political power grows out of the barrel of a gun'"; furthermore, "war can only be abolished through war."[13] From first to last "an independent regime must be an armed one"; that is, in addition to setting up guerrilla bands in KMT-controlled territory, the base area (or "Soviet") must possess a regular army. Although Mao is known in the West pre-eminently as the creator of modern guerrilla tactics, it was fundamental in his view that guerrilla war was auxiliary to conventional war; the revolution would not succeed until guerrilla bands had developed into, or had been superseded by, regular large-scale armies with heavy equipment. "The existence of a regular Red Army of adequate strength," wrote Mao, "is a necessary condition for the existence of Red political power."[14] By 1945, the regular Red Army (exclusive of guerrilla units) would total 900,000 men and during the ensuing civil war would grow much larger. The creation and maintenance of such a great force involved many difficulties. Not least of these was the spectre of excessive military influence over the political leadership of the revolutionary movement, or even the complete dominance of the party by its military chiefs, as in the KMT. "Our principle is that the party commands the gun and the gun must never be allowed to command the party."[15] But how can one prevent the command of the party by the gun? That Mao was always concerned about dangers of this type is shown by his attack, as late as 1937, on "a tendency toward warlordism [!] within the Eighth Route [Red] Army." Mao expended every effort to ensure that in the Chinese Communist forces, at least at the higher levels, the regular officers were reliable party members. True, he also appointed political officers, with direct access to the highest levels of the party, at various strategic posts within the army; these regimental political officers, however, were not quite like Trotsky's commissars. Soviet commissars were watchdogs set over officially unreliable commanders, whereas the principal duty of the CCP regimental political officer was not the surveillance of the commander but the indoctrination of the troops (a practice early used by the KMT, owing to Soviet influences at the Whampoa Military Academy).

Many students of guerrilla warfare stress the necessity for the guerrillas to have good *morale*. Without it, how will the members of the band endure the physical and psychological hardships involved in months or perhaps years of operation over difficult terrain against the superior resources of the state? Many factors can contribute to good morale: defense of one's hearth, religious exaltation, and personal and group loyalties. Often a primary factor is *political conviction*, the belief that one is risking one's life on behalf of a cause whose triumph is desirable and probable. Such political conviction usually requires development through systematic instruction, that is through *political indoctrination*: For what cause are we taking and risking lives? Why will the triumph of our cause represent an improvement over the present state of things? How do we know that our acts in furtherance of this cause are noble and not merely criminal? How sure can we be that these sacrifices will not be in vain? Mao sought to build and lead an army of convinced believers. If Cromwell's army was a church in arms, Mao's army would be a party in arms. There were great military dividends in this policy. Nevertheless, an appreciation of Mao's wisdom in emphasizing the role of political conviction in warfare does not require one automatically to assume that all guerrilla forces, especially Communist ones, are composed exclusively, or even mainly, of highly motivated ideologues. In analyzing the ability of some guerrilla units to survive under the most adverse conditions, one must take into account other factors: pride in one's unit, fear of reprisal for desertion or substandard performance, a feeling of having been cut off from society at large, above all the sense of invincibility that results from the fact that well-led guerrillas are permitted to go into combat only when victory is nearly certain. One would expect none of these morale-building factors to survive even the shortest period of confinement behind barbed wire, an expectation borne out in the behavior of Vietcong prisoners, for example, who would betray their comrades with amazing facility, especially for material bribes.[16]

Whatever his level of political sophistication, "the guerrilla moves among the people," wrote Mao, "as the fish through the water." A good deal of instruction time for regulars and guerrillas was devoted to teaching them how to behave toward civilians ("Return borrowed articles, be sanitary, be polite").[17] The leaders of Chinese Communism were determined to create armed forces that would enjoy the genuine sympathy and support of the civil population among whom they operated, and certainly Mao believed that such a situation was absolutely vital to the triumph of his revolution. But in the decades since the end of the Chinese civil war, serious disagreement has developed over the question of whether active (as opposed to passive or coerced) civilian support is a *necessity*, or merely a great *advantage*, to guerrillas. One distinguished authority has written:

> only when the people provide intelligence, guides, recruits, and labor can the rebels set ambushes, avoid mopping-up campaigns, and exercise their extreme mobility. While a rebel army may be able to obtain supplies at gunpoint, it cannot get this positive support from people if it behaves like a bunch of bandits.[18]

This is a reasonable proposition, and it seems to receive direct confirmation from the triumph of Mao and indirect confirmation from the complete eradication of Che Guevara's Bolivian expedition after his ignominious failure to obtain civilian support. But the self-evident validity of the statement that guerrillas benefit enormously from a friendly civil population, and hence should not behave "like bandits," does not prove that all protracted guerrilla operations *by definition enjoy uncoerced civilian support*, with the implication that the government against which a guerrilla struggle is being waged must necessarily be repressive and unpopular. Even well-disciplined guerrillas may use threat or force against the civil population. To discount, or even to deny a priori the effectiveness of using terror against civilians, to obtain recruits or intelligence or anything else (not to mention the resigned belief on the part of these civilians that the rebels are probably going to win and therefore must be placated) would constitute a serious impediment, especially in light of the Algerian and Vietnamese experiences, to a broader understanding of guerrilla war.[19] The exact relationship between a given guerrilla movement and its noncombatant environment is a subject for investigation, not pontification.

At any rate, Mao firmly grasped the truth that nothing attaches a soldier to his cause more firmly than the conviction that it is going to win. Von Clausewitz taught that the morale of guerrillas must be built up by winning early victories against very small numbers of government troops. The first duty of the guerrilla unit is to survive. There must be no needless heroics and absolutely no staking of the survival of the guerrillas on one throw of the dice. The second duty of the guerrilla unit is to win, no matter how minor the encounter. Guerrillas must therefore never be led into combat unless victory is mathematically certain owing either to their locally overwhelming numbers or to other factors, such as notoriously poor enemy morale. Mao insisted on this principle whether in regard to a small guerrilla band attacking an isolated Japanese outpost or the regular Communist army attacking KMT main-force units. Whatever the overall strategic situation, however badly Mao's forces might be outnumbered in the big picture, he always strove to achieve *local* superiority, to have more men (many times more) at the particular point of action. This proved not very difficult to achieve against the ponderous and less-than-brilliantly led KMT forces after the end of World War II. In Mao's summary, "the enemy advances, we retreat. The enemy camps, we harass. The enemy tires, we attack. The enemy retreats, we pursue."[20]

Propaganda was not only for one's own soldiers, but also for the enemy's, and Mao insisted that "the most effective method of propaganda directed at the enemy forces is to release captured soldiers and give the wounded medical treatment."[21] This was a profound insight. Clearly, KMT soldiers who knew that capture by the enemy meant decent treatment and eventual release could hardly be counted upon to fight to the death or even to the point of serious danger.

The development of these concepts — the secure territorial base, the central role of regular armed forces, party supremacy over the army, constant indoctrination of troops, no battle without overwhelming superiority, careful treatment of the civil population, leniency toward prisoners — and their effective application would one day bear much fruit for the Communist forces confronting a war-battered and demoralized KMT. In the early 1930s, however, the picture was very depressing. The large and self-confident KMT army was on the offensive. By the fall of 1934, the fifth of Chiang's "annihilation campaigns" placed the very survival of communism as a viable military force in question. At that time, the CCP decided to save what could be saved by embarking on the famous Long March: 100,000 Communists set out on the journey from Kiangsi province. One year later, after meandering 6,000 miles through swamps and across mountains, decimated by hunger and KMT troops, perhaps 5,000 survivors reached what was to become the new base area in Shensi province. Chiang was preparing another annihilation compaign for these remnants late in 1936 when a revolt broke out among some of his generals. They demanded that Chiang give up his obsession with exterminating the CCP and turn his attention more fully to the growing menace of Japanese aggression. The nucleus of a Communist China thus was spared, and the history of the world was changed.

THE JAPANESE INVASION AND THE KMT

In 1931, the Japanese had taken over Manchuria and set up a puppet state called Manchukuo. This was a substantial enterprise, with 500,000 square miles and nearly 40 million inhabitants. The government of Japan also wished, however, to bring China proper into its political and economic orbit. Its efforts to penetrate China diplomatically ran into increasingly strong resistance by the middle 1930s, and the prospect of a China unified under the nationalist (and xenophobic) Chiang filled wider and wider circles in Japan with alarm. On the other hand, certain elements in Japan were gravely worried about the consequences for Japanese influence, or even Japanese security, if the Communists should triumph on the Chinese mainland. These factors helped convince the Japanese, especially the semi-independent armed forces, to enter north and central China in strength in the summer of 1937.

It would be difficult to exaggerate the catastrophic effects — military, political, economic, and moral — of this invasion on Chiang Kai-Shek's government. The backbone of the KMT was the progressive elements in the great coastal cities: merchants, professionals, students. These people were by no means democrats, nor did they look with enthusiasm on the prospect of social revolution in the countryside, whence many of them derived much of their real income. They were also very distrustful, in the Chinese manner, of grass roots movements. What they did want, and were willing to work for, was a strong and modern Chinese state, able to maintain internal order, deter or repel external aggression, and build the infrastructure of a modern and developing economic life. China had been making real progress toward these goals when the Japanese, invading the coastal areas, severed the KMT government from its natural supporters. Driven back into western rural China, with his capital now at Chungking, Chiang was forced to rely for support on the local landowning class. Not only did the KMT regime now have uncongenial supporters; it was also extremely short of revenue. It therefore made the fateful (if understandable) decision to finance the anti-Japanese war through inflation. This policy encouraged corruption, always a problem within the KMT and destined henceforth to become very severe. Inflation also broke the back of the middle class, the KMT's natural constituency.

The Japanese war also did severe damage to the KMT army. Between 1929 and 1944, the Whampoa Academy graduated the enormous number of 146,000 officers. The quality of many of these was gravely reduced as a result of the Japanese invasion: the three-year academy course was, in the face of the emergency, cut to one year. Moreover, during the war many candidates were admitted who in normal times would not have met the educational qualifications. Thus, by war's end, when Chiang was confronting a civil war with the Communists, he was in command of forces in which many of the officers were simply not proficient.

Nor did KMT officers always demonstrate the virtue of political reliability. The Japanese invasion offered to outlying provincial commanders an alternative to following Chiang's orders; they could make deals, explicit or implicit, with the Japanese. "The question of what troops would obey whom under what circumstances could not be answered with any certainty."[22] The natural effect of this on Chiang was to make political reliability more important than professional competence in the choice of commanders. But, in the last analysis, Chiang could count completely only on those troops he commanded directly.

While the Japanese war undermined the quality of the KMT officer corps, the rank and file also deteriorated. To meet the Japanese threat, the KMT armies of World War II had to rely on conscription. The conscripts were rarely well supplied, received scanty medical attention, and were often under the dirction of officers who were less than able. Under these conditions, obtaining and retaining a sufficient number of troops became a problem in itself. "A large proportion of the Nationalist KMT conscripts, often to be seen in Chinese wartime towns roped together to prevent their escape, died *even before reaching their assigned units.*"[23]

Resting on a conservative rural base, fighting one war against the Communists and another against the Japanese, the KMT regime in Chungking failed not only to address itself to land reform but even to hold down the usurious interest rates with which peasants were confronted so often. Thus, it never had a chance to attach to itself the great peasant masses; after the invasion began, the tendency of the KMT to devote less attention to anti-Japanese than to anti-Communist operations gradually alienated those elements of the educated classes who had not already lost faith in the ability of the KMT to save China.

It is easy to heap condemnation on Chiang and the KMT for their weaknesses and failures. But in simple fairness, one must admit that efforts to unify China, create a modern civilization, and spur economic development would have taxed, even in peacetime, the abilities of any leader and any party to the limit and beyond. It is certainly no mystery that the Chiang regime failed to accomplish these monumental tasks while at the same time it was faced with Communist rebellion and Japanese invasion. (For comparative, not polemical, purposes we might also note that today, after forty years of Communist control, China remains among the poorest nations of the earth.)

As the war went on, the Japanese began setting up puppet regimes in northern China, each under the tutelage of a different Japanese army. In March 1940, these separate principalities were combined into the National Government of China, with its capital at Nanking. The leader of this new regime was Wang Ching-Wei, a close disciple of Sun Yat-Sen and a former leader of the left wing of the KMT and longtime rival of Chiang. Wang's government was not initially without prospects of attracting popular support in largely apolitical north China[24]; it could offer the people peace and economic cooperation with Japan instead of interminable war, and Wang's ideological stance of uniting exploited East Asia under Japanese leadership against Western imperialism had great potential appeal. The Wang regime used the same party name, the same slogans, and even the same flag as the KMT, which caused great confusion among many of the people who lived in Japanese-occupied areas, indirectly aiding penetration by the Communists.

Japanese economic activities in north China, including labor conscription and large-scale immigration of Japanese civilians, were clearly exploitative. Japanese pacification efforts in particular (especially the notorious "mopping-up campaigns" discussed in following paragraphs) infuriated great numbers of people and created many recruits for the now rapidly growing Communist forces.

JAPANESE AND COMMUNIST EXPANSION

By 1937, the Communists had been at war with the KMT in north China for a decade. They had an army of no more than 50,000 men and few real contacts with the peasantry.[25] Communists forces were "concentrated in central Shensi province, a backwater of China in the loop of the Yellow River."[26] Prior to the Japanese invasion, the peasantry was a passive element in political affairs; even the Communists' appeal to its most basic economic interests "was a conspicuous failure."[27] The year before, Mao had embarked on the Long March to Shensi to save his decimated followers from total destruction at the hands of the conquering KMT. All this was changed by the coming of the Japanese. "The actual source of the Communist party's authority in China today dates from the wartime period when it led the mobilized masses of previously non-Communist areas in their struggle with the Japanese army,"[28] and

> there is no very good reason to believe that the CCP and the Red Army would have triumphed had it not been for the Japanese invasion of China and the methods of pacification adopted in support of the consolidation of Japanese politico–military power.[29]

In summary, "Communism in China has very little meaning apart from the trials China experienced during the war of resistance."[30]

As a profound student of non-Western politics pointed out years ago,

> one of the central features of the great revolution of our times which has brought the modern world into being is that peoples of mankind in successive stages have been swept into a vivid and sometimes all-consuming sense of their existence as nations — or at least the desire to create nations where none existed before.[31]

But why has it only been in our own era that countries like China, India, Vietnam, such very old societies, have been swept by these nationalistic convulsions? Part of the answer is that it is very difficult to make a revolution without the "revolutionary alliance" of intellectuals, with their schemas and their rhetoric, and the peasants, with their great numbers *and* their apathy. Revolutions — in the sense of violent, profound and lasting change in the power structure of a society — are rare, largely because of the great obstacles in the path of this union of ideas (intellectuals) and numbers (peasants). The urban intellectual disdains the peasant as superstitious, ignorant, and dirty; the peasant fears the intellectual as contemptuous, unrealistic, and dictatorial. Each group has some good reasons for holding its unflattering view of the other. Some very powerful catalyst, therefore, is necessary to overcome the mutual distaste of peasants and intellectuals and to allow a revolution, Communist or otherwise, to occur. This catalyst has in our time been almost exclusively *outraged national feeling.*[32] The Communists have become well aware of this truth: indeed

> the primary political tactic of communist revolutionaries since the time of Lenin has been the attempt to forge a "united front" with genuine nationalist movements, thereby hoping to gain mass support for a communist organization not on the basis of the organization's *communist* values and goals but on the basis of its tactically adopted *nationalist* values and goals. [italics added][33]

Since the days of the Napoleonic invasion of Spain at least, the best way for guerrillas to gain the support of the local population has been on the basis of "the defense of the fatherland against alleged domestic traitors or foreign invaders" or both.[34] Nonetheless, for politically alienated intellectuals in general, and for the leaders of a given Communist party in particular, to make effective contact with the peasants in the name of vindicating the outraged motherland, foreigners must cooperate by carrying out (or at least appearing to be getting ready for) an invasion. *This signal, essential service the Japanese performed for the Chinese Communists.*

> From 1921 to 1937 communism failed in China because the Chinese people, in general, were indifferent to what the Communist party had to offer. After 1937, it succeeded because the population became receptive to one particular kind of political appeal, and the Communist party—in one of its many disguises—made precisely that appeal: it offered to meet the needs of the people for leadership in organizing resistance to the invader and in alleviating war-induced anarchy in rural areas.[35]

Lenin wrote:

> The fundamental law of revolution is as follows: for revolution to take place it is not enough for the exploited and oppressed masses to realize the impossibility of living in the old way, and demand changes; for a revolution to take place it is essential that the exploiters should not be able to live and rule in the old way. It is only when the "lower classes" *do not want* to live in the old way and the "upper classes" *cannot carry on in the old way* that a revolution can triumph. This truth can be expressed in other words: revolution is impossible without a nationwide crisis . . . that the ruling class should be going through a governmental crisis, which draws even the most backward masses into politics . . . weakens the government and makes it possible for the revolution to rapidly overthrow it.[36]

The Japanese militarists forced great segments of the peasantry to see that they could not go on in the old way any longer and simultaneously made it impossible for the ruling KMT to continue to rule, in the old way or any other.

More than anything else, it was Japanese brutality against the peasants that opened the path to the Communists. In late 1940, the CCP in northern China launched its Hundred Regiments Offensive. This operation did extensive damage to the Japanese occupation forces. In response, the Japanese under the command of General Okamura began to carry out the "three alls" campaign: "Kill all, burn all, destroy all." The object was to "dry up the water in which the guerrilla swam." In carrying out this "policy," the Japanese would surround an area, kill or scatter everyone within it, then burn everything to render the area uninhabitable. Thus, the Japanese themselves created the conditions for the alliance between the CCP and increasing numbers of peasants. Communist guerrillas, following Mao's injunction to run away from superior forces, were rarely encountered. What the Japanese did encounter was the defenseless and hitherto inactive peasant. Indiscriminate Japanese terror taught the peasants that there was no safety, no living, with the Japanese, even if the peasants did not help the guerrillas, *even if the peasants were opposed to the guerrillas.* The terror compelled even the most parochial and pacifist peasants to think anew, to conclude that the only viable course lay in armed resistance, and to concede that the best organizers of armed resistance in northern China were the Communists. (The CCP attracted far fewer recruits in central China because in those parts they lacked the strength to launch Hundred Regiment drives and thereby bring down Japanese retaliation on the peasants.) Instead of breaking the tie between the Eighth Route Army (the name of the Red Army after 1937) and the peasantry, Japanese policy drove the two into a closer alliance.[37] For a while, however, it looked as if Japan's deliberately brutal policy would work: "even given their lack of understanding of what was politico–military good sense in northern China, the Japanese and their puppet forces came close in 1941–1942 to breaking the links between the Red Army and the peasantry."[38] But the major effect of the "three alls" campaign was to turn the Communists into a powerful force: membership in the CCP was 40,000 in 1937; by 1945 it was 1.2 million. "The masses were mobilized for war."[39]

The superiority of the Japanese enemy clearly influenced Mao's theory of protracted guerrilla war; it also forced him to invent new political "expedients." After 1937, wishing to stress the need for unity among all classes in the countryside against the hated invader, the CCP downplayed agrarian radicalism and abandoned the class war and compulsory redistribution of property in favor of national resistance. Class compromise became the order of the day in Communist-controlled areas; to be sure, landlords had to lower rents and interest charges, but peasants still had to pay them. Landless peasants were supposed to sublimate their economic desires through being hailed as the real force of the Red revolution and by accepting political pre-eminence in the party, from which landlords were excluded. Of course, social harmony was an anti-Japanese tactic; once the Japanese were visibly losing the war, Mao became much more radical in his land policy.

The Chinese Communists, because they were not the government and because they controlled relatively small territories, did not have to bear the brunt of the war against the Japanese. The war gave them time to consolidate previous gains, train new leaders, acquire experience, and test and indoctrinate soldiers. The KMT, on the other hand, was faced with trying to maintain order over vast areas it nominally controlled, fight the superior Japanese army, and guard against the Communists all at the same time. Thus, by the early 1940s, Japanese intelligence observed that despite inferiority in armaments, the discipline and training of the Communist army was superior to that of the KMT forces.[40]

The Japanese army attempted to conquer and hold more of China than its human and material capacities warranted. The KMT forces retreated, and the local gentry fled before the advancing Japanese, who lacked the numbers and the technology to maintain order behind their lines. Anarchy and chaos among the peasantry resulted, for which the Japanese could find no better solution than "Kill all, burn all, destroy all." Confusion and terror created a vacuum for the Communists to fill; in many areas to the rear of the Japanese forces the CCP became the real government. When the war finally came to an end, northern China had become the stonghold of the Communists because the Japanese army and the Communist guerrillas had between them succeeded in squeezing out the KMT forces.

POSTWAR MISTAKES OF THE KMT

In contrast to the experience of the Communists, the war had been very hard on the KMT. Its forces had been "taxed by eight years of supreme effort against imperial Japan and betrayed from within by corruption, maladministration, and dissension in high places."[41] And as the KMT returned to take over control of the coastal areas and Formosa, it did enormous damage to its cause. KMT plans for administration and economic recovery were inadequate. Those who, for whatever pressing reasons, had remained behind under Japanese occupation were treated with condescension at best.[42] Widespread and shameless looting took place; in part, this can be explained by the wartime inflation, which made the pay of the KMT soldier worthless and led him often to extort food from civilians. The stealing was no doubt stimulated by the suspicion on the part of many who served the KMT that the regime was not going to last very long. At any rate, the abuses that accompanied the KMT return to power in the former Japanese-occupied areas dissipated much of the prestige of the recent victory. Mao, on the other hand, had long labored to inculcate into the Communist forces "a respect for the civil population and abstinence from plunder which distinguished the Red Army from all other armies which the Chinese peasantry had seen in the past and contributed greatly toward winning the support of the population."[43] (During the subsequent civil war, Chiang's troops occupied all the great cities, which were often blockaded by guerrillas. This caused the price of food and other commodities in urban areas to skyrocket and thus aggravated the tendencies of KMT troops to engage in extortion.

Nevertheless, Stalin did not believe that the Communists had a serious chance of winning a civil war with Chiang's Nationalists. Hence, the Russians, as well as the Truman administration, exerted pressure on both sides to work out some sort of compromise settlement. Between August and October 1945, Mao himself spent six weeks in Chiang's capital, negotiating and banqueting with him. That Mao was allowed to enter the Nationalists' den and then leave was a sign of Chiang's confidence in an ultimate KMT triumph.

Two de facto governments and two claimants to ultimate power could not coexist peacefully within the same country for long. In July 1946, the leadership of the CCP announced from Yenan, which had been their capital ever since the days of the Long March, that the Eighth Route Army, the New Fourth Army, and various CCP forces in Manchuria were being combined to form the People's Liberation Army (PLA). It was a proclamation of civil war.

Throughout the struggle that followed, morale within the PLA seems to have been relatively high, even when the civil war was not going as well as it might have. In part, this was a result of the PLA's emphasis on good relations between officers and men; Mao insisted that an officer must lead by example, not by fear and punishment, as in the Japanese and Tsarist armies. And it must have been very important in sustaining Communist morale (as perhaps it has been in all Communist insurgencies since that time) to know that ultimately the PLA had behind it the power of the Soviet Union. Watchful of the morale of its own troops, the leaders of the PLA were untiring in seeking to undermine that of their opponents. Ceaseless propaganda was directed at KMT soldiers, already aware that if they were taken prisoners they would not be shot and might be released after a short time.[44] The Communists also enjoyed success in their efforts to convert KMT prisoners and enlist them in the PLA.

Above all, the level of morale on both sides depended on the fact that most of the time it was clear to everyone that the KMT was not winning the civil war and might actually be defeated. This depressing situation stemmed directly from a fundamental strategic decision by Chiang. Because the KMT claimed to be not just *a* government of China but *the* government, Chiang believed it essential to take control of as much territory as possible after the Japanese surrender. This decision was one of the major factors in the undoing of the Nationalist cause. The Reds cared nothing for holding territory per se, as their abandonment of Yenan proved. They operated against the thinly spread Nationalist forces according to Mao's fundamental principle of always having superior numbers at the point of combat: "the major objective is the annihilation of the enemy's fighting strength, not the holding or taking of cities and places"; hence, "in every battle, concentrate absolutely superior forces — double, triple, quadruple, and sometimes even five or six times those of the enemy — to encircle the enemy, and strive for his annihilation, with none escaping from the net."[45] KMT positional warfare, against which the Reds used concentration of forces at one particular spot after another, had catastrophic consequences for the Nationalists in Manchuria.

THE NATIONALIST DEBACLE IN MANCHURIA

Manchuria, the first major battleground of the Nationalist–Communist civil war, became the graveyard of KMT military power.

As World War II ended, Chiang felt it was politically essential for him to take over as much territory from the defeated Japanese as possible. This was especially the case with Manchuria, long a locus of Japanese occupation and aggression. But Russian troops had overrun Manchuria in the waning days of the war; the PLA was now pouring its best units from northern China into Manchuria, and with Russian help was seizing enormous amounts of equipment. The KMT wanted to reach Manchuria before the Communists had established their complete domination there, but the center of KMT strength was far away in southwest China, and they lacked sufficient transport to move large enough bodies of men in the required time. Many Nationalist units, as a result, were flown into Manchuria aboard U.S. aircraft. Chiang also took the desperate expedient of using surrendered Japanese and puppet troops on the scene to maintain order and keep the Communists at bay until he could arrive there in strength, a decision that undermined Chiang's credentials as a nationalist leader. Moreover, when large numbers of KMT soldiers began to arrive in Manchuria, they treated the puppet troops there badly. Consequently, about 75,000 of the latter eventually joined the PLA.[46]

At the same time, the KMT government had decreed, for purposes of economy, a sweeping postwar demobilization, just as civil war loomed on the horizon. Over 1.5 million troops, including 200,000 officers, suddenly found themselves dismissed from the army. Many of these men, jobless and deeply embittered, joined the PLA.[47]

The Nationalists made a large military investment in Manchuria, but they fought their typically defensive and stationary war there, playing into the hands of Mao and his tactics of concentration of forces. The struggle for Manchuria was the first in which the Communists were able to use tanks and artillery in significant numbers; Chiang, on the other hand, sought to conserve the strength of his best units rather than to use them aggressively.

The confusion and disorder within the Nationalist high command made a bad situation worse. The cliquishness of the older Whampoa graduates undermined unity of command. Chiang's cronies insisted on reporting directly to him instead of to their nominal superiors. Chiang also issued orders over the heads of those responsible, compounding the chaos. In addition, omnipresent corruption had bedeviled the KMT for years; now certain generals were pocketing funds that were intended to purchase supplies for their illtended troops and even selling equipment to the PLA. (A considerable portion of this equipment had been furnished by the U. S. taxpayer.)

Realizing that the Nationalists were on the edge of disaster, in March 1948, U.S. Major General David Barr advised Chiang to cut his losses and evacuate Manchuria. Chiang refused, and the battle continued. KMT losses, through combat and defection, mounted into scores of thousands. Finally, in October 1948, Chiang himself undertook to direct the struggle for Manchuria from his headquarters in Peking. It was too late. A major KMT army, with all of its American equipment, surrendered to the PLA on October 15, and the Manchurian capital of Mukden fell on November 1.

The Communist conquest of Manchuria was the beginning of the end for the Nationalists. Not only had the KMT lost nearly 400,000 troops,[48] but the Communists now had 360,000 men free to send into the battle for China proper.[49]

THE VICTORY OF THE PLA

The KMT disinclination to coordinate movements or to take the offensive, which allowed their units to be defeated piecemeal by the Communists, together with major defections of KMT units at decisive moments, had made 1948 a year of Nationalist disasters. General Barr ascribed most of the responsibility for the rapid decay of the KMT military position to "the world's worst leadership."[50]

Immediately after the fall of Manchuria to the Reds, the battle for central China (the battle of Hwai-Hai) began. Approximately 1 million men took part on both sides. Once again, the KMT command played into Mao's hands, allowing him to use his favorite tactic of crushing the dispersed Nationalist forces in segments. When, by January 12, 1949, this phase of the war came to an end, the KMT had lost roughly 550,000 troops,[51] including the last of their American-equipped divisions. Now the KMT had no really first-rate soldiers left with which to prevent the Communists from crossing the Yangtze River (even if they had had the heart for the job). "The way to Nanking was now open to the Communists."[52]

After the fall of Mukden, General Lin Piao moved his Red Army with unexpected rapidity from Manchuria to the gates of Peking. The plans for the defense of this great city had been betrayed to him, and thus Peking fell to the Communists on January 22, 1949.[53] That same disastrous month, Chiang surrendered his office of president to Vice-President Li, a redoubtable figure who wanted to make a stand on the banks of the Yangtze; if the enemy should nevertheless succeed in crossing the river, Li intended to create a bastion in southwest China. By the spring of 1949, Communist forces had increased within six months from 1.2 million to almost 2.8 million, while KMT forces in the same period had fallen from 2.7 million to 1.5 million; nevertheless, the Nationalists still had sufficient troops with which to continue the struggle.[54] Chiang, however, undercut such plans; he had already secretly decided to abandon the mainland for the island of Formosa, to which he began moving men and supplies without informing all the relevant commanders. Hence, Li was deprived of the strength he needed to prevent a Communist crossing of the Yangtze, while the normal disarray and confusion within the Nationalist armies increased.[55]

Even at this point, all was not necessarily lost. KMT General Pai struck boldly at Lin Piao's army and inflicted a costly defeat on it. But Chiang, for reasons that can only be guessed, caused essential forces on Pai's flanks to be withdrawn, making further aggressive action on Pai's part impossible.[56] On the night of April 20, 1949, therefore, Communist units crossed the Yangtze, assisted in this endeavor by a suitable bribe to the commander of the key Nationalist fortress at Kiangyin.[57]

Nanking, capital of the Nationalists, fell to the Red Army on April 22, and Shanghai fell one month later. The collapse of KMT rule continued during the summer, capped by the surrender of a large Nationalist army in Shensi province on September 19. This event made the cautious Mao confident enough to proclaim at Peking, on October 1, 1949, the birth of a Communist government of all China. Meanwhile, after the fall of Nanking, the KMT government had fled to Canton, a city with matchless historical associations for them. Even this last mainland bastion was lost on October 16. By the end of 1949, Nationalist rule existed only on Formosa.

The causes of the defeat of Chiang and his Nationalists are complex, some going back deep into Chinese history (and thus outside the scope of this chapter). They include grave political shortcomings of the KMT as well as profound political insights of Mao and his collaborators. But few scholars and historians, if any, would care to deny that military blunders on the part of KMT leadership and especially of Chiang—retention of incompetent generals, confusion in command structure, overextension of forces, mistreatment of the civil population, tactics of static defense against a mobile enemy—must take a prominent place in a full explanation of the outcome. Many, indeed all, of these military defects and errors were correctable in principle; if they had been corrected, even in part, it is uncertain that the civil war would have ended at the time and in the way it did.

The KMT would not have had the opportunity to make all these serious military blunders—or at least the cost of them would not have been so high—if no major civil war had occurred. If we ask, what made the conflict after 1945 possible, the answer is the Japanese invasion, the most fundamental reason for the Maoist triumph.

The lack of enthusiasm in the KMT for serious land reform made it all the more imperative that the party deliver, or seem to deliver, on its basic program: independence and unity. In a China so long invaded, defeated, and degraded by its neighbors and other imperial powers, so often torn by peasant rebellion and warlord extortion, any leadership group that managed to achieve independence and unity would have assured itself of historical significance and political popularity. In the 1930s, unity meant bringing all China under KMT rule, which in turn meant the final extirpation of the Communists. Chiang was arguably on the verge of achieving this very aim when the conquering Japanese burst in. Thus, after 1937, the KMT could deliver *neither* independence *nor* unity. It lost the "Mandate of Heaven," the all-important aura of the eventual winner. On the other hand, between 1937 and 1945, the fight against the Japanese presented the CCP with scope to develop from a relatively small and ragtag force on the edge of the country and on the verge of extinction into a major contestant for power and a plausible claimant to the title of defender of Chinese nationalism. The Japanese invasion, in sum, both made a post-1945 civil war inevitable and insured that the KMT would fight it under seriously disadvantageous conditions.

Finally, the worldwide mystique of Mao was based on his (deserved) reputation as the theorist and practitioner par excellence of guerrilla warfare. Today many commentators and revolutionaries think that they see in this mode of fighting the ultimate, invincible weapon that can be used anywhere against anybody. In fact, however, the Maoist victory over Chiang's force, badly mauled for years by the Japanese, was won not by guerrilla bands but by regular armies, enormous in size and equipped with modern Russian, Japanese, and American weapons.

NOTES

1. Lucian W. Pye, *Warlord Politics* (New York: Praeger, 1971), p. 3.
2. F. F. Liu, *A Military History of Modern China, 1924–1949* (Princeton, NJ: Princeton University Press, 1956), p. 7.
3. O. Edmund Clubb, *Twentieth Century China*, 2d ed. (New York: Oxford University Press, 1972), p. 122.
4. James E. Sheridan, *China in Disintegration: The Republican Era in China, 1912–1949* (New York: Free Press, 1975).
5. Liu, *A Military History*, p. 11.
6. Stuart Schram, *Mao Tse-Tung* (Harmondsworth, England: Penguin, 1966), p. 165.
7. Sheridan, *China in Disintegration*, p. 230.
8. See Arthur N. Young, *China and the Helping Hand, 1937–1945* (Cambridge, MA: Harvard University Press, 1963).
9. Henry McAleavy, *The Modern History of China* (London: Weidenfeld and Nicolson, 1968), p. 267.
10. Tang Tsou, *America's Failure in China, 1941–1950* (Chicago: University of Chicago Press, 1963), p. 51.
11. Chalmers Johnson, *Autopsy on People's War* (Berkeley: University of California Press, 1973), p. 13.
12. See Samuel P. Huntington, *Political Order in Changing Societies* (New Haven, CT: Yale University Press, 1968), chap. 5.
13. Mao Tse-Tung, *Selected Military Writings* (Peking: Foreign Language Press, 1966), pp. 274–275.
14. Mao, *Selected Military Writings*, p. 14.
15. Mao, *Selected Military Writings*, p. 274.
16. Geoffrey Fairbairn, *Revolutionary Guerrilla Warfare: The Countryside Version* (Harmondsworth, England: Penguin, 1974), p. 298.
17. Chalmers Johnson, *Peasant Nationalism and Communist Power* (Stanford, CA: Stanford University Press, 1961), pp. 82–83.
18. Chalmers Johnson, *Revolutionary Change* (Boston: Little, Brown, 1966), p. 163.
19. See Lucian Pye in Harry Eckstein, *Internal War* (Glencoe: Free Press, 1964), pp. 159–160.

20. Mao, *Selected Military Writings*, p. 72.
21. Mao, *Selected Military Writings*, p. 33.
22. Tang Sou, *America's Failure*, p. 50.
23. Clubb, *Twentieth Century China*, p. 234.
24. Johnson, *Peasant Nationalism*, chap. 2.
25. Johnson, *Peasant Nationalism*, pp. 72–73.
26. Johnson, *Peasant Nationalism*, p. 94.
27. Johnson, *Peasant Nationalism*, p. 69.
28. Johnson, *Peasant Nationalism*, p. 49.
29. Fairbairn, *Revolutionary Guerrilla Warfare*, p. 118.
30. Johnson, *Peasant Nationalism*, p. 155.
31. Rupert Emerson, *From Empire to Nation* (Boston: Beacon Press, 1963), p. 89.
32. Huntington, *Political Order*, chap. 5.
33. Johnson, *Autopsy*, p. 12.
34. Johnson, *Revolutionary Change*, p. 161.
35. Johnson, *Peasant Nationalism*, p. 4.
36. Lenin, "Left-Wing Communism: An Infantile Disorder," in Robert C. Tucker, ed., *The Lenin Anthology* (New York: Norton, 1975), pp. 602–603.
37. Johnson, *Peasant Nationalism*, p. 59.
38. Fairbairn, *Revolutionary Guerrilla Warfare*, p. 118.
39. Johnson, *Peasant Nationalism*, p. 16.
40. Johnson, *Peasant Nationalism*, p. 143.
41. Liu, *A Military History*, p. 270.
42. Suzanne Pepper, *Civil War in China: The Political Struggle, 1945–1949* (Berkeley: University of California Press, 1978), chap. 1.
43. Schram, *Mao*, p. 242.
44. Liu, *A Military History*, pp. 243–244.
45. Liu, *A Military History*, p. 250.
46. Liu, *A Military History*, p. 229.
47. Liu, *A Military History*, p. 229.
48. Clubb, *Twentieth Century China*, pp. 289–290.
49. Liu, *A Military History*, p. 260.
50. Tang Tsou, *America's Failure*, p. 483.
51. Clubb, *Twentieth Century China*, p. 291.
52. Clubb, *Twentieth Century China*, p. 291.
53. Liu, *A Military History*, pp. 263–264.
54. Liu, *A Military History*, p. 245.
55. Liu, *A Military History*, p. 267.
56. Liu, *A Military History*, pp. 268–269.
57. Liu, *A Military History*, p. 266.

6

Caribbean Upheavals: Cuba and Nicaragua

CUBA

When princes think more of luxury than of war, they lose their states.
— Machiavelli

The flight of Fulgencio Batista out of Havana in the waning hours of the year 1958 signaled not only the complete collapse of his dictatorship but the beginning of a transformation of the politics of the Western Hemisphere. This transformation had three main aspects. First, the triumphant rebels thoroughly dismantled the old society, drove out almost the entire middle class, and created a social and economic upheaval never before witnessed in this part of the globe, and in few other parts. Second, Cuba developed into that previously unthinkable entity, a Soviet ally in the very center of what Americans had long imagined to be their special sphere of influence, and consequently preoccupied Washington administrations for a quarter-century and more. Third, the Cuban Revolution became a model for all those who sought to spread revolution throughout Latin America. Many years would elapse and much blood would be shed and much egregious nonsense written before the total absence of success for Cuban-inspired revolts (including the spectacular and fatal failure of Che Guevara in Bolivia), along with certain finally undeniable shortcomings of revolutionary Cuba (Batista's Cuba was a sugar island dominated by a foreign power; after three decades, Castro's Cuba is still that) would begin to restore the Cuban Revolution and its leaders to realistic proportions.

BATISTA'S CUBA

Roughly the size of Pennsylvania, Cuba on the eve of the Castro takeover had a population of about 6.5 million. The country was really two societies: "one urban, educated, and well-off, the other rural, illiterate and poor."[1] The most fundamental myth surrounding the Cuban Revolution, the myth that cost Guevara his unhappy life, was that of a mass rebellion of poor peasants rising in their wrath against intolerable poverty. Quite to the contrary, "the Cuban experience belies the thesis that poverty alone is sufficient to cause revolutionary upheavals."[2] It was not from the peasantry but from the urban middle classes that the thrust and leadership of the revolution derived, that is, from that sector of Cuban society that was, by Latin American standards, well advanced economically. In 1958, Cuba was fifth among all Latin American nations in manufacturing, fourth in per capita income, 60 percent urbanized, 75 percent literate. There were more Cadillacs per capita in Havana than in any city in the United States, more television sets per capita than in any country south of the Rio Grande.[3] But Cuba had reached the dangerous condition for any society, in which expectations had outrun achievement.

> The Cuban Revolution was born not so much out of grinding poverty, racial hatred, economic underdevelopment, or United States imperialism [although these factors were certainly present to some degree] as out of the fact that the development of a more modern Cuba was not proceeding fast enough to satisfy rising expectations. . . . Revolution came to Cuba not because it was a poverty-ridden, traditional society but because it was a transitional nation which had "taken off."[4]

It was also, for complex reasons, a society that nobody much wanted to defend.

Cuba was the last of the Spanish colonies in this hemisphere to attain its independence (1902). In the nineteenth century, there had been several bloody efforts to end Spanish rule on the island, as well as major slave revolts and race wars (until this century, most Cubans were of African heritage). The Spanish administration, especially in its last years, tended to rely more and more on a system of repression as ineffective as it was provocative. After independence, repression and revolt continued to characterize Cuban politics, with the political arena often resembling a bloodsoaked battleground. In perhaps no other Latin American nation did violence play so prominent a role in political and social life.

Other deeply rooted factors contributed to Cuban instability. Colonial Cuba was almost entirely given over to the cultivation of sugar, and sugar plantation owners were often foreigners and almost always absentee. The Roman Catholic Church on the island was served by a clergy totally inadequate in quantity and often in quality; in the days of the Spanish empire, Cuba had been used as a dumping ground for troublesome priests from all over Latin America. Whole districts lacked churches or even temporary chapels. Again, in contrast to other Spanish-speaking republics, Cuba had no heroic traditions embodied in an army; Cuban independence had not been won from Spain but received from the United States, and the Cuban national army was created *after* independence, with U.S. assistance. Thus, the "holy trinity" of Latin American society—the landed aristocracy, the church, and the army—was absent in Cuba or at most present in an attenuated and distorted form. However we may evaluate these institutions, it cannot be denied that aristocracy, church, and army gave structure, style, and stability to Spanish-American society, for good and ill. Cuba lacked these elements, and was therefore an invertebrate, artificial, and profoundly vulnerable society.

After two generations characterized by turmoil, dictatorship, and incipient civil war, the Cuban republic seemed, in the 1940s, to be entering a new era of maturity and stability. The administrations of Presidents Grau San Martin (1944–1948) and Carlos Prio Socarras (1948–1952) were the most open and democratic in Cuban history. But they were also identified by middle-class Cubans as among the most brazenly corrupt in the country's experience, and Fulgencio Batista was able to overthrow President Prio in 1952 with hardly a shot fired. "It is indicative of the failure of liberal, pluralist democracy in Cuba that at least initially the bulk of the population welcomed Batista back with a sense of general relief."[5]

Fulgencio Batista had started his political career many years before, when as a sergeant in the Cuban army he led his fellow noncommissioned officers in supporting the democratic revolt against the dictator Gerardo Machado, thereby becoming "the outstanding revolutionary of 1933."[6] Known as a progressive, a populist, a friend of the downtrodden blacks, with many contacts in the army, Batista was elected to the presidency in 1940. In that contest, he enjoyed the fervent support of the Cuban Communists, and he displayed throughout his administration a notable benevolence to that party, allowing them, among other privileges, unlimited authority over the vital Havana dockyards.[7] But after returning to power in 1952, Batista sought to take more and more control into his own hands, at the same time turning the state into a sort of full-time extortion racket. These trends stirred up opposition and criticism, which Batista met with a harshness previously uncharacteristic of him, provoking more opposition, requiring more repression, in a vicious circle. Within a few years of Batista's initially popular coup, many Cubans were longing for a new leader. Among those who were preparing to assume this role was a young law school graduate named Fidel Castro.

THE BEGINNING

Fidel Castro was born in 1926 on his father's estate, a plantation that employed hundreds of sugar workers. Educated in private schools, young Castro received a law degree in 1950 from the University of Havana.

Castro, like almost all well-to-do Cubans, was intensely interested in politics from a very early age. He was known at the university as a critic of Batista; indeed, in July 1953, he and some associates staged an armed uprising that the government crushed in a few hours. An amnesty proclamation by President Batista in May 1955 released Castro from prison; shortly afterward he arrived in Mexico, where he was joined by some of his friends and other Cuban revolutionaries. The little band studied political philosophy, along with the rudiments of warfare, under Colonel Alberto Bayo, a guerrilla leader in the Spanish Civil War.[8] They soon attracted the attention of the Mexican government, and it was time to return home. Thus, on December 2, 1956, Castro landed in Cuba accompanied by about eighty armed followers, most of whom were quickly rounded up by the security forces. The rest escaped with Castro into the mountains of the Sierra Maestra in the extreme southeastern section of the island.

In those days, Castro had not proclaimed, or even hinted, that he was a Communist; only much later would he decide that "a select core of intellectually superior and proven revolutionaries has to lead the masses."[9] Nor did the Cuban Communist party commit itself to helping the rebels until the summer of 1958, after it became clear that Batista was losing. Castro's announced program in the Sierra was the overthrow of Batista and the restoration of free and democratic elections. In his remote mountain fastness, without power and without responsibility, Castro quickly became a symbol of resistance to tyranny, the embodiment of all virtues and the repository of all hopes. In contrast to this, the thieving, prosaic Batista made a poor show indeed. Soon press reports, very sympathetic to Castro, especially those of Herbert Matthews in the *New York Times*, began to appear regularly in the United States, bringing in much-needed money and arms from American sympathizers.

In the initial stages of the rebellion, Castro and his men would attack small patrols and isolated army outposts, withdrawing immediately to prepared positions from which their pursuers could be ambushed. Besides the "propaganda of the deed," the main purpose of these early raids was to procure weapons; the proportion of Castro's weapons that was brought from outside has been estimated at as low as 18 percent.[10]

According to the *Statesman's Yearbook* for 1958, the army that opposed Castro consisted of 946 officers and 14,000 enlisted men. The army had serious problems. It was equipped with artillery like that which had defended Verdun; many of its rifles were 1903 models.[11] But a more difficult problem than that of armaments, which is easily solved, was the grave question of personnel. Batista's army was no fighting force:

> the Cuban army, after all, had no experience, and therefore no traditions of combat; the wars of independence had been fought by amateurs before the army was founded. No regiments had battle-honours, none had captured flags to flaunt in regimental chapels.[12]

Promotions depended almost exclusively upon political favoritism. "Officers regarded commands merely as means of enrichment by the use of intimidation. The army was rotten and became more so as time went on."[13] It was by understanding and manipulating the nature of this army that Batista had come to power, but even Batista did not understand his army well enough.

Because of the poor condition of the national army, and the small size of Castro's forces, which could disperse and hide easily, the Sierra that sheltered them was not attacked for a long time; Batista evidently hoped the rebels would go away or give up. Thus, Castro was given invaluable time in which to build up a good base area. Eventually, Batista realized he had a serious challenge on his hands, and ordered the Sierra to be cordoned off. But the mountains ran 100 miles east to west, and from 15 to 25 miles north to south, and no one in the Cuban army had ever had any anti-guerrilla training; thus, the 5,000 troops assigned to this job faced an impossible task, quite aside from their previously mentioned disabilities.[14]

Castro continued his effective tactics of attacking only isolated government posts; in response, the Batista troops fell back to larger and larger fortifications, abandoning the countryside and undermining their own morale. When the army tried to make thrusts against the rebels, the brutality and inefficiency of the troops alienated increasing numbers of initially neutral Cubans. Batista and his commanders failed to realize that guerrilla war is at least as much a political as a military phenomenon, and so is counterguerrilla warfare. When the army treats the civilians among whom it operates like enemies (or like prey), the civilians become just that. Soldiers of the Soviet army in Afghanistan who were fighting against an alien, primitive people ignored by the outside world—by the United Nations, by the "peace movement," even by their Third World and Muslim "brothers"—and who were under orders to win the struggle at any cost, even if it meant turning the country into a depopulated desert, may have been able to forget the political dimensions of counterguerrilla warfare. Batista, however, waging a campaign in his own country less than 100 miles from Florida and under the eyes of the *New York Times*, could not afford to act this way even on a restricted scale; to do so was a very costly mistake for him and for many of the Cubans.

So the Castro rebellion took root, and grew. In September 1957, some young naval officers engaged in a brief but violent pro-Castro rising at the Cienfuegos base, an event that should have alarmed and galvanized the regime, but did not. Then, on February 16, 1958, Castro forces destroyed the small garrison at Pino del Agua. "After this date it began to be evident to all the people of the hills that Castro and his men were there to stay and that therefore they had nothing to gain in the long run from working with Batista's army."[15] Displaying increasing confidence and boldness, Castro decreed from the Sierra that after April 1, 1958, Cubans should cease to pay their provincial and municipal taxes, because they would only have to be paid again as soon as the revolution triumphed. Anyone serving in the executive branch of the government after April 5 would be guilty of "treason"; anyone who joined the armed forces after that date would be considered a "criminal." Judges had to resign their posts if they wished to be able to continue practicing law after the revolution.[16] Later, Castro forbade anyone to participate in the presidential elections scheduled for November and caused a prominent politician to be executed to give point to his admonition.[17]

But it was May 13, 1958, when the real thunderbolt struck the Batista regime: the Eisenhower administration proclaimed an embargo on arms shipments to Cuba. Arms embargoes, like that of the Roosevelt administration during the Spanish civil war, by forbidding transfers of arms to either side in an insurrection, work in fact against the incumbent government, placing it on a moral level with the insurgents and preventing it from strengthening its armed forces. "No step by Castro could have so disheartened Batista."[18] The arms embargo, along with restrictions on credit and discouragement of investment in Cuba, "put a severe strain on the regime and [caused] gradually a failure of nerve within the administration that spread to the military and made it practically impotent long before most of the troops had ever heard a rifle shot."[19] Before the embargo, "Batista could suggest in a hundred small ways that behind him stood if need be the armed might of the world's most powerful country."[20] Now Batista and his regime were isolated. In the dictator's own words: "The prohibition of the sale of arms to the Cuban government weakened the faith and the will to fight in many of our men."[21]

THE COLLAPSE

In the same month, May 1958, the Batista regime launched its only serious offensive operation in the Sierra Maestra. It turned into a complete disaster. Castro possessed the army code. This enabled him to send false information to the Batista air force, which consequently dropped napalm more often on Batista's men than on Castro's. Nor did the government have any helicopter gun ships, vehicles that might well have been very effective in the mountain war. Eventually, regular bombings had to be stopped because Castro had kidnapped a number of U.S. private citizens in Oriente province, announcing that the prisoners would be released when the bombing ceased. U.S. pressure on Havana caused the bombing to be halted, while the rainy season hampered the movements of motorized detachments and armored units. The ground fighting was a series of shocks for the regime. On June 29, the Eleventh Battalion was badly cut up by a much smaller force of Fidelistas. Through bribery, an entire armored train was betrayed to the rebels under Guevara.[22] Batista noted that "other units had been needlessly surrendered without combat through the strange conduct of their chiefs, who let themselves be cut off so easily."[23] One result of these conditions was that 85 percent of the arms now possessed by the rebels had originally belonged to the regular army.[24]

Batista later complained bitterly, "how strange it was that military units were being continually surrendered without combat to an enemy who, in number and military capacity, could not possibly possess the strength necessary to immobilize the army."[25] In part this collapse resulted from sending inadequately trained draftees into combat while elite units were kept in Havana.[26] But the truth was even simpler than that; as one of Batista's own officers told him during the offensive, "the soldiers are tired and the officers do not want to fight."[27] Many of these officers were receiving letters from brother officers who had gone over to Castro, urging them to defect.[28] In August, therefore, the high command, "a demoralized gaggle of corrupt, cruel, and lazy officers without combat experience" ordered a general retreat.[29] As the meaning of all this began to sink in, Castro carried out a move reminiscent of Maoist tactics during the Chinese civil war: he released 400 Batista prisoners taken during the offensive. This "expression of utter contempt for the fighting potential of the defeated"[30] weakened even further the self-confidence both of the army and the regime. Raul Castro said to one group of captured Batista soldiers:

> We took you this time. We can take you again. And when we do we will not frighten or torture or kill you, anymore than we are doing to you at this moment. If you are captured a second time or even a third time by us, we will again return you exactly as we are doing now.

The effect of such words on the fighting edge of those who hear them can only be imagined.

Shortly after the failure of the offensive, Castro made a radio broadcast in which he appealed to the younger officers to forsake the regime: "We are at war with the tyranny, not with the armed forces. . . ."[31] This supremely clever effort to convince lower ranking officers that they might have a future separate from that of a sinking Batista had a powerful effect.[32] Numerous officers began making plans to remove Batista, plans that were supposed to ripen around mid- or late December. The fighting qualities of the troops deteriorated even further; as one high-ranking officer wrote later:

> Our army, tired and decimated by two years of fighting without relief had completely lost its combat power. Desertion to the enemy increased daily. We lacked reserves and a great part of the officers confined to barracks were in contact with the enemy.[33]

Meanwhile, by late summer, Castro was levying and collecting a tax on each bag of sugar milled, including that milled by U.S.-owned firms. In autumn, the United States evacuated fifty-five of its citizens from the town of Nicaro, a sure sign of disbelief in Batista's ability to win.[34]

Yet even now, "the civil war was far from lost, if only Batista could have brought himself to admit that a civil war, properly speaking, was in existence."[35] Batista still had cards to play, the area of Cuba under control of the rebels was quite small, the bulk of the population still lived in government-held areas, and certainly "Castro did not expect Batista to collapse as fast as he now did."[36] But Batista did not want to make the effort required, assuming that he knew what was required, which would have included cleaning out all the rotten wood from the top of the army down, men such as General Francisco Tabernilla, "the real author of the army's defeat," who was preparing to enter negotiations with Castro.

Another thunderbolt from the north struck on December 10: the State Department told Batista that it would not accept his duly elected successor, Rivero Aguero: in effect, the United States was withdrawing its recognition from Batista's government.[37] Three weeks later, on New Year's Eve, 1958, with Santa Clara having just fallen to the rebels and Santiago under close seige, Batista fled the country. The war was over.

RETROSPECT

Undoubtedly, Batista was badly shaken by the arms embargo, and so were many of his followers. It seemed to mean that the United States was betting against him, perhaps even *siding* against him. This suspicion, combined with the increasing defection of most of the upper and middle classes, caused the leadership to have serious doubts about the long-term chances of the regime to endure, and these doubts infected the army.[38] Batista's officers, without combat experience or even simple esprit de corps, also lacked accurate information on the numbers and location of the rebels. When the United States withdrew its support and the offensive failed, panic set in.

However doubtful or insecure an army may be, surely it must be defeated by *someone*. Clearly, the rebels were both brave and intelligent, but the scope and scale of the fighting during the rebellion was embarrassingly small. The only serious encounters were the 1958 summer offensive and the battle of Santa Clara in December 1958, during which the rebels suffered the loss of six men.[39] Throughout the two-year conflict, the Batista forces probably lost no more than 300 men.[40] On the day that Batista fled his country, whole units of the Cuban army had not yet fired a shot in anger, indeed had not even glimpsed the enemy. Rather than a bloody death struggle, "the Cuban civil war had really been a political campaign in a tyranny, with the campaigner [Castro] being defended by armed men."[41] But the officer corps was not loyal to Batista; on the contrary, it was riddled with his would-be rivals and successors and their plots and schemings. And the willingness of Batista commanders to make deals with the enemy, so that Fidelistas could go almost anywhere they wished whenever they wished, rivals the most egregious episodes of betrayal from the history of classical Greece or Renaissance Italy. Beyond the alienation of high society (on one notable occasion, President Batista, partly and unmistakably of African heritage, entered an exclusive

Havana restaurant, whereupon every other client got up and walked out), beyond the small number of casualties it suffered, beyond even the undeniable severe blow of the arms embargo, the Cuban army collapsed because of "its own weaknesses, divisions, jealousies, and errors."[42]

All of this, of course, amounts to a profound and protracted failure of leadership at the top. The army could never have been so corrupt, so ineffective, so disinclined to any physical activity whatsoever if the highest political levels had not been complaisant. The rottenness of the army reflected that of the regime. How could it have been otherwise? If Cuba had possessed an efficient, well-turned-out army with at least a minimum of ideological coherence, no one like Batista could have come to power in the first place. Beyond the activities of Castro's miniature army, "Batista's laziness and weakness damaged morale more than anything else; the president played canasta when he should have been making war plans; as his press secretary put it in exile, 'Canasta was a great ally of Fidel Castro'."[43] Many would agree with the succinct summation of the fall of Batista offered by one Latin American expert: "He was not forced out—he simply abdicated."[44]

Two conclusions immediately suggest themselves. First, the well-known and widely accepted principle that a regime defended by an intact army cannot be overthrown by makeshift forces has perhaps been damaged but not refuted by the Cuban case. Batista fled the stage well before the last curtain. Besides, one might argue, with only slight exaggeration, that Batista did not possess an army as the term is commonly understood, but rather a sort of uniformed collection agency.

A second conclusion is much more important. If our description of these Cuban events is relatively accurate, any attempt to put the "Cuban model" of revolution to work elsewhere, against a Latin American country with a real army, especially one seriously supported by the United States, should meet with failure. In Venezuela, in Bolivia, and elsewhere, failure of Cuban-inspired rebellions is exactly what we encounter. On the other hand, we have no clear-cut case of the Fidelista experience being successfully imitated anywhere else in Latin America, not even in Nicaragua, to which we now turn.

NICARAGUA

One does not establish the dictatorship in order to safeguard the revolution; one makes a revolution in order to establish the dictatorship.
—George Orwell

The defeat of the Somoza dictatorship in Nicaragua provides us with what appears to be another challenge to the principle that rebellion cannot succeed against a regular army not previously defeated in war or paralyzed by political decision makers. Furthermore, Nicaragua, with a population of less than 3 million in an area the size of the state of Iowa, reminds us of an important rule: the magnitude of events often has little relationship to the size of the country in which they occur. The Sandinistas had hardly come to power before they established the second pro-Soviet state in the Western Hemisphere and initiated a chain of events that could someday involve the United States in a Central American war.

Such an American military involvement would be ironic in the extreme, because two prime factors converged to produce the Sandinista triumph in 1979. One was a series of deplorable and inexcusable mistakes on the part of the eventually defeated government. The other factor, equally important, was the intervention in the Nicaraguan conflict, not once but twice, by the U.S. government, against the incumbent regime, on the side of the Sandinistas, and in the name of human rights.

THE UNITED STATES AND NICARAGUA

Nicaragua's achievement of independence from Spain in the 1820s removed such restraints as had previously existed on domestic violence and external interference. For about 100 years, independent Nicaragua was the scene of endemic civil conflict, especially warfare between the Liberal and Conservative parties (which often was a cover for rivalry between the cities of Léon and Managua).

In 1912, President Adolfo Díaz, faced with yet another of his country's innumerable rebellions, requested that the United States help restore order. U.S. sailors and marines landed in Nicaragua soon thereafter, there to remain most of the time until the 1930s (although at times the U.S. presence was as small as a 100-man detachment guarding the U.S. legation). Why, beginning in the administration of President Taft and continuing through the administration of President Wilson, were U.S. troops stationed in Nicaragua? The least important reason was to protect American investments there, which were very small. Of more importance was a (naive) belief that American occupation would result in a stable democracy. The most important reasons of all were providing security for the Panama Canal Zone and preventing construction of any future interoceanic canal in Nicaragua from falling to a German or a Japanese firm.[45] In spite of these plausible justifications, U.S. presence in Nicaragua caused much adverse criticism at home; thus, Washington faced a problem in January 1925 when newly inaugurated Nicaraguan President Carlos Solorzano requested the State Department to keep U.S. troops in his country. The problem was resolved by a Washington commitment to train a nonpartisan, professional constabulary to keep peace in Nicaragua and perhaps to serve as a model for other countries in the Caribbean area.

The State Department submitted to the Nicaraguan government a plan (which was accepted) for the training of a force of 410 men, with retired U.S. Army Major Calvin Carter (who had experience training soldiers in the Philippines) as commander. All recruits were to be volunteers. They would wear uniforms and receive regular pay, training, and discipline. Most of all, they were to be loyal—not to this or that regional caudillo but to the nation—and above politics. But no party or faction in Nicaragua, then or thereafter, ever really accepted the nonpartisan nature and purpose of the constabulary, *and that is the essential reason why things went wrong.* Indeed, by 1926 the U.S. minister in Managua reported that the new constabulary, the Guardia Nacional, was disintegrating into a partisan force in the service of conservative President Emiliano Chamorro. The Guardia was thereupon disbanded. Nevertheless, pressure to develop a reliable force continued both in Nicaragua and in Washington, and fresh recruiting for a new Guardia began in May 1927 under the supervision of Marine Colonel Robert Rhea.

THE PROGRESS OF THE GUARDIA NACIONAL

Why did the U.S. government take responsibility for building up a new Guardia Nacional? It wanted first, against all local tradition, "to transform Nicaragua's armed forces into a nonpolitical force, dedicated to defending constitutional order and guaranteeing free elections."[46] Second, it wanted a body of men capable of restoring order in the northern countryside by defeating the Liberal party insurgent leader Augusto Sandino (see below).

It was soon found necessary to send several specially trained medical personnel to help with the Guardia. Syphilis and malaria were rampant in the country. Recruits often suffered from various venereal diseases, whose symptoms they stoically accepted as a part of life. Neither lectures nor U.S. Marine Corps prophylactics were able to accomplish great changes in this department. The marines, however, were far more successful in their national campaign against smallpox and typhoid.[47]

Originally all recruits into the Guardia had to be at least 18 years old and literate. This second requirement had to be dropped if enough men were to be obtained to maintain order in the 1928 presidential elections. (U.S. supervision of these elections was desired by the opposition Liberal party, several elements of which had openly rebelled against the Conservative regime of Emiliano Chamorro.)

In the early years of the Guardia Nacional almost all the officers were U.S. Marines. The author of the major study on the Guardia (and a critic of U.S. policy in Nicaragua) wrote: "The marines did surprisingly well, transforming their raw recruits within a few months into the best trained, disciplined and equipped force in Nicaraguan history."[48] Life in the Guardia was no bed of roses for the enlisted men, but the regular pay, uniforms, food, and medical treatment, together with the respect for Nicaraguan fighting qualities that many Marine officers developed, made conditions highly acceptable for most recruits.

In the late 1920s, the Guardia under its marine officers found it necessary to take over many police duties, especially in the city of Managua. They acted with great efficiency in making arrests and in collecting fines. Undoubtedly, the Managua municipal treasury benefited from this, and street crime was kept to a minimum, but the Guardia's efficiency probably did not endear it to every element of the population.

Guardia supervision of the presidential elections of 1928 was impeccable. To prevent multiple voting, the fingers of electors were dipped in mercurochrome; the followers of Sandino (who, unlike most of the other Liberals, did not accept U.S. supervision of the election) told the people that the mercurochrome was poison. Ninety percent of the eligible voters went to the polls anyway, and Liberal candidate General José María Moncada won a clear victory. Even the Conservatives acknowledged that they had lost fairly. *For the first time in Nicaraguan history, the ruling party had lost an election.* Nevertheless, the Sandinista revolt continued.[49]

Despite their good work against disease and election disorders, the presence of Americans in Nicaragua was being denounced throughout Latin America and in the United States as well. In the Senate, the attack on American involvement was led by the country's leading isolationist, William E. Borah of Idaho. Another isolationist, Burton D. Wheeler of Montana, advised his fellow senators that if the marines were going to be used to fight bandits, they should be sent into Chicago. Increasing pressure in the United States for the marines to withdraw forced the Guardia into combat on its own before it was ready; the marines simply had not had enough time to train a sufficient number of officer replacements. Thus, the door was left wide open for the politicization of the Guardia once the marines left. All parties agreed that the marines would go home as soon as the 1932 presidential elections were over. (Once again, in honest elections, the Liberals won a clear victory.) The leadership of the two parties then entered into a fateful agreement: once the marines were gone, officerships in the Guardia were to be divided equally among the two parties (this was absolutely contrary to the aims of the American advisers to produce not a bipartisan but a nonpartisan constabulary). Anastasio Somoza García, a leading Liberal, a general in the old army, and a protegé of outgoing Liberal president Moncada, was designated as commander-in-chief of the Guardia Nacional. The long-standing animosity between the two parties, however, was soon to make even Guardia bipartisanship an impossibility. In 1936, Somoza, with Guardia backing, ran for the presidency and won. He then combined the presidential office with the command of the Guardia, and the Somoza dictatorship had truly begun.

SANDINO

Augusto Sandino was born in 1895, the illegitimate son of a local landowner and a young Indian woman. As a young man, he had to flee the country for Mexico after he wounded someone in a brawl. While in Mexico, he became a member of the fiercely anti-Catholic Freemasons. He returned to Nicaragua in 1926 and, joining the rebellion of the Liberals against President Chamorro, soon rose to an important position. Sandino apparently wanted U.S. supervision of the 1928 elections,[50] but did not like the agreement under which it was to be obtained; Sandino subsequently led his men in an attack against the Guardia Nacional post at Ocotal on July 16, 1927. So began the conflict that was to shape so much of Nicaraguan politics for the next sixty years.

In time, Sandino's men engaged in further skirmishes with the Guardia, but a new stage in the conflict was reached in April 1931, when Sandinistas seized the headquarters of the Bragman's Bluff Lumber Company, "massacring the American and British employees and sacking the company town."[51]

As soon as the Marines had left Nicaragua, negotiations began in earnest between the Managua government and Sandino, who came to the capital city by plane early in February 1933. A signed agreement provided for a cease-fire, an amnesty for Sandino's men, and the handing over by them of a certain number of their arms. In addition, Sandino retained the right to keep a force of 100 armed men in his northern border base, these men to be paid by the government. Sandino publicly embraced Guardia commander Somoza.[52]

Yet all was not sweetness and light. It soon became clear that Sandino's men were not handing over the arms as had been promised in the agreement; Sandino also began speaking of the Guardia Nacional as an unconstitutional body. When the treaty was nearing its expiration date (February 1934) General Somoza declared that the Sandinistas must give up all their arms, whereupon many of them would be incorporated, if they wished, as regular members of the Guardia; then everyone would live in peace. Sandino ignored these proposals.

Liberal President Sacasas invited Sandino to come again to the capital and discuss matters. Sandino arrived on February 16, 1934, without incident, and remained in the city for several days. But on February 21, members of the Guardia removed Sandino and some of his aides from the car in which they were traveling; they were then driven to their airfield and killed. Apparently, some bitterly anti-Sandinista officers had forced Somoza to consent to these murders, which were publicly criticized by the U.S. ambassador.[53] At the same time, the Sandinista camp at Wiwili was surrounded, and the troops there were disarmed. Many must have believed at the time that the Sandino episode was over, but in fact "Sandino's ghost . . . haunted the Somozas ever since."[54]

THE SOMOZA DYNASTY

As noted previously, the Somozas came to power in 1936, when the commander of the Guardia Nacional, Anastasio Somoza García, won the presidential election. Assassinated in 1956, he was succeeded in office by his son,

Luís Somoza Debayle. Luís's brother, Anastasio "Tachito" Somoza Debayle, held the presidency from 1967 to 1972 and again from 1974 to the fall of the regime.

During this remarkably long reign, the Somoza family became the richest in the country, and probably the richest in all Central America. The family acquired controlling or part interest in every major and almost every secondary economic enterprise in Nicaragua. As one observer has tartly noted: "For a system such as that maintained in Nicaragua by the Somozas to succeed, there must be great numbers of those willing to be corrupted as well as a dominant family willing to do the corrupting."[55] The Somozas did not hoard their wealth; instead, they channeled some of it, along with a good deal of tax revenue, through the old Liberal party, which served for many years as an effective patronage machine, to those numerous Nicaraguans found deserving by the Somozas. Until the early 1970s, the dynasty also cultivated the Roman Catholic clergy, whose attitude toward the Somoza regime, running from acquiescence to open support, was not the least of the props on which it rested.

The most important key to retention of power by the Somoza family was its control of the Guardia Nacional. Anastasio had become commander of the Guardia in a deal worked out between the Liberal and Conservative parties in the early 1930s, and the family control over the Guardia was jealously protected and assiduously improved. The Somozas devoted much attention to the selection of higher officers, with preference being given, when feasible, to members of the family. As a protection against possible coups, officers were constantly transferred from post to post; officers who became too popular might be retired or sent on a mission overseas. In later years, the Guardia was kept increasingly isolated from the general community, with special medical, housing, and clothing subsidies, special educational arrangements for children, steady pay raises, and tax privileges. None of these policies were particularly exceptional or deplorable in themselves; the governments of all Latin American countries, especially those with histories of civil strife and coups d'état, are well advised to keep the army as happy as possible. But with time, the Guardia was permitted activities and privileges that went beyond the necessary or the admissible: guardsmen were free, even encouraged, to supplement their incomes through extortion, and crimes committed against civilians by guardsmen rarely were tried in a civil court. Thus, the morale of the Guardia Nacional *as a fighting organization* was slowly but effectively undermined.

But beyond graft and patronage, beyond the support of the church and the control of the Guardia, the long tenure of power by the Somozas derived from the fact that through the 1960s their rule was neither too harsh nor completely without benefit to large segments of the population, especially if Nicaragua is compared with certain other states in Latin America, not to speak of the wider Third World. As one long-time student of Central American affairs states: "Somoza moderation [was] clearly one of the major factors behind the family's long stay in power."[56] Under Luís Somoza, whose administration coincided with the launching of the Alliance for Progress, some real improvements were made in public housing, health care, and education, and some steps were taken toward agrarian reform. Luís did not want his brother "Tachito" to become president, but the latter commanded the Guardia and so had his way. It is with the administration of "Tachito" Somoza that the regime entered its crisis, because he eventually "deviated from the family tradition of restraint."[57] Press censorship under his administration became far more heavyhanded and civil rights violations more widespread. Thus, support for the regime began to erode both at home and abroad.

THE BREAKDOWN

During the 1970s, while the Somoza regime was in its fourth decade, a series of events alienated even conservative public opinion and shook the confidence of the leadership in its ability to survive. These events were the Managua earthquake of 1972, the aftermath of the Sandinista hostage affair of 1974, the coming to power of Jimmy Carter in 1977, and the murder of Pedro Joaquin Chamorro in 1978.

On December 23, 1972, an earthquake destroyed almost the entire downtown area of Managua, resulting in the deaths of many and in destitution, injury, or illness for thousands more. Here was a golden opportunity for Anastasio Somoza to play the statesman-benefactor by dipping into his enormous private fortune to succor his afflicted countrymen. Instead, Somoza and his henchmen sought to make a profit from the calamity, even going so far as to interfere with the distribution of internationally donated emergency relief. Even many of the commercial and industrial elite turned in revulsion from this cesspool of graft amid an inferno of misery, and began to speak openly against the president. The adverse publicity resulting from accusations and revelations of corruption surrounding the Managua tragedy badly damaged Somoza's image in Nicaragua, Latin America, and the United States.[58]

The disaffection of Managua's elite class was a severe blow, but others were to follow in rapid order; 1974 was an especially bad year for the regime. The opposition Conservative party, led by Pedro Chamorro, declared that the upcoming presidential elections would be a sham. The Roman Catholic bishops signed a joint pastoral letter condemning the unrepresentative nature of Nicaraguan politics. Worst of all, the long-comatose Sandinista National Liberation Front (FSLN) began carrying out notable raids in Matagalpa province. The FSLN had been founded in 1962 by Carlos Fonseca Amador and others, with moral and material assistance from Fidel Castro. Their attempt to ignite a guerrilla war in 1963 failed completely. Another effort in 1966–

1967 sank against the rocks of peasant apathy and Guardia vigilance; even the illegal Nicaraguan Communist party refused to support the guerrillas (just as, at about the same time, the Bolivian Communists would have nothing to do with the Guevara expedition). In 1974, however, the rebels began to make themselves felt, and on the night of December 27 they staged a big raid on the house of former Minister of Agriculture Castillo, capturing many important persons, including the minister of foreign affairs, the Nicaraguan ambassador to the United States, and the mayor of Managua.

On December 30, in exchange for their hostages, the Sandinistas were permitted to fly to Cuba (with the papal nuncio and the Mexican and Spanish ambassadors along for security); the government had also had to pay a huge ransom, and perhaps worst of all, had had to permit the reading over national radio of a violently anti-Somoza tract.

The December 1974 raid of the FSLN and its aftermath seriously undermined the prestige of a regime obviously no longer invulnerable. Worse, a furious Somoza "unleashed" the Guardia Nacional in the countryside: searching for Sandinista supporters, they pillaged and raped at will throughout large areas of the country, doing no harm to the rebels but instead a great deal of good. The Somoza dictatorship provides us with a textbook example of a regime that, displaying a truly perverse stupidity, plays into the hands of the rebels and uses completely inappropriate punitive tactics against the civil population, turning its supporters into neutrals, neutrals into critics, and critics into recruits for the guerrillas.

The year 1977 was to be another signally bad one. In January, the Nicaraguan bishops issued a severe criticism of the regime. Much worse, newly inaugurated President Jimmy Carter, determined to make Nicaragua a showplace of his new human rights policy, announced that the United States would not renew its security pact with Nicaragua. This was crushing news for Somoza. The Guardia Nacional was still a very good fighting force in the Central American context, but at the time of Carter's announcement it had only about 8,000 men, with perhaps another 4,000 reserves.[59] It was one of the smallest constabularies in all Latin America.[60] In view of the increasing activity of the latter-day Sandinistas, the Guardia would have had to be built up substantially to reach the ratio of ten to one that many consider essential for waging a successful large-scale anti-guerrilla war. Carter's abrupt reversal of U.S. policy meant that Nicaragua could not count on getting training or all-important equipment for the necessary expansion of the Guardia. In the midst of these reverses, on July 25, 1977, President Somoza suffered a heart attack that necessitated his being flown to Miami for treatment. This medical emergency, perhaps more than anything else, suggested to many inside the regime that its days might be fewer than anyone had hitherto imagined. And by the end of the year Sandinista attacks on outlying garrisons, although small in scale, were increasing in number.

In the midst of this disintegrating situation came the explosion caused by the murder, in January 1978, of Pedro Chamorro, Conservative party leader and internationally respected Managua publisher, an authentic member of the nation's elite and a prominent critic of the regime. It is not inconceivable that Somoza told the truth when he said he was not involved in this shameful killing, which he certainly had to know would damage his already shaky regime. However, when it became apparent that the government investigation into Chamorro's death was going to be not much more than a whitewash of the structure of the whole regime, a remarkably effective general strike, led by the Managua chamber of commerce, closed down much of that city and several others. Such general strikes are historically considered a fatal augury for Latin American dictators, and Somoza was to prove no exception. Henceforth it was clear that the only remaining support Somoza had in the country was the (still formidable) Guardia Nacional. Thus, on June 9, 1978, Somoza announced that on completion of his presidential term in 1981, he would retire from politics. This declaration failed to have the hoped-for sedative effect on the nation, however. The Sandinistas smelled victory, and the fighting increased.

The disaffection of the Nicaraguan elite with the Somoza regime was reflected in the country's deteriorating relations with other Latin states. Charges and countercharges about Costa Rican border and neutrality violations became numerous and bitter. Venezuela actually offered Costa Rica aircraft and troops with which to defend her territory in case of a Somoza invasion. At home, the myth of Somoza power continued to crumble. In March 1978, in an act of "revolutionary justice," the FSLN murdered General Reynaldo Perez Vega, Somoza's chief military adviser and second in command of the Guardia Nacional. Then in August, some Sandinistas, disguised as presidential bodyguards and led by soon-to-be-famous Edén Pastora, were able to seize the national palace and hold it for almost 48 hours. In the next month, attacks by rebels escalated in number and seriousness. At last, physically ill, tired of fighting, aware that the old order would have to change, Somoza offered to hold a plebiscite on the future of Nicaragua, the balloting to be under the supervision of the United States, Guatemala, and the Dominican Republic. No one, least of all the FSLN, was interested in this proposal. The fighting continued.

At the beginning of June 1979, the Sandinistas launched their long-awaited grand offensive. Heavy fighting engulfed the towns of Chinandega and Naranjo, raged along the Costa Rican border, and burst forth in the slums of Managua itself. A Guardia counteroffensive in the second half of June gained back some ground. Nevertheless, in September, the rebels took the sizable town of Masaya, 20 miles from Managua, and held it through several days of heavy fighting.

Meanwhile, the Carter administration continued its two-year practice of tightening the noose around Somoza. On February 8, 1979, Carter ordered most of the Americans in Nicaragua to leave and announced the suspension of all aid to the country. Still Somoza and the Guardia Nacional held on. Finally, on June 22, 1979, Secretary of State Vance, in an address to the Organization of American States, called for Somoza's ouster, and the OAS voted in favor of his resignation two days later. (The FSLN had promised the OAS that, in return for its help in overthrowing Somoza, the Sandinistas would hold free elections as soon as possible.) Mexico had already broken relations with Nicaragua, denouncing the government's "horrendous genocide."

But resolutions and speeches could not bring the fighting to an end; neither, for all the friendly publicity that they received in the United States, could the Sandinista forces. The Guardia, bloody and battered, was still probably the best fighting force in Central America. In the summer of 1979, it was clear that the Guardia's 13,000 men were not nearly numerous enough to wipe out the 5,000 Sandinista fighters, especially as many of the latter now possessed modern weapons. It was equally clear that the Guardia could, and almost certainly would, go on fighting indefinitely and effectively. The officers and men of the Guardia kept fighting partly from loyalty to the Somozas, partly in hatred of the Sandinistas, but most of all because they feared what would happen to them if they laid down their arms and the FSLN took power. In light of the mass executions that destroyed the Cuban army after Castro's victory, they had good reason to be afraid. Thus, the combat could drag on for years.

The Gordian knot was cut by the Carter White House, which again, as with the arms embargo, intervened unexpectedly and effectively in the Nicaraguan civil war. President Carter sent a special envoy, W. G. Bowdler, to the Costa Rican capital of San José, where he entered into negotiations with the FSLN. In an agreement signed on July 12, 1979, the Sandinistas renounced all plans of bloody vengeance against the Guardia; indeed, they promised to allow those Guardia members who so desired to join the new Sandinista-run national army after Somoza had fallen.[61] In the face of such United States-blessed guarantees, the Guardia gave up the fight. Thus, the last obstacle to the Sandinista conquest of power was removed not by military victory but by the intervention of Jimmy Carter. As in Iran, President Carter had succeeded in neutralizing the army of a long-time U.S. ally so that rebel forces could come to power, rebels who almost immediately bared the fangs of profound hostility to the United States.

Five days after the Bowdler agreement, Somoza resigned the presidency and left the country.

But neither free elections nor peace came to Nicaragua.

NOTES

1. Howard J. Wiarda, "Cuba," in Ben G. Burnett and Kenneth F. Johnson, eds., *Political Forces in Latin America* (Belmont, CA: Wadsworth, 1970), p. 241.
2. Wiarda, "Cuba," p. 233; see also Theodore Draper, *Castroism: Theory and Practice* (New York: Praeger, 1965).

3. Ramon Eduardo Ruiz, *Cuba: The Making of a Revolution* (New York: Norton, 1968), pp. 9–10.
4. Wiarda, "Cuba," p. 235.
5. Wiarda, "Cuba," p. 239.
6. Hugh Thomas, *The Cuban Revolution* (New York: Harper and Row, 1977), p. 263.
7. Ruiz, *Cuba*, p. 127 and *passim*.
8. D. E. H. Russell, *Rebellion, Revolution and Armed Force* (New York: Academic Press, 1974), p. 116.
9. Harvey F. Kline, "Cuba: The Politics of Socialist Revolution," in Howard J. Wiarda and Harvey F. Kline, eds., *Latin American Politics and Development* (Boston: Houghton Mifflin, 1979), p. 452.
10. D. Chapelle, "How Castro Won," in Franklin Mark Osanka, ed., *Modern Guerrilla Warfare* (New York: Free Press, 1962), p. 334.
11. Thomas, *The Cuban Revolution*, p. 258.
12. Thomas, *The Cuban Revolution*, p. 259.
13. Thomas, *The Cuban Revolution*, p. 257.
14. Robert Tabor, *The War of the Flea*, quoted in Geoffrey Fairbairn, *Revolutionary Guerrilla Warfare: The Countryside Version* (Harmondsworth: Penguin, 1974), p. 271.
15. Thomas, *The Cuban Revolution*, p. 196.
16. Thomas, *The Cuban Revolution*, p. 202.
17. Thomas, *The Cuban Revolution*, p. 229.
18. Thomas, *The Cuban Revolution*, p. 203.
19. Tabor in Fairbairn, *Revolutionary Guerrilla Warfare*, p. 276.
20. Thomas, *The Cuban Revolution*, p. 258.
21. Fulgencio Batista, *Cuba Betrayed* (New York: Vantage, 1962), p. 43.
22. Batista, *Cuba Betrayed*, p. 101n.
23. Batista, *Cuba Betrayed*, p. 89.
24. Thomas, *The Cuban Revolution*, p. 261.
25. Batista, *Cuba Betrayed*, p. 102.
26. Louis A. Perez, Jr., *Army Politics in Cuba, 1898–1958* (Pittsburgh, PA: University of Pittsburgh Press, 1976), pp. 155–158.
27. Batista, *Cuba Betrayed*, p. 99.
28. Ray Brennan, *Castro, Cuba, and Justice* (Garden City, NJ: Doubleday, 1959), pp. 232–233.
29. Thomas, *The Cuban Revolution*, p. 215.
30. Thomas, *The Cuban Revolution*, p. 217.
31. Thomas, *The Cuban Revolution*, p. 218.
32. Batista, *Cuba Betrayed*, p. 107n.
33. Batista, *Cuba Betrayed*, p. 105n.
34. Thomas, *The Cuban Revolution*, p. 228.
35. Thomas, *The Cuban Revolution*, p. 240.
36. Thomas, *The Cuban Revolution*, p. 241.
37. Thomas, *The Cuban Revolution*, p. 236.
38. Edward Gonzalez, *Cuba Under Castro: The Limits of Charisma* (Boston: Houghton Mifflin, 1974), p. 91.
39. Thomas, *The Cuban Revolution*, p. 256.
40. Thomas, *The Cuban Revolution*, p. 258.
41. Thomas, *The Cuban Revolution*, p. 256.
42. Thomas, *The Cuban Revolution*, p. 258.
43. Thomas, *The Cuban Revolution*, p. 259.
44. Wiarda, "Cuba," p. 244.

45. Thomas W. Walker, "Nicaragua: The Somoza Family Regime," in Howard J. Wiarda and Harvey F. Kline, eds., *Latin American Politics and Development* (Boston: Houghton Mifflin, 1979), p. 321.
46. Richard Millett, *Guardians of the Dynasty* (Maryknoll, NY: Orbis, 1977), p. 70.
47. Millett, *Guardians*, p. 77.
48. Millett, *Guardians*, p. 71.
49. Millett, *Guardians*, p. 106.
50. Millett, *Guardians*, pp. 63–64.
51. Millett, *Guardians*, p. 94.
52. Millett, *Guardians*, pp. 147–148.
53. Millett, *Guardians*, pp. 158–159.
54. Millett, *Guardians*, p. 160.
55. Millett, *Guardians*, p. 252.
56. Walker, "Nicaragua," p. 316; see also Martin C. Needler, *An Introduction to Latin American Politics: The Structure of Conflict* (Englewood Cliffs, NJ: Prentice Hall, 1977), pp. 186–187.
57. Walker, "Nicaragua."
58. Somoza denies any wrongdoing on his part in his memoirs, *Nicaragua Betrayed*, one of the most incredibly ineffective attempts at self-justification I have ever encountered.
59. John Paxton, ed., *Statesman's Yearbook, 1979–1980* (Boston: St. Martin's Press).
60. Alfred G. Cuzan and Richard J. Heggen, "A Micropolitical Explanation of the 1979 Nicaraguan Revolution," *Latin American Research Review*, 27 (1982): 156–170.
61. *New York Times*, July 12, 1979.

PART

4

Armies Versus Governments

In the third quarter of the twentieth century, national armies played the decisive role in reshaping the political structures of several countries, from the toppling of the Fourth Republic in France to the reintroduction of parliamentary democracy in Portugal. Invariably, the armies viewed their moves against their respective governments as a defensive reaction.

In 1954, the French army was deeply humiliated by what it viewed as its politically contrived defeat in Vietnam. When in that same year a nationalist rebellion broke out in Algeria, a land that possessed an old and deep emotional significance for the army, it vowed that it would win the struggle at all costs.

Early French counterguerrilla tactics in Algeria were poor, but the army eventually evolved a strategy whereby with limited numbers of soldiers and limited destruction of life and property it reduced the guerrillas to the edge of extinction.

French Algeria is an illustration of how a nationalist guerrilla movement can be defeated and how, in a democracy, a successful counterguerrilla effort can be extremely costly for the army and for the constitutional system.

In Brazil, we encounter the intriguing institution of the constitutional coup: the army's acknowledged right to remove a government that acts contrary to the national interest.

The dominant figure of twentieth-century Brazilian politics was Getulio Vargas, whom the army twice removed from the presidency. In the early 1960s, Jango Goulart, a lieutenant of Vargas', became president by accident, and proceeded to distort the economy, frighten the middle class, and challenge the army's control over its chain of command. The army's eventual move against Goulart, the most massive deployment of troops in the Western Hemisphere since the U.S. Civil War, succeeded in a few days at the cost of a handful of casualties.

The charismatic Sukarno led Indonesia to independence after World War II. He then gradually assumed the powers of a dictator, and his policies produced foreign war and economic stagnation. Indonesia's Communist party, the largest in any non-Communist state, feared a clash with the army if Sukarno died too soon. Party leaders (along with elements of the Indonesian air force) therefore supported an attempt to murder all the principal army generals. Two of the surviving generals rallied the army against the coup, and, unleashing the widespread popular hatred of the Communists, presided over a general massacre.

In Portugal, Dr. Salazar rescued his country from economic and political chaos in the 1930s and thereafter remained in office for decades with the silent support of the army. By 1974, Salazar was gone. His successors seemed prepared to make the army the scapegoat for the interminable wars in Portugal's African empire, and announced an ill-advised move to interfere with seniority in the officer corps. As in the Brazilian model, the Portuguese army exercised its "moderator" function and removed the regime in a swift and nearly bloodless coup.

7

French Algeria: The Victory and Crucifixion of an Army

If one is to sacrifice one's own life and that of others, it is essential that the cause be simple.

—De la Gorce

"The Algerian War was to be the last, probably, and certainly the greatest and most dramatic of the colonial wars."[1] Algeria was the scene of a double revolt: one by a Muslim-based nationalist organization against France, the other by the Algeria-based French army against the French government. The Algerian War would encompass the almost complete defeat of the Muslim rebels by the French army, the handing over of Algeria to these defeated rebels, and the immolation of the victorious French army and its numerous Muslim allies.

FRANCE, ALGERIA, AND THE ARMY

Algeria once had been the home of the Barbary corsairs (from the Roman word *barbari*) and the scene of the heroic 19th century exploits of young Stephen Decatur. French armies entered the area in 1830, but France did not decide seriously to subdue the entire region until about 1840, and total control was not achieved before the end of the century. During and after the conquest, large numbers of Europeans, mainly French but including many Italians, emigrated to Algeria and made their homes there. The Second Republic declared all Algeria to be an integral part of France and divided the country into three departments. Thus, the flag, and the prestige, of the French nation was irrevocably planted on the North African shore. Moreover, the European settlers and their descendants believed that because they had found Algeria a desert and made it a garden, they should be forever recognized as the dominant element there. They bitterly opposed any idea of giving political equality to the Arabs, and the concept of an independent Algeria under Muslim control was to them preposterous and infuriating. Thus, in a true sense, "Algeria was France's Ireland, almost as closely linked to the homeland as Ireland had been to Great Britain until 1922, and with the same problems of a minority population implanted by colonization."[2] The Irish Question poisoned British politics for generations, plunged Ireland into a bloody civil war, and ultimately caused a grave constitutional crisis at Westminster. Algeria would be even more painful for the French.

An essential element of the complicated and eventually tragic Algerian Question was this: much of the professional French army of the 1950s was based in Algeria, and felt that the land could not be relinquished. This attachment of the army to Algeria had three principal sources. First, the army had been deeply impressed with the liberation of France and Europe during World War II, partly from bases in North Africa; from this point of view, to abandon the country would be a strategic as well as a symbolic catastrophe.

Second, the French army was attached to Algerian soil for psycho-sociological reasons. Algeria was perfect for the army: here it had space and scope to pursue its vocation. If the politicians were to lose Algeria or give it away, the whole army would have to be domiciled permanently on metropolitan territory, where it felt unwelcome and uncomfortable. Based against its will in a bourgeois, uncomprehending, indifferent and inhospitable France, the army would lose its soul.

Last, the outburst of serious violence in Algeria began only a few months after the last French forces had withdrawn from Indochina. During the southeast Asian conflict, the French army had promised its hundreds of thousands of native supporters that it would never abandon them. But, in the army's view, the pusillanimous politicians in Paris, having cast the soldiers into a hell in Indochina, starved them of the supplies and men to fulfill that promise, causing the army to lose some of its finest men, along with its reputation and, to a degree, its honor. Then the French army had been forced to witness the plight of 1 million Vietnamese refugees fleeing southward from the areas that had been handed over to the Communists at the war's end. From these dreadful experiences, many professional French soldiers conceived a real contempt for and real fear of the Fourth Republican establishment, and indeed all politicians. "This was the cancer that took root and grew, until it would shock the world."[3] Heartsick and humiliated after the Indochina inferno, now confronted with another challenge in Algeria, many officers identified the Algerian struggle as the war that "even against the will of God or man, must not be lost."[4]

Thus the flag was nailed to the Algerian mast.

GENESIS OF THE MUSLIM REBELLION

The belief that revolutionary wars "erupt spontaneously out of conditions grown socially and economically intolerable — and can only erupt out of such conditions — is a very important propaganda weapon in the hands of sympathizers with revolutionary warfare."[5] In the view of many contemporary analysts, however, revolutions, especially in peasant countries, are never spontaneous, and almost always are organized by elite groups of urban intellectuals intent on transforming their societies through the accumulation of total power within their own hands.

The idea that revolution is the creation not of the masses but of the elite has a venerable lineage. Vilfredo Pareto defined revolution itself as "the circulation of elites": would-be or counterelites challenge the incumbent power-holders by mobilizing mass support to their side, promising fraternity and equality, but meaning something rather different from the understanding of those terms common among the masses.[6] And Lenin himself, who knew a thing or two about revolution, baldly declared: "No revolutionary theory, no revolution." This meant that the unaided masses by their own efforts could engage in violence but not in lasting social transformation; for that, a comprehensive analysis of society and a comprehensive plan for changing every salient aspect of it is required; *that* requires the leadership of people who know how to create and manipulate theory: an educated elite. Hence, Lenin organized his vanguard party of professional revolutionaries to give a few well-aimed nudges to Marx's historical inevitability.[7] The party becomes the advance guard of the proletariat and acts *in the name of* the proletariat.[8] Whether or not one fully accepts the elitist concept of revolution, it certainly dominates the thinking of professional revolutionaries (Lenin, Mao, Guevara, Debray) and students of revolution alike.[9]

In Algeria, the stage had been partially set for an attempt at revolution early in the century by a puritanical Islamic revival that called for a total rejection of European culture and physical isolation of the French. Subsequently, "the revolution [of the 1950s] was not born in the hearts of the peasantry and proletariat, nor was its ideology directly derived from their deepest concerns."[10] Instead, the Algerian uprising was led mainly by middle-class intellectuals, described rather harshly by one scholar as "a small group of power-hungry men, shrewd, ambitious, and ruthless, who had little in common with the half-starved Algerian peasant."[11] In the early years of the revolt, many Muslims, peasant or urban, supported the revolution not spontaneously but "through fear of reprisal from their nationalist rulers-to-be" or otherwise "leaned in the direction where real power seemed to exist at the moment."[12]

A notable example of the elite nature of the Algerian revolution's leadership was Ferhat Abbas. Educated in Europe and a great admirer of French culture and French power, he began and remained for a long time a moderate, seeking true integration of the Algerian Muslim population into the French nation. He believed that before the arrival of the French no such thing as an Algerian nation had existed.

> When the French crossed the Mediterranean to North Africa in 1830, they were confronted, not with a nation, but with a nest of pirates. Algeria had no demarcated boundaries, no national history, no effective government, and no name.[13]

Such resistance to French rule as there had been up to 1940 occurred almost exclusively in the name of religion, not nationalism. Then came World War II. France suffered a crushing defeat in Europe, while many Algerian Muslims were mobilized for the war and received military training. Despite some vague phrases enunciated during the wartime crisis about a postwar "French community," it eventually became apparent even to such assimilationist advocates as Ferhat Abbas that no Fourth Republican cabinet was going to make any serious changes in the general status of Algerian Muslims vis-à-vis the hard-fisted and ever-watchful European settlers (*colons*). Thus, Abbas joined the *Front de Libération National* (the FLN; the military arm was the *Armée de Libération National:* ALN) and announced a new executive committee of that group, with himself as the head, in September 1957.

Another aspect of the elite nature of the Algerian revolutionary leadership is illustrated by Frantz Fanon. "Violence is a cleansing force," proclaimed Fanon, through which the "manhood" of the colonialized peoples could be "restored." Fanon disseminated these interesting ideas in the FLN newspaper, of which he was editor (in Tunis) and in several books, of which perhaps the best known is *The Wretched of the Earth* (1965). It is perhaps less well known that Fanon was born not in Africa but in the French West Indies, received a splendid education in France (medicine and psychiatry), and did not so much as set foot in Algeria until 1953.

The Algerian revolution was elitist but not Communist. Indeed, "Communist influence barely touched the FLN war effort."[14] Algerians returning home from the cities of France after World War I found the local Socialist and Communist parties and unions dominated by Muslim-hating colons. Hence, they had to form their own organizations. The methods used by the FLN during the revolution won it no friends in the world of Algerian Communism: Communist railway workers, for example, did not like to see their co-workers blown up by terrorist bombs. During the early years of FLN violence, in fact, bloody fighting took place between it and the Algerian Communists. The FLN also bitterly fought a rival Muslim organization, the *Mouvement National Algérien.*

VICTORY OF THE FRENCH ARMY

The armed revolt of the FLN erupted on the night of October 31, 1954. Perhaps 500 insurgents attacked or committed arson against some 60 French military posts and police stations in eastern Algeria. Few authorities, however, took the outbreak seriously, and this, along with the inadequate numbers of French troops in North Africa at the time and significant support from Egypt's dictator, Gamal Abdel Nasser, enabled the revolt to develop rapidly.

Writers on guerrilla war maintain that in order to defeat guerrillas, the government forces need a ratio of ten men to one (this ratio of course would not in itself be a *sufficient* condition for victory). This great disproportion is necessary for good reasons. Although the guerrillas need only strike here or there, now or then, as the spirit or the opportunity moves them, and can then fade back into the bush or the villages, the government must maintain order in populated areas, keep highways open, guard strategic installations such as oil fields, airports, power facilities, government buildings, etc. It must provide some sort of security for the sometimes widely scattered population in rural areas. Beyond these tasks, the government must use mobile strike forces so that the guerrillas will not only be resisted where they attack, but be sought out and pursued. When the rebellion began, there were fewer than 50,000 French troops in all Algeria, a territory larger than Norway, Sweden, Finland, Denmark, France, West Germany, Portugal, and the United Kingdom combined. For almost a year after the outbreak of violence, there were never enough soldiers to mount a serious counterguerrilla effort.

It was partly owing to the inadequate number of troops available that early French counterguerrilla tactics were very poor. For example, the army would move into a village known to have been visited by guerrillas, stay for a short time, interrogate some villagers, and then move on. Thus, those villagers who had given information to the army or even the entire village, were exposed to immediate and grave reprisals when the guerrillas returned. In fighting guerrillas, the essence of the whole activity is to separate the guerrillas from the support, voluntary or extorted, of the rural population. To accomplish this, the peasants must be convinced that the government is going to win, or at the very least, that the government is going to *be in permanent control of the particular province or region.* No village once occupied by government forces must ever under any circumstances be permitted to fall back into the hands of the guerrillas. So-called search-and-destroy tactics are therefore utterly misdirected and negative. To fight guerrillas effectively, a government must spread steadily outward from base areas that have been thoroughly cleared of guerrillas and that are visibly under its control. The French forces in Algeria eventually adopted these tactics, and with them they defeated the guerrillas.

By April 1956, having learned to take the Algerian insurrection very seriously, the French had mobilized 450,000 men. They used the *quadrillage* (checkerboard) system, a variant of successful tactics used against royalist guerrillas during the French Revolution.[15] The essence of this system is as follows: hold the cities in strength, but also occupy many smaller places in the hinterland with light garrisons, restricting the guerrillas to movement in an ever-narrowing field. Meanwhile, mobile elite formations (in this case, paratroopers and Foreign Legionnaires) raid the hinterland, keeping the guerrillas off balance, depriving them of a secure base, and inflicting casualties on them.

Revolutionary guerrilla warfare is an attempt to prove wrong Trotsky's principle that a revolution cannot be made against an entrenched elite's armed forces. It is a strategy designed to answer the question: "how does a rebel party make a revolution against a regime protected by a professional army?"[16]

From von Clausewitz to Mao, students of guerrilla warfare have laid down certain general principles by which those who would oppose the power of the state and its professional army should guide themselves. The most important among these principles are: (a) the guerrillas should operate over a wide area, so that their movements do not become stereotyped and they cannot be surrounded easily; (b) guerrillas should stay away from the seacoast, so that the government cannot make use of amphibious operations against them; (c) they should choose as the center of their activity an area of rough terrain, thus impeding the movements of the heavily armed and well-equipped government troops (the Roman word for an army's baggage was "impedimenta") while rewarding the lightly armed guerrillas. So-called urban guerrillas, whether by ignorance or by design, violate all these rules; for the consequences of such violation, we have no better example than the Algerian insurrection. For instance, the FLN chose to make the Muslim quarter of the city of Algiers, the famous Casbah, a center of its operations. They infiltrated the Casbah, recruited thousands from the proletariat of that section, and from within it began engaging in a massive terrorist campaign against the French civilian population and France's numerous Muslim sympathizers. The French army responded intelligently and efficiently, throwing a noose of well-trained and tough troops around the constricted area of the Casbah and then tightening that noose: thus "between February and October 1957 the 10th Paratroop Division commanded by General [Jacques] Massu effectively destroyed the terrorist organization in Algiers."[17] At the end of that period "the terror had been effectively lifted."[18]

In the countryside, anti-guerrilla operations became ever more effective and ever more massive. From *protecting* civilians from the guerrillas, the French Army moved toward *separating* civilians from the guerrillas. Between 1955 and 1961 nearly 2 million Muslims (of a population of perhaps 12 million) either moved or were moved out of the war zones. The main purpose of regrouping the Muslims was surveillance, but the army began to provide social services for them on a very large scale; officers found themselves totally responsible for all aspects of life in their areas, including medical care, education, public hygiene, police and political activities, and even employment for large numbers of Muslim civilians. Thus, the moral and psychological involvement and commitment of the officers to the Algerians was immeasurably deepened, over and above the remarkable fact that the French army employed nearly 180,000 Muslims as auxiliaries, persons who could expect little mercy from the FLN if the French ever left the country.[19] On the other hand, during most of the war, many French officers in Algeria were remote from, and unsympathetic to, the colons, whom the army viewed as the major obstacle to its plan for converting the Muslim population into loyal, or at least acquiescent, citizens of French Algeria.

This was not a farfetched aim or one limited in its attractions to "the military mind." In 1954, in a speech to the National Assembly, François Mitterand (no less) declared: "Algeria is France, and who among you would hesitate to employ every means to preserve France?"[20] Many metropolitan politicians compared Nasser, the FLN's benefactor, to Hitler, and when Nasser seized the Suez Canal in August 1956, Mitterand compared it to Hilter's taking of Czechoslovakia.[21] Indeed, in the summer of 1956, the politicians hatched a plan for an invasion of Egypt that would settle Nasser (and the FLN) once and for all. The French army found itself committed to the Suez operation by the politicians and, when this battle was on the verge of victorious completion, the French army was pulled out again. The cycle of commitment and capitulation was all too reminiscent of what had happened in Vietnam, and the stock of Fourth Republican politicians declined, if possible, among the officer corps.

Nevertheless, with the war going well, with the politicians proclaiming Algeria to be irrevocably "France," with the care and feeding of millions of Muslims well in hand, and with the military collaboration of a large section of the Muslim population, it seemed that "everything combined to reinforce, in the minds of the military cadres, the conviction that French authority in the Maghreb was both natural and necessary.[22]

From the guerrilla viewpoint, the action in Algeria was indeed going very badly. Stymied inside the country, the rebels sought help from the outside. Morocco and Tunisia, independent and sympathetic neighboring states, provided the FLN with supplies and sanctuary. The French, however, were equal even to this challenge. By the fall of 1957, the army had completed construction of the Morice Line; this was an impressive barrier extending all along the Algerian borders with Morocco and Tunisia. With its watchtowers, electrified wire, alarm systems, and mine fields, the Morice Line effectively slowed traffic across the borders to an inadequate trickle. Late in April 1958, the ALN mounted a desperate attack in strength on the line; the attack failed, and the ALN sustained enormous casualties.

By the end of 1957, the French had almost completely eliminated terrorism in the large towns, effectively interrupted transit between Algeria and her neighbors, and choked off outside assistance. The quadrillage system kept the rebels in the countryside away from the cities and towns, while the regroupment of the peasants into protected areas broke the ties of the ALN with the peasantry and starved it of food, recruits, and intelligence. There were perhaps 25,000 rebels outside Algeria, only 15,000 within it. The guerrilla organization was split by jealousies and rivalries both within Algeria and between the rebels inside and those outside the country. In short, by the beginning of 1958 the war was, by every intelligent measure, clearly being won by the French army. To have suggested to the army at this point that it should give up the struggle, that Algeria, the 1 million colons, the millions of Muslims who did not want to support the rebellion, that all this should be handed over to the visibly losing FLN, would have seemed either totally ridiculous, or the malicious scheme of a profoundly diseased mentality.

THE QUESTION OF TORTURE

The late Raymond Aron once observed that "pacification cannot be imagined without torture, just as the war of liberation cannot be imagined without terror." Perhaps this is true. Whatever one's views on the inevitability or the morality of torture, there can be little doubt that its use in the Algerian context gravely undermined the ability of the French army to hold onto the victory it had so clearly attained.

The fact of torture — physical punishment by the authorities of captured terrorists to extract information about future terrorist activities — must be linked to the fact that urban and rural terrorism was a basic technique of the FLN. Bombs were placed near bus stops and in restaurants; the maiming and massacring of European and loyal Muslim civilians became an every-day occurrence. In this war, characterized by brutality and even savagery on both sides, the rebels concentrated on killing, often in grisly fashion, Muslims who cooperated with the authorities; even the nephew of Ferhat Abbas himself was murdered in retaliation for helping the government. In this grim context, many found the standard justifications for the forced extraction of information from known terrorists to be very compelling. As one French officer anonymously wrote: "between two evils, it is necessary to choose the lesser. So that innocent persons should not be put to death or mutilated, the criminals must be punished and put effectively out of harm's way."[23] Or in the more succinct phrase of General Massu: "the innocent [i.e., the next victims of terrorist bombs] deserve more protection than the guilty."[24] And had not François Mitterand said "employ *every means*"?

"It would be wrong," writes one student of this sad and complicated subject, "to infer that torture gangrened the Army as an institution."[25] These acts "being inadmissible, they were compartmentalized and secreted — known to all but apprehended by few, a dark cloud floating over the operational landscape."[26] General Pierre Billotte wrote: "regarding torture, I am categorical: whatever its form and whatever its purpose, it is unacceptable, inadmissible, condemnable; it soils the honor of the army and the country. The ideological character of modern war makes no difference."[27] (To which Massu replied: "torture is to be condemned. But we would like a precise answer as to where torture begins."[28] Many others in the army establishment besides General Billotte condemned torture for any purpose, no matter how grave the provocation. Nevertheless, torture existed:

the well-established fact that certain members of the French military service, on their own initiative or on orders from above, methodically tortured FLN sympathizers and agents *contributed little to the unity of the army* and much to its anguish [italics added][29]

Torture undermined the French effort in Algeria in three ways. First, the discovery of its existence shocked many of the finest junior officers. These young men, inexperienced, idealistic, with a romanticized view of their profession, often possessed an image of themselves as knights heroically defending the far-flung ramparts of a valid civilization against a barbarous and perhaps dishonorable foe. This self-image, and the morale that it sustained, could hardly survive intact a confrontation, even at second hand, with the practice of torture, no matter how officially condemned, cleverly justified, and discreetly practiced. Second, the use of torture, however overdramatized its scope and severity may have been in the French press, played directly into the hands of those French groups whose opposition to the war did not stem from a concern over torture per se, especially those for whom politics is not a systematic effort to find workable solutions to complex problems but a splendid arena in which to display one's moral superiority to one's fellows, and who are never more certain they are doing so than when publicly excoriating their own civilization and its underlying values. In the absence of torture, the dogmatic anti-patriotism and reflex anti-militarism of these persons could have been dismissed, or at least contained; the torture issue gave them a matchless weapon with which to destroy support for the war among groups who had not already been disaffected by the squalid demands of the colons or the mounting casualty lists. Third, and perhaps most important, the fact of torture contributed directly to the ripening view within the army in Algeria that collective military mutiny would be preferable to politically imposed surrender. The French officer corps (and not that element alone) in Algeria resisted the idea of a negotiated settlement not only because they knew themselves to have won on the field of battle, not only because they had become deeply committed to the army's educational and medical work among the peasants, not only because they knew what would happen to the scores of thousands of Muslims who had cooperated with them, but also because if the war had been for nothing, *then so had been the dishonor they had incurred from the means used to root out the terrorists.* That so many good officers should have implicated themselves in illegal and unethical procedures *for nothing*—this was intolerable. In order for the torture to have been more than a mere crime, or a shameful weakness, the war *must have been worth it*; that is, the army simply could not afford to have the politicians pull the rug out from under them yet again, as in Vietnam and at Suez.

The damage that the use of torture inflicted on the French army appears all the more a tragedy when one reflects that relatively little more information was obtained by this method than could have been derived from use of the more usual and infinitely more acceptable techniques of bribery, surveillance, and civilian cooperation.

OPINION IN METROPOLITAN FRANCE

As the war continued, FLN elements inside Algeria found themselves in a position subordinate to those outside. In part, this was because of the success of the French anti-guerrilla effort, which had destroyed many ALN units and chased others over the frontiers; in part it was because while the military struggle inside Algeria was being lost, the FLN was winning one diplomatic and psychological victory after another in the wider world, including Paris.[30]

Along with a rising tide of success for the French army in its struggle against the FLN went a rising tide of disenchantment with the war within France itself. Numerous streams came together to feed antiwar sentiment. Many in France were still spiritually exhausted after the traumatic events of defeat and occupation by the Nazis. The recent ignominious loss of Vietnam had soured many French citizens on any kind of overseas military involvement. The growing demands of the draft increased the unpopularity of the war. The gross intransigence of the colons, opposed to any concessions to the Muslims, even to those whose loyalty to France was indisputable, offended many, especially when they considered that many of these colons were Italians or Corsicans or Alsatians; it seemed ridiculous that one should be called upon to make sacrifices to preserve the outmoded caste privileges of a settler population not even composed of true Frenchmen. The FLN terror network among the 400,000 Algerian Muslims resident in France killed more than 1,700 of them during 1957 and 1958 alone; this carnage caused many Frenchmen to want to extricate their country from the North African morass. The rising technocratic elite, which would come into its own under Charles de Gaulle but had already heavily infiltrated the corridors of power in the Fourth Republic, wanted France to play a big role in the Common Market and therefore desired to cut French losses by amputating bleeding Algeria.

All these forces together, however, would not have compelled a French surrender to the FLN, especially when it was becoming more and more apparent that the war was being won. A crucial impetus was imparted to the process by which metropolitan France was moving toward the decision to abandon Algeria, a process reaching its culmination at the turn of 1957–1958, by the very effective propaganda efforts of the French intellectual class. Vast strata of this group, especially in the educational system, the mass media, and the arts, had long since become thoroughly imbued with an anti-military, anti-Western, and anti-democratic ("mere bourgeois democracy") vocabulary, ritual, and reflex. For many of them, Western society was beyond redemption; hence, no war waged by it could be a good one. Thus, influential sectors of the French intelligentsia lent themselves with gusto to propagating two extraordinary ideas: first, that the FLN, founded and controlled by a cosmopolitan and educated elite, was actually the unanimous Muslim population that had finally risen up, spontaneously and in desperation, against intolerable oppression (in 1957 more Algerian Muslims wore the French uniform than served with the FLN both inside and outside Algeria); second, the whole French military effort, which in the long run was doomed to failure because it ran counter to the tides of history, was garnering its deceptive and ephemeral successes through the wholesale use of unspeakable torture against defenseless patriots and even randomly selected civilians of both sexes. The torture issue was especially effective within the Catholic community; even if the war was not actually being waged for intrinsically bad purposes, the totally unacceptable means by which it was fought polluted it and therefore rendered it insupportable. Thus, even though many Catholic chaplains defended the army's integrity, young Catholic militants and pacifists grew intoxicated with indignation against their own country.

While the French army continued to reduce the FLN in Algeria to ineffectiveness, and while French opinion wavered in support of the war, in Tunisia an event occurred that shook the French political class like nothing since the fall of Dien Bien Phu. In January 1958, 300 FLN troops crossed into Algeria from Tunisian territory with the support of Tunisian army units; they ambushed a French patrol, killing 15. In the days that followed, two French aircraft, on different days, were shot down by fire from the village of Sakiet, just inside the Tunisian border. Soon after, a flight of French air force bombers struck the village, causing considerable damage. The so-called Sakiet Incident raised a tremendous outcry, from the United Nations to the U.S. Congress. Even French politicians who favored the war were surprised and alarmed at these demonstrations of the increasing isolation of France in the world. Thus, the Fourth Republican leadership moved ever closer to entering negotiations with the FLN, a process that could end only with the FLN coming to power, with all the consequences that would entail for the French army and its scores of thousands of Muslim supporters.

NEW DOCTRINES IN THE ARMY

While these fateful changes were taking place at home, equally portentous developments were occurring within the mind of the French army in Algeria. Before the Algerian war, the army had an "ingrained propensity to neutrality" in politics; an instance of even a serious plot against the state would be difficult to find in the history of the modern French army. But the desperate events that would soon occur in Algeria have been described as the results of a sort of "nervous breakdown" that affected all French society to a degree, but the army above all.[31] In the army's attempts to understand and to defend the war it was waging lay the seed of the most dramatic confrontation between a major European government and its armed forces that anyone could remember.

On the army's side, the principal thrust for this confrontation came from a set of ideas called the theory of revolutionary war (*guerre révolutionnaire*). From out of the savage and bitter experiences of Indochina came not only a determination on the army's part not to be caused to fail again, but also the foundations of the guerre révolutionnaire theory formulated by officers who had served there and had been reflecting upon their experiences, comparing them to the situation in Algeria. Guerre révolutionnaire theory began with two related beliefs: (a) guerrilla warfare reverses the normal pattern of war; the guerrillas aim not at military or even geographical objectives but at the *mind of the civil population*; an inferior force could defeat a modern army if it could gain at least the tacit support of the civil population in the contested area; (b) guerrilla war stems from the will of an organization, not from the grievances of the population; to be sure, friction and sometimes blatant injustice exist in colonial areas, but these are not the causes of guerrilla warfare; rather, the exploitation of these grievances by a revolutionary elite, for the elite's own purposes, is the root cause. From this it follows ineluctably that a guerrilla movement cannot successfully be fought against (or averted) by social reforms alone: the revolutionary elite makes the revolt because of its political aspirations, not because of the people's socio-economic deprivation. More and more the French army's understanding and conduct of the Algerian war would come to conform to these principles of guerre révolutionnaire.[32]

The viewpoint of guerre révolutionnaire dovetailed beautifully with the already widespread suspicion among many officers that so-called Algerian nationalism was really only the cat's paw (or *antechambre*) of Soviet expansionism; knowingly or not, the elite directory of the FLN was part of a far-reaching scheme to turn Algeria eventually into an outpost of Soviet power, thus outflanking NATO and posing a mortal threat to European freedom. The fate of France, and perhaps of the entire West, was thus bound up with the outcome of Algeria: "our last, our ultimate line of defense is Algeria."[33]

In this way, the French army came to view its mission in Algeria more and more in moral terms: to protect the French community in Algeria and the loyal Muslims from criminal terrorists, to protect the soil of France from charlatan agitators, and to protect the West from Soviet encirclement.

And if, as most advocates of guerre révolutionnaire maintained, such conflicts could not be successfully fought by means of social reforms or political concessions alone, it was nevertheless imperative to recognize that the pacification of rebel-infested areas would be made much easier through programs aimed at the civil population, and all military commanders should be totally alert to their duty to approach the population under their jurisdiction with deeds as well as words. If the Muslims were going to accept French authority as a positive good, then those on the spot—that is, the army—would have to engage in programs that, if carried out in a European context, would be tantamount to a social revolution. Officers would have to take the lead in uprooting ancient injustices, cruelties, and inefficiencies. "They wanted to show beyond a doubt that the army had turned its back on social conservatism and it became fashionable in military circles to talk of experiments undertaken in Yugoslavia and Israel."[34] Many were caught up in the intoxication of the hour: "countless officers gave freely of their spare time to assist educational and charitable works. General Massu and his wife themselves adopted two Muslim orphans. The motives were mixed and various, often highly confused, often extraordinarily honorable."[35] Added to these activities was the undeniable fact that many Muslims supported the French even to the extent of donning the uniform and fighting the FLN. Estimates of the numbers of these Muslims in the French armed service vary, but 150,000 is a widely accepted figure.[36] Surely, some of these Muslims joined the French colors just for the regular pay, some were doubtless FLN infiltrators. Nevertheless, "the presence of tens of thousands of armed Moslems under the tricolor gave credence to the French claim to fight for Algeria rather than against it."[37]

The theorists of guerre révolutionnaire searched for an ideology with which they could effectively counter the illusory but undeniable appeals of communism. Some advocated Western humanism, others preferred "integral Catholicism," many were moving toward a sort of anti-Marxist, anti-capitalist "national collectivism," a sort of barracks socialism using the army as the model for society.

The search for an effective ideology, and the fervent discussions this search produced, led to, or perhaps brought to the surface, profound dissatisfaction on the part of many officers with political life in contemporary France. The Indochinese debacle still rankled; the Suez operation of November 1956, in which French troops (including the 10th Parachute Division of General Massu) had done very well, only to be unceremoniously yanked out by the politicians, had done nothing to stimulate respect for the Fourth Republic among officers. Most of all, the army was hurt, embittered, and alarmed by the growing strength, or at least vociferousness, of the antiwar movement at home. There are grounds for believing that as late as the spring of 1958 most French citizens were on the side of the policies of the army.[38] But the number of editorials and articles, speeches and demonstrations against the war increased, and began to take on not only a pro-FLN but definitely anti-army tone. But, demanded many officers, how could the Muslims be kept loyal unless they were convinced that France would be loyal to them? Demands to negotiate with the FLN or to abandon Algeria altogether undermined Muslim belief in the permanence of the French presence. Hence, many officers concluded that the war would be won or lost *not in North Africa but in France itself.*

The contempt, the hatred poured out against the army by the intelligentsia, was especially galling to many; one officer wrote a piece significantly entitled "The France of Pontius Pilate," in which the bitter bafflement of many officers was distilled: "the university professors, the students, the journalists and the writers offered their cheeks to those who were striking us, and brandished their ridiculous little fists and screamed like little girls at us, who were defending their freedom to scream."[39] (The growing rancor of the intellectuals toward the army may have been stimulated by the fact that fewer and fewer officers were being drawn from prestigious institutions like the Polytechnique or even St. Cyr, but more and more from the ranks of the noncommissioned officers, a phenomenon sneeringly referred to as "military poujadism.")

It was becoming all too apparent to many officers that multiparty, liberal France could not effectively wage protracted counterguerrilla war; French-style democracy, the democracy of the parties, press, and pressure groups, produced a weak state and a confused public opinion. Officers in Algeria began to draw Rousseau-esque contrasts between the "real will" of the nation as opposed to the ill-informed will of this or that transient majority, or rather, collection of minorities. To win in Algeria and save the West, the army would first have to win in Paris. "Not only was Algeria to be saved from Pan-Arabism, France was to be saved from inefficiency and corruption and turned into a disciplined, progressive power."[40]

With the army's growing commitment to social transformation in Algeria, its anti-Communist obsession, its increasing tendency to view the French public as something the army must propagandize and mobilize—with, in a word, the army's growing totalitarian stance—a collision between it and the regime was now unavoidable. All that was lacking was a suitable occasion.

THE ARMY REVOLTS

The occasion presented itself in May 1958, with the designation of Pierre Pflimlin as head of the next revolving-door cabinet. Pflimlin was known to have expressed views favorable to negotiations with the FLN. Consequently, on May 9, the military commander in Algeria, General Raoul Salan (the most decorated officer in the French army and supreme commander in Indochina from 1952 to 1954), General Massu, and several others signed a telegram to the war minister, General Ely. The signers declared in terms just short of a proclamation of mutiny that, having made certain promises to the Muslims and the Europeans of Algeria, "the French Army, as one man, would look on the abandonment of this national heritage as an outrage, and it would be impossible to predict how it might react in its despair."[41]

Four days later, the same suspicions of Pflimlin's intentions triggered a massive uprising of colons in Algiers; they took over the principal government buildings, proclaimed a Committee of Public Safety, and invited General

Massu to become its head. In order "to avert further disorders" Massu accepted the invitation. (A few months later, Massu would receive an order from de Gaulle to leave the Committee; he would obey.)

The army in Algeria, especially the younger officers, was now ready to descend upon France itself, confident that the metropolitan army would not fire upon brother soldiers. They were probably right; in perhaps the worst day in Fourth Republican history, units from Algeria landed on the island of Corsica and took control of that significant territory without a hitch or a shot. The Corsican operation demonstrated for all to see how easy it would be to invade metropolitan France. It also broke the back of the Fourth Republic. Knowing that their game was up, the politicians summoned General de Gaulle, the only national figure the Algerian army would respect, out of his watchful semiretirement to save them from their own soldiers. On June 1, 1958, Charles de Gaulle became the (last) prime minister of the Fourth French Republic. He requested and received plenary powers, and sent the parliament on a six-month holiday while he tried to straighten out the mess he had inherited. On September 28, de Gaulle submitted his new constitution to the voters, including those in Algeria. Even there, where voters had to go to the polls in the face of FLN threats, the "no" vote was negligible and so was abstention. Thus, the army showed that it could "marshall and protect the bulk of the Muslims."[42]

Numerous colons had greeted the return of de Gaulle to power with something less than enthusiasm. During World War II, many of them had been *Pétainistes*, and the Pétain government had proclaimed de Gaulle a mutineer and a traitor. The army, however, almost all of it, was deeply reassured: de Gaulle, a soldier like themselves, was an authentic national hero, indeed the greatest Frenchman of his age, precisely because in France's darkest hour he had known how to discern and obey the true needs of France rather than the letter of the law. Therefore, for these entirely inadequate reasons, the army concluded that French Algeria was safe, the sacrifices of the army had not been in vain, and its victory was secure. So it seemed.

All went well at first. De Gaulle appointed Air Force General Maurice Challe to the task of the final clean-up of the reeling ALN. The Challe Plan fulfilled everybody's brightest hopes. Challe improved the quadrillage system by reducing the forces in permanent occupation of strategic sites and augmenting the number of men in the attack units. He also increased the number of Muslims in French uniform, making them a personal promise that France would never desert them. Beginning in the west, Challe methodically cleared the civilians out of one zone after another, driving the rebels ever closer to the Morice Line. By October 1959, the ALN was short of arms, losing up to 500 men a day (including those who deserted), and, no longer able to operate in units of battalion size, was reduced to the most primitive stages of guerrilla warfare.[43]

But many forces were working, even at this late hour, to bring about a decision by de Gaulle on Algeria totally at variance with the army's expectations. During 1958, de Gaulle concluded that peace could not be made with the FLN short of independence; the rebels could be reduced from the status of threat to the status of problem but never totally extirpated. But if the war, in however attenuated a form, went on indefinitely, de Gaulle would never be able to bring the French army totally under his control; de Gaulle was keenly aware that the army of Algeria, having swept aside his constitutional predecessors, could one day turn against him as well.

Even more important: two schools of high strategy had long contended for the soul of French foreign policy: the "Neo-Carolingians" and the "Neo-Romans." The first saw France's destiny in Europe, the latter in the Mediterranean, or "Eurafrica." De Gaulle, in spite of his experiences during World War II, was definitely a Neo-Carolingian. He wanted France to dominate "Little Europe" (the original six Common Market countries) and saw Algeria, even a relatively pacified Algeria, as at best a distraction from essential, that is European, affairs. The difficulties presented by an intransigent FLN merely confirmed this basic orientation.[44]

Therefore, on September 26, 1959, de Gaulle offered to negotiate "self-determination" for the Algerians. A few months later, partly in response to this visible turn in de Gaulle's policy, partly in response to increased FLN terrorism in Algiers, came the Affair of the Barricades, in which great numbers of colons, under the not unsympathetic eyes of many military units, set up street barricades and for a while took over physical control of key sectors of Algiers. In reply to these challenges, de Gaulle delivered an address on January 29 in which he was understood by many to say that he would not negotiate with the FLN.

Then, in September 1960, the so-called Jeanson case resulted in the publication by many well-known intellectuals of a manifesto proclaiming the right, indeed the duty, of Frenchmen to refuse to serve in the army.

> Military men were infuriated by the thought that the most elementary principles of duty to the state could be challenged with impunity [especially by that] already detested milieu of atheist writers, amoral women novelists, cinema actresses and leftist professors. . . . The bitterness of the army was proportionate to its feeling of isolation.[45]

Finally, on November 16, 1960, the government announced that a referendum on self-determination in Algeria was imminent. This announcement set in motion the second and final major army uprising in Algeria.

DE GAULLE DEFEATS THE ARMY

General Challe himself agreed to accept leadership of the forthcoming coup, because in his eyes de Gaulle was getting ready to give away the army's victory, and along with it the army's pledges to its Muslim dependents. The plan was to take over Algeria, in which the bulk of the army was stationed, and then move to France, following the 1958 model. Then, by retaining complete control of Algeria in its own hands, the army would clean up the war once and for all, probably within three months.

The coup, which took place in April, 1961, was an utter failure for four reasons.

First, in contrast to the 1958 uprising, the coup was a purely military undertaking, the so-called "putsch of the generals": the European population of Algeria was not invited to participate, nor were sympathetic political elements in metropolitan France. Thus, the army, or rather the rebellious element of it, was seen to stand alone against the legitimate government.

Second, again unlike 1958, no group of authority, power, or prestige rallied to the coup-makers once they had revealed their hand. Quite to the contrary: Prime Minister Michel Debré began arming a Gaullist militia, and all the trade unions and most of the political parties vigorously supported the de Gaulle government.

Third, and quite crucial, the army itself was divided. Challe's principal support came from some elite parachute regiments. Most officers shied away from the coup. They shrank from an open challenge to the authority of de Gaulle, who clearly — unlike the politicians of 1958 — had public opinion in France behind him. In addition, by April 1961 communal conflict and fear in Algeria between colons and Muslims had reached unprecedented proportions, owing largely to revived FLN terrorism. Many officers saw their goal of an integrated Algeria being overshadowed by the grim prospect of race war, and they wanted no part of it. Thus, in a real sense, "the FLN had won 'the second battle of Algiers'."[46] Besides, since he had returned to power in June 1958, de Gaulle had been carefully and gingerly making changes within the army command in Algeria, removing many officers who might have made trouble for him. Most of all, his policy of moving slowly, slowly, step by step, toward negotiations with the FLN, never revealing his final intention until the very end, never bringing the army to a Rubicon, allowed important strata in the officer corps to become accustomed to the idea of an eventual betrayal of their victory that would be supported by public opinion. In such ways, those elements in the Algerian army nevertheless willing to resist de Gaulle had been diminished and isolated. And draftees, who often bitterly resented having to serve in Algeria, or anywhere for that matter, sometimes resisted officers who tried to rally to the coup-makers.

Fourth, and finally, the coup-makers failed because, unlike in May 1958, the rebellious officers of Algeria were not dealing with the political mummies of the Fourth Republic but with Charles de Gaulle. Dressed in his impressive uniform, speaking his beautiful, slightly archaic French, de Gaulle made a television and radio appeal to the troops in Algeria to resist the coup. "Once the State and the Nation have chosen their path, military duty is spelled out once and for all." (We unfortunately cannot know to what degree de Gaulle appreciated the irony of these particular sentiments being expressed by this particular man.)

The coup collapsed.

The generals' revolt of April 1961 completely discredited the army (and gave heart to the FLN) because it was manifestly a move not only against de Gaulle but the voters who stood behind him — and because it failed so miserably.

De Gaulle, having known how to defend himself, was now at last free to get rid of Algeria. Many would pay a high price for this, none more than the army. Several officers involved in the failed coup, including Raoul Salan, were condemned to death in absentia. General Challe was sentenced to fifteen years. Many other good officers were given heavy sentences; eighty were dismissed from the service, and nearly 1,000 resigned. As a cohesive, self-confident force, the French officer corps had ceased to exist.

There was an ugly epilogue to the story of the French army in Algeria. Some officers and former officers joined the die-hard, colon-based Secret Army Organization (OAS) headed by Salan. Hoping to force a partition of Algeria into Arab and European sections, the OAS tried to incite race war and anarchy. OAS terrorism for a while rivaled that of the FLN in sheer brutality. The OAS tried several times to murder de Gaulle, and then in a final paroxysm of rage and despair turned its violence against the army itself. With the capture of Raoul Salan in April 1967, the sad, misshapen thing died.

AN ACCOUNTING

The politicians of the Fourth Republic entrusted the army with the preservation of a French Algeria. They made a moral commitment, and permitted the army to make a moral commitment, to the colons and to the loyal Muslims. Then French public opinion began to tire of the war, so the politicians prepared to void the sacrifices, and the victory, of the army. The army offered an unprecedented and at first successful resistance to this development, shattering the Fourth Republic to pieces. But in the end it was outmaneuvered and broken by de Gaulle.

Paradoxically, however, precisely because "the ultimate victory of the [FLN] was not gained by a conventional battle, such as that at Dien Bien Phu, but by political and diplomatic means,"[47] the cadres of the Algerian army felt less bitterness that did those who had served in Vietnam. After all, the French army in Algeria had been able to do its job, it had won a military victory. Its strategy of occupation, observation, and quick movement had made a guerrilla victory in the field impossible, so that victory eventually came to the FLN only "through the strains which the war had produced in the foundations of the French polity."[48]

Algerian independence day was July 4, 1962. By that date, 1.5 million persons, including many Muslims, had left the country. The French had lost 18,000 soldiers, including Muslims. European civilian casualties amounted to 10,000. The rebels had killed 16,000 Muslim civilians, and nearly 50,000 others were listed as "missing." The French army claimed to have killed 141,000 rebels, with another 12,000 rebels dead in internecine fighting. Estimates of the number of *Harkis* — Muslims in French uniform — killed by the FLN after independence range from 30,000 to 150,000.[49]

NOTES

1. Paul-Marie de la Gorce, *The French Army: A Military–Political History* (New York: George Braziller, 1963), p. 447.
2. Michael Carver, *War Since 1945* (New York: G. P. Putnam's Sons, 1981), p. 120.
3. George T. Kelly, *Lost Soldiers: The French Army and Empire in Crisis, 1947–1962* (Cambridge, MA: MIT Press, 1965), p. 75.
4. Kelly, *Lost Soldiers*, p. 145.
5. Geoffrey Fairbairn, *Revolutionary Guerrilla Warfare: The Countryside Version* (Harmondsworth, England: Penguin, 1974), p. 71.
6. See especially Vilfredo Pareto, *I sistemi socialisti* (Turin: U. T. E. T., 1963).
7. For an excellent treatment of a revolutionary movement frustrated through lack of sophisticated leadership, see John Womack, *Zapata and the Mexican Revolution* (New York: Vintage, 1969).
8. See especially V. I. Lenin, *Selected Works* (Moscow: Progress Publishers).
9. For example, Mark N. Hagopian, *The Phenomenon of Revolution* (New York: Dodd, Mead, 1974), pp. 296–307; Samuel P. Huntington, *Political Order in Changing Societies* (New Haven, CT: Yale University Press, 1968), pp. 288–307.
10. Kelly, *Lost Soldiers*, p. 152.
11. Edgar O'Ballance, *The Algerian Insurrection, 1954–1962* (Hamden, CT: Archon, 1967), p. 202; see also Hugh Seton-Watson, *Nations and States* (Boulder, CO: Westview, 1977), pp. 263–267.
12. Kelly, *Lost Soldiers*, pp. 155, 154.
13. Alvin J. Cottrell and James E. Dougherty, "Algeria: A Case Study in the Evolution of a Colonial Problem," in Robert Strausz-Hupé and Harry W. Hazard, *The Idea of Colonialism* (New York: Praeger, 1958), p. 76.
14. O'Ballance, *The Algerian Insurrection*, p. 213.
15. Peter Paret, *French Revolutionary Warfare from Indochina to Algeria: An Analysis of a Political and Military Doctrine* (New York: Praeger, 1964), p. 35.
16. Chalmers Johnson, *Revolutionary Change* (Boston: Little, Brown & Company, 1966), p. 160.
17. Eric R. Wolf, *Peasant Wars of the Twentieth Century* (New York: Harper and Row, 1969), p. 239.
18. Kelly, *Lost Soldiers*, p. 194.
19. Carver, *War Since 1945*, p. 131.
20. Carver, *War Since 1945*, p. 128.
21. De la Gorce, *French Army*, p. 431.
22. De la Gorce, *French Army*, p. 412.
23. Kelly, *Lost Soldiers*, p. 202.

24. Kelly, *Lost Soldiers*, p. 201.
25. Kelly, *Lost Soldiers*, p. 204.
26. Kelly, *Lost Soldiers*, p. 204.
27. Kelly, *Lost Soldiers*, pp. 200–201.
28. Kelly, *Lost Soldiers*, pp. 200–201.
29. Kelly, *Lost Soldiers*, p. 198.
30. Kelly, *Lost Soldiers*, p. 171.
31. Kelly, *Lost Soldiers*, p. 22.
32. Paret, *French Revolutionary Warfare*, p. 8.
33. Paret, *French Revolutionary Warfare*, p. 25.
34. De la Gorce, *French Army*, p. 479.
35. Kelly, *Lost Soldiers*, p. 260.
36. Paret, *Revolutionary Warfare*, p. 41.
37. Paret, *Revolutionary Warfare*, p. 41.
38. Kelly, *Lost Soldiers*, p. 236.
39. De la Gorce, *French Army*, p. 487.
40. Paret, *Revolutionary Warfare*, p. 28.
41. De la Gorce, *French Army*, p. 464.
42. Kelly, *Lost Soldiers*, p. 229.
43. O'Ballance, *The Algerian Insurrection*, p. 209; Carver, *War Since 1945*, p. 141.
44. Kelly, *Lost Soldiers*, pp. 255–256.
45. De la Gorce, *French Army*, p. 523.
46. O'Ballance, *The Algerian Insurrection*, p. 11.
47. Kelly, *Lost Soldiers*, p. 303.
48. Wolf, *Peasant Wars*, p. 242.
49. Carver, *War Since 1945*, p. 147.

8

Brazil: The Army and the Conservative Revolution

Revolutions in democracies are generally caused by the intemperance of demagogues.

—Aristotle

One often hears it observed that "Brazil is a big country." This is an understatement of Amazonian proportions. Brazil's more than 100 million citizens make her seventh in population of all the world's nations. But it is the sheer expanse of the country that often surprises people. Within Brazil's capacious borders one could place Indonesia, Burma, Thailand, and the Philippines, along with Vietnam, Cambodia, Laos, North Korea, South Korea, Malaysia, Singapore, Taiwan, and Japan; one could then throw in *all of India*—and still have room left over for Israel, Jordan, Cyprus, and Lebanon.

The coup of 1964 was suitably Brazilian-sized. The Western Hemisphere had not witnessed the deployment of so many troops over so broad an area for more than a century nor the confrontation of so many armed men for fifty years. The coup was of great magnitude in its political effects as well; among other things, the resulting regime held Brazil firmly in the Western camp while the United States suffered and recovered from its Vietnamese agony, a fact of incalculable importance for the entire Latin American strategic picture.

BACKGROUND OF LATIN MILITARISM

"The coup d'état is now the normal mode of political change in most member states of the United Nations."[1] This has always been the case in Latin America and continues so today: "militarism is not simply an accident of history or the curse of our time but is endemic and intrinsic to the structure of Latin America."[2]

Latin American militarism—that is, the tendency of soldiers to interfere directly and corporately in politics—has its roots in pre-independence times. The Spanish colonial system combined civil and military authority in the same person, and Spanish rule was often ineffective outside the major metropolitan areas, forcing the rural population to rely for protection on local strongmen. The long and sanguinary wars of independence produced a new leadership class, men who enjoyed power and wealth because they successfully combined the fields of arms and politics. Independence, moreover, decapitated civil authority in Spanish America: with the destruction of royal rule, no one could establish a compelling claim to civil legitimacy, and so power was up for grabs. "The real choice usually was not between constitutionalism and dictatorship, but between dictatorship and anarchy."[3] New rules had to be made, and the men who made them were the victorious commanders of the independence armies. Thus, politics became the arena of the military heroes of independence and their heirs. Latin American armies usually faced no real threat from outside, so commanders had plenty of time to devote to domestic politics. Neither were the civilian institutions that remained after independence (such as the Roman Catholic Church) able to offer any real and sustained competition to the soldier-politicians. Finally, coup-making is a habit; there are countries that have never in modern times experienced a coup, there are countries that experience coups on a regular basis, but there is no country that has experienced only *one* coup.

In vivid contrast to that of her Spanish-speaking neighbors, however, Brazil's experience with militarism for the first six decades of her independence was almost a nonexperience. Brazil obtained her independence from Portugal bloodlessly; thus, there were no military heroes to claim rewards. Equally important, the chain of civil legitimacy remained unbroken because newly independent Brazil retained a monarchical form of government, with a member of the Portuguese royal house on the throne of the new Brazilian empire. Because the country was not a republic, there were no presidential elections after which the loser, in the highly stylized manner of Spanish America, could proclaim fraud and lead an armed uprising. Neither did the less-than-glorious record of the Imperial Brazilian Army during the savage Paraguayan War (1865–1870) do anything to stimulate anybody's desire to see the country ruled by its military.

ARMIES AND STATES

Latin America has not been the only locus in which militarism has been a major feature of political life. From the late Roman republic to today's Soviet empire, the tension between the necessity of the state to maintain armed forces for its defense and the possibility of those armed forces taking over control of the state has preoccupied leaders and scholars. Over the centuries, four classic models or patterns have evolved in the search for ways to eliminate or reduce this tension. Following closely the excellent work of Alfred Stepan, we will call these models the aristocratic, the liberal, the communist, and the professional.[4]

The Aristocratic Model has been the most successful in controlling militarism; it is also the simplest. Leaders of the armed forces are drawn almost exclusively from the ruling class, and they identify with that class and not with the officer corps or the military service per se. (The sale of military commissions in eighteenth century England is a manifestation of the aristocratic approach to preventing military coups.)

The Liberal Model seeks to preserve the state from militarism by keeping the regular army small and completely depoliticized. The army faces countervailing forces, such as state militias; in wartime, the nation drafts citizens, thus filling the enlarged army with persons whose values and loyalties and futures are civilian, not miliary; as soon as the war is over, demobilization occurs, and the army resumes its small size. This model has worked best in countries with strong civil institutions and mild external threats, such as the United States in the nineteenth century and Canada today.

The Communist Model completely rejects the depoliticization of the army that is the heart of the liberal model. The army must not be politically neutral; on the contrary, it must be thoroughly indoctrinated with the vision of the ruling party and ever prepared to do its bidding. The great majority of the officers, especially at the higher levels, are party members (here the Communist model resembles the aristocratic); further safeguards against army interference with the political leadership include the use of political commissars, secret surveillance, and periodic purges.

The Professional Model (the principal American theoretician of which has been Samuel P. Huntington) attempts to protect the state from militarism by teaching soldiers to seek gratification and rewards through increasing competence in their own profession. Ideally, the state does not monitor the political activities of officers; rather, officers per se are indifferent to, or too busy for, political activity.

Some countries have combined aspects of more than one model, such as the liberal and professional (twentieth century United States) or the aristocratic and professional (pre–World War I Germany and Austria–Hungary).

It becomes apparent that Latin America, including Brazil, does not fit any one or any combination of these models very neatly. We therefore must express the Latin American experience in terms of a fifth model, which Stepan calls the *moderator model*.[5] Behavior seen as pathological in the liberal or professional models *becomes the norm* in the moderator model, where the military repeatedly enters into the political arena, usually at the call of civilian politicians, to straighten out a crisis. Among the key components of the moderator model:

- A politicized military is the norm, and all major civilian groups attempt to use the military for their own purposes;
- The main political activity of the army (the "moderator") is to check or remove the chief executive;
- Both civil and military elites believe in the legitimacy of military intervention but do not believe in *extended military rule*;
- The army views the maintenance of a minimum level of institutional cohesion within itself as absolutely essential to its ability to fulfill its moderator role; hence, the army will intervene in politics *only when its internal cohesion is not thereby threatened.*

In this model,

> the military in a sense assumes constitutional functions analogous to those of the Supreme Court of the United States: they have a responsibility to preserve the political order and hence are drawn into politics at times of crisis or controversy to veto actions by the "political" branches of government which deviate from the essentials of that system.[6]

In the Brazilian case, the army fulfilled the role that formerly belonged to the emperor. It was in concordance with these basic assumptions that the Brazilian army came to power in 1964.

Keen observers (whether or not they have used the term moderator model) have always been struck by one aspect of this model: the intervention of the army in politics is almost always precipitated by civilian politicians themselves, often to remove their political rivals, who are seen as perverting or destroying the system.

Throughout the Latin American region, and in other areas as well, military intervention has facilitated entrance into politics of new or hitherto-excluded elements of society, especially the rising middle classes, and has often acted as a stimulus to social and economic development.[7] "In this sense, the military coup is part of the democratic process, and has been freely acknowledged as such in Latin America."[8]

We should not, moreover, automatically condemn all Latin American military interventions as anticonstitutional and illegitimate; the military sees itself as exercising an implied prerogative not against but in defense of the constitution[9]; indeed, "*it is often the constitution itself that gives the military the right, even the obligation, to intervene* in the political process under certain circumstances [italics added]."[10] The Brazilian constitutions of 1891, 1934, and 1946 recognized this role of the military. The 1946 constitution contained two clauses extremely relevant to the process culminating in the 1964 coup: the military is charged with *guaranteeing the normal functioning of the con-*

stitution, and is also enjoined to be obedient to the president of the republic *"within the limits of the law."* The constitution thus called upon the army to exercise its collective political judgment in the most delicate constitutional areas, just as does the U.S. Supreme Court (another body that, like the Brazilian army, is neither elected to office nor directly answerable to the citizenry).

This moderator model, not very surprisingly, has drawn severe criticism from students of government. Samuel P. Huntington, for example, has labeled the moderator model (which he calls the system of "institutionalized coups") as profoundly corrupting because it divorces responsibility from power. That is, the civilian leaders have the responsibility for running the country, but not the real power, because the army can step in and veto their policies or end their incumbency. This awareness of the tentativeness of their terms and powers of office sometimes encourages Latin American leaders to turn away from the hard work of governing restless societies to the less taxing and more exciting activities of phrasemaking and rabble-rousing. The army, on the other hand, can take over to prevent things from happening of which it disapproves, but knows that when the problems of governing become too tough it can always hand power back, in an act of "selfless renunciation," to the hapless politicians.[11]

Many Brazilians, civilian and military alike, undoubtedly were becoming aware of these debilitating features of the moderator model, under which their country had operated for decades (since the revolution of 1889). In addition, powerful elements within the armed forces and in civilian political life began to convince themselves that what Brazil needed was not *temporary military intervention* but *long-term military government*. The Brazilian coup of 1964, sanctioned by the moderator model, would result therefore in a major alteration of that model.

To appreciate how and why this transformation in the thinking of the Brazilian military regarding its moderator role occurred, we must consider the overwhelming influence in modern Brazilian politics of Getulio Vargas. His name and personality dominated his country for more than thirty years, and although he died in 1954, it was against Vargas that the 1964 coup truly aimed.

THE VARGAS ERA

For the first sixty-seven years of its independence, Brazil was an empire ruled by a branch of the Portuguese royal house. By the last decade of the nineteenth century, it was clear that the imperial institution was in difficulty. Emperor Pedro II was a man of great personal probity but he had been long on the throne, and several groups that might have been expected to be staunch supporters of the monarchy, such as the great sugar planters and the bishops of the Roman Catholic Church, had become alienated from him for various reasons. A growing republican movement, which felt that Brazil's imperial institutions were behind the times and out of place in the Americas, made many converts among younger army officers, and, in 1889, a nearly bloodless revolution in which officers played a prominent part abolished the empire and proclaimed a republic.

During the Old Republic (1889–1930) politics became fragmented, with Brazil resembling less a united country than a loose federation of states. The political bosses of the principal states passed the presidency back and forth among themselves through deals in which manipulation of the ballot box figured prominently. This boss system became more and more outdated as Brazilian society increased in size and complexity. The end came in 1930: the world depression, dissent within the ruling elite over who would receive the presidency that year, and smoldering dissatisfaction within the army officer corps all combined to bring swift victory to the revolutionary coalition united behind the governor of the state of Rio Grande do Sul, Getulio Vargas. The army mostly supported Vargas's rebellion once it became clear how very strong it was; this marked the first time the Brazilian army had participated in overthrowing a president.

Vargas held the presidency for the next fifteen years, until 1945. During his long rule, he reversed the centrifugal tendencies of the Old Republic. Economic development and national self-assertion became the goals, centralization and velvet-glove authoritarianism the means. The central government in Rio de Janeiro assumed more and more initiatives and powers and lavished attention on key groups: coffee barons, industrialists, labor leaders, army officers. Money, contracts, protection, promotions, decorations, and promises flowed out of the capital in ever-increasing abundance. The Vargas system offered something nice for almost everyone—everything except the opportunity to choose a president.

Several factors eventually joined to put an end to the rule of Vargas. Principal among these: (a) the growing resemblance, especially in vocabulary, between the Vargas regime and Mussolinian fascism became ever more embarrassing to many Brazilians, especially when it became clear that the Axis was definitely going to lose World War II; (b) the rising middle classes were restless under Vargas's paternalism, and jealous of the money and attention he began to lavish on the growing labor unions; they thought that under a post-Vargas system of free elections the middle classes would elect one of their own to power; (c) many people, especially in the army, began to suspect that Vargas was preparing organized labor as a counterweight to the army's moderator role and thus as an instrument for an indefinite prolongation of his presidency; everyone could see the prototype of this kind of politics being developed right across the border, in the Argentina of Juan Perón.

All this combustible material awaited any random match, which Vargas provided when he seemed to be getting ready to postpone the presidential elections he had promised. In October 1945, therefore, the army removed Vargas politely and bloodlessly, just as they had removed the emperor half a century before. Thus, the Vargas era came to an end—or so most people believed at the time. The middle classes were elated: "for the liberal constitutionalists [middle-class politicians], the armed forces' action to end the dictatorship . . . both justified their institutionalized role as holder of the moderating power and was justified by it."[12] Thus appeared the open alliance between the army and the middle classes, an alliance based simultaneously on a dedication to constitutional government and on fear of Vargas and the increasingly proletarian coloration of his backers. The growing animosity between these two coalitions, the army–middle-class alliance and the heterogenous Vargas supporters, would shape and define Brazilian politics from the end of World War II right up to the coup of 1964 and beyond.

The bloodless removal of Vargas by the army had widespread civilian support, but it did not bring the Vargas era to an end. The free elections of 1950 saw the ex-dictator Vargas return to power on a plurality vote, to the dismay of the officer corps and to the disgust of middle-class constitutionalist elements, who had imagined that free elections would put men of their choice in power on a semipermanent basis. Probably nothing did more to undermine the faith of the Brazilian middle classes in electoral democracy than the triumph through free elections of their detested adversary, the archcorruptor himself.

The new Vargas administration assumed a more and more pro-labor and anti-American posture; conservative and even moderate elements became increasingly alarmed at the influence in the administration of such figures as Labor Minister "Jango" Goulart. Political rhetoric became more inflamed and political violence more common. The crisis came in August 1954 with an assassination attempt against Carlos Lacerda, prominent Rio politician and bitter critic of Vargas. Lacerda himself was only wounded, but his companion, an air force major named Vaz, was killed. Subsequent investigations implicated members of Vargas's personal bodyguard and led to sensational revelations of corruption on the part of several close associates of the president. For the second time in less than a decade, the heads of the armed forces informed Vargas that he must step down from the presidential office. Thereupon President Vargas shot himself to death.

All those who imagined that now at last the Vargas era was at an end were soon undeceived by the presidential elections of 1955. The Vargas coalition, grouped around the candidacy of Juscelino Kubitschek, again won a plurality of the vote against a divided opposition; adding insult to injury, the vice president (elected separately from the president in Brazil) was Jango Goulart. Finally, in 1960, the anti-Vargas coalition found a winner in the popular mayor of São Paulo, Janio Quadros. At last the "constitutional liberals" had come into their own! But the quixotic Quadros found his measures frustrated by Congress and, in an ill-advised power play a few months after his inauguration, he offered his resignation. To his consternation and that of many others, Congress accepted. Now there ascended to the presidency none other than the very symbol of Vargas populist rabble-rousing and election-rigging: Vice President Goulart.

Having been defeated at the polls twice by Vargas and his heirs, having finally won the presidency that they considered theirs by a sort of moral preemption, only to see it snatched from their grasp and handed over to the incarnation of all their fears, the middle classes of Brazil (and their numerous sympathizers within the armed forces) had reached the end of their democratic and constitutional rope. Within three years, the armed forces were to remove Goulart from power. The key to the fall of Goulart lay in the army's conviction that it could carry out a move against Goulart in the classic moderator-model style: broad army cohesion and widespread civilian support. How the army leadership came to this conclusion—how President Goulart lost the ability to control or even influence the armed forces—is the burden of the remainder of this chapter.

GOULART IN POWER

The story of the fall of the Goulart administration suggests two general precepts: (a) regimes usually fall at least as much from their internal weaknesses as from external opposition; and (b) diffuse, generalized problems are constantly stressing all regimes, working against their popularity and stability, but regimes *actually fall* because of a crisis generated by the specific actions of specific persons.[13]

The Brazil over which Goulart presided had been changing from an overwhelmingly rural and agricultural country to an urban and industrialized one. Between 1950 and 1960 Brazil experienced a phenomenal population increase of 20 million, most of which took place in the cities. The country had inadequate and deteriorating systems of public education and health care, and a long and sometimes violent history of regional rivalry. The man who in 1961 had to deal with this configuration of stresses, opportunities, and dangers was an extremely controversial politician who had become leader of his nation quite by accident. On the other hand, Brazil's armed forces had a tradition of respect for the constitution; the removal of President Vargas in 1945 and 1954 did not violate this tradition to the mind of most Brazilians. Both times, the army had acted with wide public approbation and had handed power back to duly chosen civilians within a very short time. It was, in brief, by no means a foregone conclusion that the army would move against Goulart.

As president, Goulart dealt poorly with powerful state governors, and his record was no better in his relations with the congress. In part this was because of Goulart's limited and artificial experience in politics. He had never held a governorship or any state office at all, neither had he ever been a member of Congress. Instead, Goulart had gone "straight from the ranch to the cabinet"; President Vargas had made 33-year-old Goulart his minister of labor and later head of Vargas's new political vehicle, the Brazilian Labor party. Thus, Goulart had been "manufactured by Vargas as an instant national political figure."[14] Labor Minister Goulart's open admiration for Juan Perón fed the army's fears that Vargas was getting ready to imitate the Argentine dictator and break the moderating power of the Brazilian military. These fears played no small part in the final army decision to remove Vargas in 1954.

> In sum, there is considerable justification for terming Goulart a second-rate Vargas and ersatz Perón, both of whom understood military values and mentality much better than did the young rancher turned leader of a labor movement and head of a political party by the will of his mentor rather than by his own efforts.[15]

Complicating these serious weaknesses was the fact that people openly spoke of the amatory adventures of the president's wife and of Goulart's knowledge of these escapades. Such stories would undermine anybody's prestige, but especially that of the leader of a Latin country.[16]

THE PATH TO CONFRONTATION

From the first hours of his presidency, both supporters and opponents of Goulart said openly that the regime would not last as it was, that Brazil was on the verge of great changes. Major leaders of the radical parties began to proclaim that when the new day came the new order would include not a single "bourgeois reformer." This kind of vaguely menacing declaration may have been nothing but rhetoric, but it was ill-advised, because it scared off many potential Goulart supporters and hardened the attitudes of those who were initially skeptical of him. The first year of the Goulart presidency was 1961, when the Cuban revolution had entered a truly radical phase; many in Brazil began to draw lessons from events on the island, appropriately or not. For the army, Cuba raised the specter of a Moscow-oriented elite that destroyed the Cuban army as an institution and executed in cold blood many of its officers; for many Brazilian leftists, the big lesson of the Cuban revolution was the efficacy of violence in bringing about social change.[17]

Goulart and his allies and lieutenants not only indulged in rhetoric that offended and frightened many; Goulart also began to turn more and more to the apparatus of the Brazilian Communist party for the purpose of arousing the politically listless Brazilian proletariat. This tactic not only prematurely alarmed conservative and moderate elements; Goulart's implicit alliance with the Communists deprived him of the support of many who were willing to back a radical and nationalist program but who remained fundamentally anti-Communist. The ironical aspect of Goulart's maladroitness lies in the fact that while his overtures to the Communists deprived him of many potential allies and made him implacable enemies, the Communists themselves did not trust Goulart and at the hour of crisis deserted him totally.[18] Indeed, the entire "left" that looked so formidable and menacing to ever-increasing segments of Brazilian opinion was actually quite fragmented by rivalry and mutual suspicion. "In their flush of self-confidence they failed to appreciate that they were even more seriously divided than their enemies."[19] Thus, Goulart was actually mobilizing his opponents while his own alleged supporters were in serious disarray.

When Goulart succeeded to the presidency in 1961, most army officers took a traditionally "legalist" stance; that is, Goulart was and would be president unless he caused a crisis so serious and so unmistakable that public opinion demanded that the army do something. But these legalists were not permitted to get off so easily. Leonel Brizola, brother-in-law of Goulart and former governor of Rio Grande do Sul, conceived the bright idea of politicizing the army's noncommissioned officers. Soon labor unions became actively involved in the project. The purpose was to make clear that the chain of command between officers and enlisted men could be broken in case the army ever tried to move against Goulart. Naturally, nothing could have proved more scandalous, frightening, and provocative to army leaders, including the legalists. Their worst fears seemed to be confirmed by events in Brasilia in September 1963. A group of noncommissioned officers in the capital city took over some key buildings and held several hostages in protest against a recent court ruling that noncoms were not eligible to hold elective civil office. It became clear that the rebels were in contact with radical union leaders close to Brizola. Worse still, President Goulart declined to condemn the revolt, therefore stimulating suspicions in the minds of many officers that the president himself was involved with a plot to break the chain of command, a break that would result first in the isolation of the officer corps and then in its destruction, à la Cuba.

In the superheated atmosphere of autumn 1963, Governor Carlos Lacerda, perhaps the most vitriolic critic of Goulart's administration, was the object of a kidnapping plot that failed due to traffic tie-ups in downtown Rio de Janeiro. Lacerda and many others believed that the plot against him was directed from inside the presidential palace.

Serving as a backdrop to these disturbing events was the grave economic decline being experienced by the country. The growth rate in the gross national product declined in 1962, and Brazil actually suffered negative growth in 1963. By March 1964, the inflation rate was running at 100 percent annually.

To meet this deteriorating situation, Goulart proposed a long list of economic measures. These proposals, centering on land reform and the nationalization of the oil industry, were not very radical in themselves, but the atmosphere in which they were presented had become electric. Goulart's opponents feared not so much what he actually said as what he was leading up to, which might include a suspension of the constitution and an open alliance with the Communists. Goulart did not fail to lend all possible credence to these worries; as one authority has concluded, "the final causes of the revolution [against Goulart in 1964] were intimately related to questions of the strategies and tactics that Goulart used. . . . "[20] At a huge meeting on March 13, 1964, Goulart spoke vigorously in favor of his reform program, but the highlight of the evening was a speech by his brother-in-law Brizola in which, in the presence of the president, he denounced Congress and called upon the people to rise up and take what was rightfully theirs. Moved by the excitement of the occasion, Goulart himself declared that "I am not afraid of being called a subversive for proclaiming that it is necessary to revise the constitution."[21]

That remark, more than any other single event, probably sealed the doom of the regime. But as though he were obediently following a script written by his enemies, Goulart three days later demanded that Congress legalize the Communist party. Further, he insisted that his reform program be submitted to a national plebiscite, a blatantly unconstitutional and bonapartist posture.

GOULART'S ENEMIES MOBILIZE

In one sense, the coup against Goulart (which would eventually take on the dimensions of a real revolution) was the culmination of a decade-old feud between him and the military. The Brazilian army above all feared the emergence of a Brazilian Perón: a popular demagogue backed by powerful labor support who could reduce or destroy the army's role as guardian and moderator; Goulart seemed to many officers to be preparing himself for just that role.

On another level, the anti-Goulart move was the expression of the army's frustration with efforts to keep the Vargas coalition out of power.

> Having ousted Vargas in 1945 only to see him elected President in 1950, subsequently driving him to suicide in 1954 only to have his political heirs triumph in the 1955 elections, and finally witnessing the defeat of the Vargista forces at the polls in 1960 only to watch them come back to power the next year, the armed forces would act decisively to end this Vargas succession in 1964, destroying in the process Brazil's experiment with a competitive democratic regime and an open political system.[22]

Goulart for his part never wanted a nonpolitical military; like every other Brazilian politician, he wanted to use the military to achieve his own purposes. In his endeavors to instrumentalize the Brazilian armed forces he failed utterly, so much so that one cannot resist the suggestion that Goulart's undoing should be laid less to his radicalism than to his ineptitude.[23] Goulart's plans (if this is the right word) for using the army had three aspects: (a) he counted on the legalist scruples of the broad center of the officer corps to protect him while he tried to (b) place his supporters in the army in key positions, and (c) detach the noncommissioned officers from regular military discipline, thus breaking the chain of command. Everything backfired. The sergeants whom he courted did almost nothing to help him when the crisis came, and his counterdisciplinary moves thoroughly alienated the mass of legalist officers. "Finally, the growing use of political criteria for promotions in the army in order to create an armed force loyal to the president (always a factor in the Brazilian military) was perceived by many officers to have reached alarming proportions."[24] Yet Goulart proceeded, largely unaware of the catastrophic effect his moves were having; for one thing, Goulart's chief military advisor, General Assis Brazil, was an alcoholic who commanded very little respect among his fellow officers and thus was not able to keep Goulart in touch with what the army's leaders were really thinking.

In sum, hostility to Goulart within the military spread from a hard core that was opposed to his taking office in the very beginning in 1961 to embrace two larger groups: officers frightened by Goulart's growing radicalism, and others dismayed by the erosion of the constitution and/or attacks on military discipline.

A true conspiracy within the army against Goulart did not begin until October 1963, under the leadership of newly appointed Army Chief of Staff General Humberto Castello Branco. The original purpose of the plotters was defensive; that is, they were prepared to resist a Goulart move to close down Congress or suspend the constitution. Only later did the conspirators move to an offensive scenario: the removal of Goulart.[25]

By the spring of 1964, two powerful perceptions were converging within the army. The first was a growing fear that the independence, indeed the very existence, of the army was beginning to be at risk. The second, not created by Goulart's policies but certainly stimulated by them, was an increasingly widespread belief among the officer corps that it possessed within itself both the doctrine and the skilled personnel required to save Brazil from chaos and place her back on the road to economic development and regional and even world influence.

This belief that the army could successfully fulfill the role, not of temporary moderator but national savior, derived its principal impetus from the activities of the Escola Superior de Guerra (ESG). Established by presidential decree in August 1949, by 1964 this higher war college had graduated hundreds of officers and numerous civilians as well. The "National Security Doctrine" expounded at the college emphasized that what Brazil needed above all was to maximize economic output and to minimize social cleavage and disunity through comprehensive planning by a strong and enlightened government. Graduates of the ESG, civilian and military alike, tended to share the conviction that they, as a group, possessed the appropriate understanding of Brazil's needs and the techniques to satisfy them.[26] At the same time, the suicide of Vargas, rampant inflation, the declining growth rate, the lack of sensible civilian plans for stabilization and development, the ridiculous resignation of Quadros after his landslide election victory, and the increasing radicalism and confusion within the Goulart administration convinced many ESG alumni that normal political processes in Brazil would produce not solutions but greater frustration and chaos.

It is customary in some circles to assume automatically that the opposition of an officer corps to a reformist or radical administration is owing to the class origins of the officers; that is, crudely, the army must have turned against Goulart because its upper-class officers did not like the president's efforts to improve the lot of the nation's poor. But this sort of explanation has been seriously questioned by some observers, who conclude that it is not possible to establish a correlation between the social background of officers and their willingness to intervene against a given regime,[27] and that in the Latin American and especially the Brazilian context, the army, particularly the corps of professional officers, is really *a class unto itself*.[28] Perhaps "the greatest myth of all is that American foreign policy is controlling the military regimes of Latin America,"[29] whereas on the contrary, "the higher the degree of military authority, the lesser (not the greater) the extent of foreign influence and domination."[30]

What has been occurring, certainly in Brazil and undoubtedly in some other countries of Latin America and the Third World, is the emergence of the officer corps, especially in the army, as a sort of political party, committed to the national interest as opposed to the interest of any particular section.[31]

> The military sees itself as protecting hardwon national gains. The bourgeoisie, proletariat, and aristocracy are each viewed with suspicion, as sectional or segmented classes without the capacity to generate either an electoral consensus or charismatic leadership.[32]

From this point of view, the rise of military intervention and then outright military rule in Brazil and in other Latin American countries "is a function of the general law of statism: the increase of centralized power at the expense of separatist class, racial, and religious interests.[33]

Right or wrong, by the end of 1963, wide circles within the Brazilian army—and not only there—had concluded that "normal" civilian politics was ruining the country, and that the officer corps and its allies among the civilian technocrats had both the ability and the moral right to step in and save the day. The penetration of elite army and civilian circles by ESG doctrine accounts to a large degree for the army's decision to maintain a long-term hold on power after the 1964 coup, thus abandoning an essential element of the moderator model.

Nevertheless, the Brazilian army would probably not have acted on its own, or even with the encouragement of the civilian graduates of the ESG. Brazilian military coups have historically occurred in the presence of two circumstances that are related but not identical: (a) a low level of legitimacy of the incumbent executive, and (b) a high level of publicly expressed civilian support for a potential coup.[34] Most officers who are normally apolitical or legalist adhere to a coup conspiracy only after it becomes clear that an army move would have powerful civilian endorsement, that a coup would be seen as a movement of the army *with* civilians rather than *against* them.[35]

The major vehicle for the expression of civilian support for an army ouster of Goulart was the National Democratic Union (UDN), the middle-class party, composed of long-time anti-Vargas elements, the party that had won the elections of 1960 by a landslide only to see Vice President Goulart elevated by miscalculation to the presidency. What the UDN's position would be with regard to an army move against Goulart was never a mystery to most officers; unlike garrison commanders in the United States, Brazilian army leaders before 1964 were always in close contact with opinion makers and civilian elite groups. They could also roughly gauge public opinion through newspaper editorials and the manifestos of parties and civic groups. Editorial demands in the great Brazilian dailies for an army ouster of the inept Goulart were reaching titanic proportions by early 1964, and mass anti-Goulart demonstrations by civilians, especially women, filled the streets of the major cities.[36] There could be no possibility of doubt in the mind of even the most politically complacent or temperamentally cautious officer that wide and articulate elements of Brazilian society would greet the removal of Goulart with acclaim.

Nevertheless, as late as February 1964, it was by no means clear that a coup, often talked about, would in fact be attempted. Indeed, many believed that Goulart still had enough support, even within the army itself, that a coup might mean the unleashing of civil war. What altered this situation of stalemate swiftly and dramatically was the combination of two unpredictable events: Goulart's speech of March 13 and the sailors' mutiny of March 26.

Goulart's March 13 address (see above) in which he called the constitution into question, was a disaster for him. For many officers, reluctance to oppose a constitutional president was the only thing keeping them from adhering to the gathering forces of the coup. But Goulart's attack *on the constitution that protected him* dissolved these scruples.[37] In that same speech, Goulart's thinly veiled threats to close down the Congress also pushed several key state governors into the camp of open resistance, because they viewed Goulart as getting ready to put aside the constitution and keep himself permanently in power and ambitious governors therefore permanently out. This adhesion of popular and powerful governors to the ranks of those calling for Goulart's ouster helped to remove the doubts further from the minds of still-wavering officers.[38]

Even then, at that late hour, when Goulart had done everything wrong and the clamor for his removal was reaching a crescendo, many officers still hung back from a coup because they feared it would provoke civil war. What finally galvanized these last reluctant officers was the incident of the sailors' mutiny.

On March 26, 1964, members of the "Association of Sailors and Marines" attended a pro-Goulart rally, against the orders of the navy minister. The meeting was sponsored by the Communist-dominated Bankworkers' Union. When some of their leaders were arrested, the remaining sailors barricaded themselves in a union hall, vowing not to emerge unless promised amnesty. Marines were dispatched to arrest these men, but they declined to carry out their orders. The navy minister thereupon resigned. Finally arrested, the mutineers were then released by the order of President Goulart, after which they paraded triumphantly through the streets of Rio.

Just before their rebellion, the sailors had been shown a Russian film, *The Battleship Potemkin*, with a running commentary provided by Goulart's minister of education pointing out similarities between Brazil and Russia on the eve of her revolution.[39] The sanctioning of this mutiny by the president made him appear not only to be outside the law, but also a direct threat to the integrity of the armed forces as an institution.

Everybody now knew that a coup was coming, including the U.S. embassy, which could see the signs in the press. (The organizers of the coup also knew that the administration of President Lyndon Johnson would not be displeased by the exercise of the moderating power against Goulart.) Although signs abounded that a military movement was underway in the large state of Minas Gerais, Goulart failed to counter it; instead, he arranged transportation for members of the "Association of Subofficers and Sergeants" of the military police to attend a big rally in Rio de Janeiro on the night of March 30. Meanwhile, fearing that a coup was indeed imminent, leaders of several labor unions called a general strike for March 30 to show support for the president. The strike was a complete flop, with almost no participation. Only then did Goulart and his intimates realize how wildly they had overestimated their strength.[40] Nevertheless, Goulart went through with his speech to the Rio rally that night. It was predictably inflammatory and, that very midnight, the military revolt broke out in the key state of Minas Gerais.

"A MASTERPIECE"

"A coup," Edward Luttwak tells us, "consists of the infiltration of a small but critical segment of the state apparatus, which is then used to displace the government from its control of the remainder."[41] This is certainly an unexciting definition, but it very accurately describes what took place in Brazil at the end of March 1964: the coup-makers, military and civilian, used one part of the armed forces to displace the Goulart administration from its control of the rest, and thus of the government.

Luttwak offers us some fundamentals on the subject of coups. First, speed is essential from the coup-makers' point of view: there are usually plenty of wait-and-see types during a coup, and they really have the effect of helping the coup-makers if the latter move rapidly enough. If the coup goes on too long — if too much time elapses between the outbreak of the coup and the final seizure of the state — it will appear to have failed, and the wait-and-see people will veer to the side of the government.

The second fundamental, a very important and perhaps the most important condition making a coup possible, is the alienation or inertia of the mass of the citizenry. If they do not believe that the regime, much less the state, belongs to them, they will not trouble themselves to defend it even in a moment of supreme crisis. This is exactly what happened in the Goulart case, and is the main reason why the coup was so quickly successful.

The strategy of the coup was simple and sound: in those commands in which legalist officers were in charge, rebel sympathizers were to spread confusion and cause delay; those commands in which rebel officers were in control were to obey government orders to march against rebel units, and then *join forces with these rebels* as soon as contact was made. Thus, the first two legalist units to encounter rebel forces went over to them without a shot; this had a devastating effect on the morale of the remaining legalist commanders.

Also operating to the benefit of the rebels was the fact that they had a cause: the removal of Goulart, enemy of the constitution and subverter of the army. The legalists, in contrast, were not fighting *for* Goulart, whom they all distrusted or despised, but for a bloodless principle — constitutional government — *in defense of which principle the rebels also claimed to be acting*. And just to make it seem as though Fortune herself was smiling on the rebels, at the crucial hour of the rebellion, the war minister, General Dantas Ribeiro, a tough legalist and a soldier of no little ability, was immobilized by intestinal surgery.

President Goulart ignored what was going on in Minas Gerais because he had been worried about possible anti-administration moves in Rio de Janeiro, São Paulo, and his home state of Rio Grande do Sul. Rio de Janeiro, whose psychological significance could not be matched by any other place in the country, was home base to the First Army, a command of great strength. There pro-coup Governor Lacerda had already mobilized the state militia on March 29. The task of Lacerda's forces would be to tie up as many legalist units as possible, thus preventing large numbers of men from being sent against the rebels in Minas Gerais. During the preceding months, as if determined to prove that his lack of common sense reached heroic proportions, President Goulart had sought to immobilize officers whose loyalty he suspected (and there were quite a few) by stationing them in Rio de Janeiro, without commands, building up by his own policy a critical mass of pro-coup officers in that key city. Thus, when the crisis came, Goulart controlled neither the Rio state government nor a majority of the regular officers there. Fort Copacabana, a place of great symbolic importance, went over to the rebel cause, and the neighboring headquarters of the coast artillery was quickly taken. The ease with which these critical victories occurred convinced remaining legalist forces in Rio de Janeiro that the game was up. Goulart prepared to leave the city.

Meanwhile, the vaunted pro-Goulart masses were doing very little; their youthful leaders had found rhetoric a joy but organization a bore. Besides, the pro-coup state militias and organized civilian supporters of the revolt would have been more than a match for any potential demonstrations by Goulart sympathizers.

The revolt in Minas Gerais state had severed communications between Rio de Janeiro and the official national capital, Brasilia. Rebel army units, along with the Minas state militia, set out toward Rio. As these troops were about to cross the state border out of Minas, a confrontation occurred with legalist regulars. But the commander of the legalist forces was convinced that the revolt had already succeeded, and by the afternoon of April 1, his troops stood aside, permitting the march on Rio to proceed.

At São Paulo, financial capital of the nation, the Second Army was under the command of General Kruel, a legalist. He was confronted, however, by the large and well-armed São Paulo state militia that supported the rebellion. Kruel hesitated, and finally negotiated the surrender of his army on April 1, when it seemed that the regime had already collapsed. (The actions of men like Kruel would perhaps be easier to understand if one keeps in mind an essential rule in the Brazilian game of military coups: officers who defend the incumbent regime, or remain neutral rather than side with the coup-makers, are never purged or punished afterwards.)

In the northeastern quarter of the country there was little activity because most of the state governors there, and consequently the state militias, openly supported the rebels.

Brasilia, legal capital of the nation, was the scene of anticlimax. Goulart was certain to fly there after abandoning Rio de Janeiro; therefore, rebel troops from Mato Grosso traveled 1,000 miles in 48 hours to intercept him. But when the troops arrived, the coup was already over, and President Goulart, having spent but a few hours in Brasilia, had fled to Porto Allegre, capital of his (and Vargas's) home state of Rio Grande do Sul.

In Rio Grande do Sul was the Third Army, largest and most powerful force in Brazil. But the state government was in rebel hands, and the state militia was quite large enough to cause much worry to the regulars. Command of the Third Army was divided over what course to take and so took no course at all. When Goulart arrived in Porto Allegre at dawn on April 2, his ever-exuberant brother-in-law Brizola tried to persuade him to make a stand in the city. Demonstrating for once a realistic appraisal of a situation, Goulart refused this bait and left for his ranch in the interior of the state. Two days later, he went unmolested over the border to Uruguay. The coup-makers had won.

Not since the revolutions of the 1820s had the South American continent seen the movement of armed men over such large areas, and not since the Mexican Revolution of 1910 had an American conflict involved such great numbers. Yet the revolt that ousted President Goulart and ushered Brazil into a new era had lasted only about three days, and had required the spilling of the minimum of blood: "from a technical viewpoint the coup was little short of a masterpiece."[42] The Brazilian Army had found the seizure of power to be no problem.

The governing of vast Brazil would be another matter.

NOTES

1. Walter Laqueur in Edward Luttwak, *Coup d'Etat: A Practical Handbook* (Cambridge, MA: Harvard University Press, 1979), p. 9.
2. Irving Louis Horowitz, *Beyond Empire and Revolution: Militarization and Consolidation in the Third World* (New York: Oxford University Press, 1982), p. 94.
3. John J. Johnson, *The Military and Society in Latin America* (Stanford, CA: Stanford University Press, 1964), p. 38.
4. Alfred Stepan, *The Military in Politics: Changing Patterns in Brazil* (Princeton, NJ: Princeton University Press, 1971).
5. Stepan, *The Military in Politics*, p. 64.
6. Samuel P. Huntington, *Political Order in Changing Societies* (New Haven, CT: Yale, 1968), p. 226.
7. Huntington, *Political Order*, pp. 201–208.
8. Johnson, *The Military and Society*, p. 123.
9. Howard J. Wiarda and Harvey F. Kline, eds., *Latin American Politics and Development* (Boston: Houghton Mifflin, 1979), p. 62.
10. Wiarda and Kline, *Latin American Politics*, p. 62; see also Huntington, *Political Order*, pp. 226–227.
11. Huntington, *Political Order*, p. 228.
12. Ronald M. Schneider, *The Political System of Brazil: Emergence of a Modernizing Authoritarian Regime, 1964–1970* (New York: Columbia, 1971), p. 50.
13. Stepan, *The Military in Politics*.
14. Schneider, *The Political System*, p. 83.
15. Schneider, *The Political System*, p. 84.
16. Thomas E. Skidmore, *Politics in Brazil, 1930–1964* (New York: Oxford, 1967), p. 284.
17. Stepan, *The Military in Politics*, p. 156.
18. Alfred Stepan, "Political Leadership and Regime Breakdown: Brazil," in Juan Linz and Alfred Stepan, eds., *The Breakdown of Democratic Regimes: Latin America* (Baltimore, MD: Johns Hopkins, 1978), p. 124.
19. Skidmore, *Politics in Brazil*, p. 277.
20. Stepan, *The Military in Politics*, p. 191.
21. Skidmore, *Politics in Brazil*, p. 288.
22. Schneider, *The Political System*, p. 57 n.
23. Stepan, *The Military in Politics*, p. 69.

24. Stepan in Linz and Stepan, *The Breakdown of Democratic Regimes*, p. 119.
25. Skidmore, *Politics in Brazil*, pp. 264ff.
26. Stepan, *The Military in Politics*, chap. 8.
27. Huntington, *Political Order*, chap. 4.
28. Stepan, *The Military in Politics*, especially chap. 3.
29. Horowitz, *Beyond Empire*, p. 106.
30. Horowitz, *Beyond Empire*, p. 106.
31. Anthony James Joes, *Fascism in the Contemporary World* (Boulder, CO: West-view, 1978), pp. 129–132.
32. Horowitz, *Beyond Empire*, p. 99. See also Kenneth Paul Erickson, "Brazil: Corporatism in Theory and Practice," in Wiarda and Kline, eds., *Latin American Politics*, pp. 173–174.
33. Horowitz, *Beyond Empire*, p. 143.
34. Stepan, *The Military in Politics*, p. 80.
35. Stepan, *The Military in Politics*, p. 97.
36. Stepan, *The Military in Politics*, chap. 5, especially pp. 108–111.
37. Skidmore, *Politics in Brazil*, p. 294; Stepan, *The Military in Politics*, p. 199.
38. Stepan in Linz and Stepan, *Breakdown of Democratic Regimes*, pp. 123–129.
39. Stepan in Linz and Stepan, *Breakdown of Democratic Regimes*, p. 137n.
40. Skidmore, *Politics in Brazil*, p. 301.
41. Luttwak, *Coup d'Etat*, p. 27.
42. Schneider, *Political System*, p. 103.

9

Indonesia: The Double Coup d'Etat

Power creates its own legitimacy.

—Henry Kissinger

At the dawn of the year 1965, Indonesia was in the second decade of leadership by President Sukarno, one of the few Third World figures who truly deserves the adjective charismatic. The country was waging continuing undeclared war against its neighbors. It was on the verge of entering into a close alliance with the China of Mao (which had already entered the period of savage convulsions known as the Cultural Revolution). And it possessed the largest Communist party, the PKI, in the non-Communist world.

On October 1 of the same year, Communist and pro-Communist elements attempted, by murdering a number of unfriendly generals, to decapitate the Indonesian army and thus remove the last important bulwark against the complete communization of the country. Poorly planned and sloppily executed, the coup totally and visibly failed within 24 hours. But that one brief day of assassination and confrontation was to have dramatic and long-term consequences. President Sukarno was slowly but inexorably stripped of his powers and offices. The nation completely reversed its foreign policy and moved closer to the West. Most of all, an eruption of popular fury against the Indonesian Communists produced one of the great bloodlettings in contemporary history, completely destroying the once-mighty PKI along with the lives of hundreds of thousands of its supporters.

THE MAKING OF INDEPENDENT INDONESIA

Ranking tenth in area among the nations of the world, Indonesia consists of numerous islands, of which the largest is Sumatra. Hot and swampy, its interior covered by jungle, Sumatra was visited by Marco Polo around 1292 and was not fully pacified by the Dutch until the early years of this century. Indonesia has the largest population of all the countries of Southeast Asia, perhaps 90 million at the time of the 1965 coup (including 2 million ethnic Chinese), of whom two thirds live on the New York State-sized island of Java.

Indonesia's islands shelter a diversity of races speaking a multiplicity of tongues (fifteen spoken languages on Sumatra alone). Although there are large non-Muslim minorities in the islands, Indonesia is the easternmost outpost of Islam, a religion that for centuries has been something of a unifying factor. Nevertheless, before the arrival of the Europeans there was no such thing as an Indonesian nation, or even an Indonesian state.[1] The Portuguese were the first Europeans to be interested in Indonesia. The Dutch ousted them early in the seventeenth century, and eventually established their capital at Batavia (Latin for Holland), calling their island empire the Dutch East Indies. Yet even under this Dutch hegemony, it was not until the early twentieth century that the islands were united for the first time in their history under one administration, and then only loosely. The Dutch made money in Indonesia and brought some improvements with them, especially in the areas of public health, but population pressure and subsistence agriculture kept the average Indonesian poor.

Early in this century, political restlessness and nationalist feeling began to grow among educated Indonesians. The successful modernization of Japan and her stunning defeat of a major European power in the Russo–Japanese War of 1904–1905; the Chinese Revolution of 1911 and its bright promises; the growth of Indian nationalism behind the Congress party; movement toward independence for the Philippines; Soviet propaganda directed at the colonial empires (Lenin said, or should have said, that "the road to Paris lies through Peking"); the feeling of moral bankruptcy experienced by many Europeans after the holocaust of the Great War; Woodrow Wilson's insistence on the right of every people to self-determination; the spread of European education among an Indonesian elite, all combined to propagate the conviction that important changes in the political status of the Dutch East Indies were desirable and inevitable.

Mohammed Hatta was typical of the elite that formed the spearhead of Indonesian nationalism. Born in 1902, a Sumatran aristocrat, Hatta attended the Rotterdam School of Economics and joined the Indonesian independence movement there. After Sukarno founded the Indonesian Nationalist party (PNI) in 1927, Hatta worked closely with him. Jailed several times by the Dutch, Hatta was released by the conquering Japanese during World War II. Later, as minister of defense in the new republic, he directed the fight against the Dutch reoccupation. Not long after, a dispute with Sukarno caused Hatta to retire from politics.

Before World War II, the ethnic, linguistic, and religious diversity of the islands, disputes between radicals and moderates, and personal rivalries among leaders inhibited the growth of a strong nationalist movement in the islands. Another major obstacle to the development of a self-confident nationalism was the belief of many Indonesians that Dutch military power was unassailable. Using the age-old tactics of *divide et impera*, the Dutch might have continued ruling their southeast Asian empire indefinitely.

The Japanese conquest of Indonesia (along with neighboring Singapore, Malaya, and the Philippines) changed everything: "the myth of colonial omnipotence was exposed both by the defeat of Western colonial powers by the outnumbered Japanese and then by Japan's own collapse."[2] The Japanese had viewed their conquest of East Asia partly in terms of a racial conflict with the Europeans and Americans ("Asia for the Asians"). They consequently encouraged the growth of nationalist organizations in many of the areas that they occupied. Sukarno, Hatta, and other leaders of Indonesian nationalism collaborated with the Japanese occupation in the belief that Japan would soon make Indonesia independent (a belief in which they were bitterly disappointed). The Japanese did provide a great deal of anti-Western indoctrination and semimilitary training mainly through an organization called "Peta," and "Peta training under the Japanese acted as a catalyst in militarizing and politicizing a whole generation of Indonesian leadership."[3]

The suddenness of the Japanese surrender after Hiroshima permitted the Indonesian nationalists to take steps toward setting up an independent government before the British (and then the Dutch) arrived to take over. Hatta and Sukarno proclaimed the Indonesian Republic in August 1945. The area claimed by the new state consisted of Java, Sumatra, and the little island of Madura; it thus included the bulk of the population of the Dutch East Indies but left out many islands that would constitute provinces of the new republic only later.

After British forces had accepted the surrender of the Japanese troops in the islands, the Dutch returned promising changes and reforms, but not independence. Tedious and lengthy negotiations between the Netherlands government and the republicans dragged on and on but got nowhere; the Dutch would not recognize an independent Indonesia, and the republicans would accept nothing less. Finally, in July 1947, Dutch military and naval units went into action against the Sukarno–Hatta forces. When this "police action" was brought to a halt by order of the U.N. Security Council on August 4, the republicans were left in control of only about a third of the island of Java and some areas on Sumatra. Nevertheless, much of their army was still intact and, after more fruitless negotiations, fighting broke out again in December 1948. This time, the Dutch forces captured Sukarno and Hatta, as well as other key leaders. But these wars had caused much damage to property and had alarmed Dutch business interests in Indonesia and back home, and many members of the United Nations were growing loud in their condemnation of Dutch imperialist violence. After more protracted bargaining and threats of more fighting, Queen Wilhelmina transferred sovereignty over the islands to the Republic of Indonesia on December 27, 1949. Within a few years, the new Indonesian state had come to rest uneasily on a tripod consisting of President Sukarno, the republican army, and the Communists (PKI).

SUKARNO

Born in 1902 and educated in a succession of European schools in Indonesia, Sukarno became an active nationalist at an early age. He suffered imprisonment and exile during the 1930s. No matter what assessment may finally be made of him, Sukarno has at least one undeniable and monumental accomplishment to his credit: after becoming first president of the republic in 1945, he succeeded in linking the explosive mixture of diverse regions, races, religions, and tongues into one more-or-less united nation. It is extremely doubtful that any other political figure in the country could have done this. An admirer of Mussolini, Sukarno borrowed many of his slogans and some of his style from the Italian fascists: but he was not at all unwilling to compare himself, at various times, with Jefferson, Stalin, Mohammed, Buddha, and Jesus. Like many leaders of revolutionary movements in Third World countries, Sukarno enjoyed the good life; at his presidential palace, he lived in opulence within view of some of the most depressing slums in all of Asia, and his pursuit of the pleasures of the flesh was legendary.

As was to be expected, political life in the multiracial, multilingual archipelago was tempestuous. Armed revolts in the name of various causes broke out in diverse places during the 1940s and 1950s. Sukarno was not, even theoretically, a believer in democratic government. Hence, few were surprised when in 1956, after an extensive tour of Communist bloc countries, Sukarno proclaimed that henceforth Indonesia would be a "guided democracy." The exact meaning of this phrase soon became entirely clear: dictatorship under Sukarno. He assumed the office of prime minister as well as president, postponed general elections to the indefinite future (in Sukarno's more than twenty years of power, parliamentary elections were held only once, in 1955), declared that members of parliament would be appointed rather than elected, and banned several troublesome political parties. Over the next few years, Sukarno pursued an increasingly radical policy: he initiated armed conflict with the Netherlands in New Guinea, began a military confrontation with neighboring Malaysia, expelled the Peace Corps and the U.S. Information Service, seized U.S. property and businesses, took his country out of the United Nations, and drew closer to Mao's Peking. In summer, 1965, Djakarta and other cities reverberated to the noise of massive anti-American and anti-British demonstrations orchestrated by the regime, while huge, brightly-colored posters showed various Communist leaders smashing a malevolent but impotent Uncle Sam. The country neared financial bankruptcy, endured the worse inflation rates in Asia, and sank deeper and deeper into international isolation.

Despite this record (in fact partly because of it), in the beginning of 1965, Sukarno appeared to be unshakable in his supremacy. Although he had never been elected to the presidency by the people, both the Communists and the army believed that he was immensely popular, and both groups feared that his removal or assassination would plunge Indonesia into civil war. Aside from his authentic charisma, Sukarno's power derived from a balancing act involving the army and the PKI: to the former, he gave plenty of money for materiel and perquisites; to the latter, he presented cabinet seats and a pro-Peking policy.

THE ARMY AND THE COMMUNISTS

With its roots in the guerrilla forces operating against the Dutch in 1946, the army was from the beginning a major political actor in Indonesia. Although the wars of independence had ended, an army career remained a wise choice for a young man with political ambitions. During the 1950s, more and more positions in the cabinet, administration, and parliament were filled with officers. The army enhanced its power and prestige by the crushing of serious regionalist revolts in 1956 and 1957.

By 1965, under Chief of Staff General Nasution, the Indonesian army was a fairly well-disciplined and well-equipped force of more than 300,000 men. Sukarno's campaign against the Dutch in New Guinea and his confrontational policy toward British-backed Malaysia contributed directly to the growth in the army's strength and influence. Yet many of its officers were increasingly uneasy about Sukarno's adventurist foreign policy and looked to the future with apprehension. There was also an open and unpleasant political rivalry with the air force. At the same time, several factors combined to weaken the army's organizational cohesiveness: personal rivalries and factionalism, the loyalty of some officers to the person of Sukarno rather than to the nation or to the army, and the development of small pockets of Communists or Communist sympathizers within the officer corps.

Challenging this less-than-monolithic army was the growing power of the PKI. Indonesian communism had quite a checkered past. It had attempted two Leninist-type revolts, in 1926 and 1948; the first had been put down by the Dutch authorities, the second by the republic. During the 1950s, however, owing to the deteriorating condition of the economy, Sukarno's slide to the left, and his wish to have a strong organization to counterbalance the army, the PKI grew powerful. By 1965, it was the largest Communist party outside the Communist bloc, with fully 3 million members, and another 15 million enrolled in front organizations. In May 1965, the party celebrated its 45th anniversary with massive demonstrations by crowds bearing huge portraits of Lenin, Stalin, Mao, Sukarno, and PKI boss D. N. Aidit. Sukarno addressed one of these monster rallies and referred to the Communists as his "blood brothers."[4] As 1965 wore on, the PKI assumed a more and more hostile stance toward the army, whereas Sukarno moved closer to the PKI.

The PKI appeared more powerful than it really was, however. Its popular base was composed of demonstrators, not fighters. It relied for its influence very heavily on the support of the press and the patronage of Sukarno; both of these props could be withdrawn at any moment. No one realized the fundamentally precarious position of the PKI better than Party Chairman Aidit. Born in 1923, he had been appointed to the party politburo at the age of 25. In 1962, Sukarno conferred ministerial rank upon him. In January 1965, Aidit told Sukarno that the workers and peasants (that is, the PKI) should be trained and armed as a "fifth force" to balance the three military services and the police; Peking promised to deliver 100,000 small arms for such an organization.[5] Aidit also wanted "political advisory boards" set up in all military units. These changes would presumably render the PKI supreme in the country. The army was of course bitterly opposed to such plans. Nothing much had been done to implement them by September 1965, but the army and the PKI had moved perceptibly closer to confrontation.

THE COUP AGAINST THE GENERALS

Toward the end of the summer of 1965, many observers began to believe that Sukarno was seriously ill. He had collapsed on a public platform on August 5, and had had other visible health problems before and after. The PKI and its sympathizers in the armed forces were afraid that if Sukarno died the army would turn on the Communists.[6] PKI fears of what the army might do focused on a body known as the "Generals' Council." This group was actually in charge of authorizing promotions to the rank of general. The Communists, however, appear to have suspected that the council was masterminding a future army strike against the PKI.[7] It is unlikely that the Generals' Council was a conspiratorial body. At the minimum, "no evidence has appeared showing that the council of generals was in fact preparing a coup at the beginning of October [1965]".[8] Nevertheless, the wheels were now rapidly turning within the PKI for a decisive, preemptive blow at the army.

Developments overseas also played a role in the decision to move against the army command. During the spring and summer of 1965, the United States carried out a massive buildup in South Vietnam. Many Communists, including those in Indonesia, feared that the Americans were preparing to resist the spread of Communism throughout Southeast Asia.[9] If the PKI did not move soon, it might never again have a good opportunity to do so. Thus, sentiment grew among party members and sympathizers for a surgical strike against the Indonesian army officer corps. The top leaders, all nationalists and unfriendly in varying degrees to the PKI, would be removed. More reliable Sukarno men, approved by the Communists, would replace them.[10]

Two key aspects of the coup have evoked much controversy. First, did

President Sukarno know about and approve the plans for striking against the top army leadership? Second, what was the exact role of the PKI in these fateful events? From circumstantial evidence, careful analysts conclude that Sukarno probably did not know what was going to happen (see below).[11] As for the Communists, two key facts seem fairly well established: (a) the top leadership of the PKI, although not in exclusive control of the coup, knew about it beforehand and approved (PKI chief Aidit, for instance, went to the headquarters of the coup-makers in the hours just before the coup unfolded); (b) individuals and groups within the PKI participated in the attack on the army from the start; it is difficult to believe that they did this without the party leadership's knowledge or against its wishes; (c) whatever the degree of Communist participation in the genesis of the coup, once the plot began its grisly unwinding, the PKI publicly and enthusiastically endorsed it. Certainly, the army perceived the coup as a mortal attack upon it launched by the PKI and quickly decided to finish the Indonesian Communist leviathan once and for all.

The actual direction of the first physical attacks on the army command was in the hands of Lt. Col. Untung, commander of the Tjakrabirawa (presidential guard). In addition to his own battalion, Untung could count on two battalions of paratroopers brought into the capital city just for this work, some air force troops, and groups from the Communist Youth Organization trained and armed by the air force.[12]

The role of the air force in this attack upon the army high command is an interesting one. The air force provided a headquarters for the plotters at its main base at Halim, outside Djakarta. It also furnished transportation for the squads that were dispatched to bring leading generals, dead or alive, back to the base. Unlike the army, the Indonesian air force had no revolutionary tradition to be proud of, and its leaders apparently sought to make up for this by assuming a pro-Communist stance in both domestic and foreign affairs.[13] Consequently, "the air force leadership was clearly on the PKI's side in the conflict with the army."[14] The air force commander, Air Vice-Marshal Omar Dhani, had gone to Peking to negotiate the arms deal for the "fifth force," and PKI leaders may have led him to believe that he was their choice to succeed Sukarno when the latter passed from the scene.[15] Dhani had repeatedly stated that if a showdown came between the PKI and the army, the air force would unhesitatingly support the Communists.[16] After the coup had taken the lives of several army generals, he made a radio broadcast placing his stamp of approval on these actions.

The group that engineered the coup called itself the "September 30th Movement." In the last minutes of that day, seven commando groups set out from Halim Air Force Base with the aim of capturing the seven top generals of the Indonesian army. Three of these generals were shot and killed in their homes. They may perhaps be considered the lucky ones. Three other generals were brought alive to Lubang Buaja (Crocodile Hole) where they were beaten to death and mutilated by members of the PKI-controlled "Indonesian Women's Movement."[17] Then the bodies of all six men were thrown into a well. During these ghoulish exercises, troops supporting the coup surrounded the presidential palace, the radio and television center, and the telephone exchange. The enlisted men participating in these events were informed that they were acting to prevent an attack on President Sukarno.

The coup-makers had seven generals on their death list, but succeeded in taking only six. The seventh was General Nasution, long-time army chief-of-staff, then serving as defense minister. Nasution, born on Sumatra, was a veteran of the anti-Dutch guerrilla effort, a major general at age twenty-eight, author of a widely-used manual on guerrilla warfare, and a devout Muslim. When the murder squad came to his house, General Nasution escaped over the wall of his garden into the grounds of the Iraqi Embassy. Those who had come to kill him instead shot to death his 5-year-old daughter.

One general whose name was not on the murder list was the 44-year-old Suharto. A Javanese who served successively in the Dutch, Japanese, and Indonesian armed forces, Suharto had commanded operations against the Dutch in New Guinea in 1962. He was now commander of Kostrad, the army strategic reserve forces. Perhaps Suharto's name was not on the coup-makers' list because they believed he would not oppose their move[18]; if so, it was an egregious error. Suharto had been aroused from sleep by a neighbor at about 5:30 A.M., October 1, and told that generals were being abducted or shot all around the capital. Suharto then made his way to Kostrad headquarters to learn what was happening and to decide what moves, if any, to make.

The escape of Nasution and the failure to include Suharto on the death list constituted the double key to the failure of the coup. Nasution soon joined Suharto at Kostrad headquarters, where they ascertained that although the PKI had indeed infiltrated the army leadership, the overwhelming majority of officers were not involved in the coup and indeed were willing to resist it. Within a few hours of arriving at his headquarters, Suharto had mobilized his Kostrad forces, along with some loyal elements of the Djakarta garrison, the paracommandos, the navy, and the capital police force. With these behind him, the calm and daring Suharto set about to reverse the tide.

Suharto soon learned that Merdeka ("Freedom") Square, location of the palace and many other key buildings, was in the hands of two battalions of rebel troops. These men were allowed by their leaders to remain in the hot sun for many hours, with nothing to eat or drink. Suharto eventually told the officers in command of these troops that they were being used in an anti-Sukarno conspiracy. He ordered them to surrender to him, in return for which they would receive food and drink. If they refused to give up, he would attack. At about 4:00 P.M., after it had been clear that no one was coming to help them, one of the rebel battalions placed itself under Suharto's command and the other left the square and retreated to Halim Air Force Base.

Thus, the strategic and symbolic center of Djakarta had fallen to Suharto's forces without a single casualty. The radio station was retaken by 7:00 P.M.; two hours later, Suharto made a broadcast in which he cleverly declared that the coup had been aimed against President Sukarno but that loyal forces under Suharto's command were in control of the situation.

And where, during all this, was President Sukarno? He had arrived at Halim at about 8:30 that morning, after having been informed that a coup was afoot and that several generals had been murdered. The fact that Sukarno went immediately to the command center of the coup convinced many Army officers that Sukarno either had previous knowledge of the coup or approved of it once it had begun. But this conclusion was not fully warranted by the evidence. Sukarno's Jet-Star airliner was always kept ready for him at Halim; it may have been mere prudence for him to go there once he learned that high-ranking officers were being killed in the night. At the base, Air Vice-Marshal Dhani asked Sukarno if he should support the coup, but Sukarno gave him an evasive answer (almost certainly Sukarno did *not* tell him *not* to support it).[19] Nevertheless, at about 3:30 P.M., Dhani made a radio broadcast that placed the air force behind the September 30th movement. Poor Dhani; within an hour of that imprudent speech, the coup was well on its way to defeat. (Dhani was condemned to death in 1966.)

On October 1, as the Pacific sun began to set, Suharto sent a message to President Sukarno at Halim, warning him that he should leave the base. Sukarno knew perfectly well what this meant, and he took Suharto's advice. (So did Marshal Dhani, abandoning his men, the guilty and the innocent, to whatever fate might await them.) Shortly after midnight, Suharto's forces surrounded Halim. It was a repetition of the events at Merdeka Square: the rebel forces surrendered without Suharto inflicting or suffering any casualties. With the heart of the capital and now the air force base in his hands, Suharto had beaten the coup-makers and everyone knew it. What was going to happen next was not difficult for anyone to guess.

THE DESTRUCTION OF THE PKI

News of what had been done to the generals at Crocodile Hole caused a shudder of horror and then a demand for revenge to run through the army. No one forgot, either, that on the morning of October 2, the Communist *People's Daily* had hailed the killing of the generals as a necessary act of revolution. President Sukarno was insisting that there should be no more violence and therefore no revenge. But the army, appalled by the fate of the murdered generals, and aware of the availability of broad civilian support, decided to seize the opportunity to cleanse the Indonesian scene of the menacing and bloodstained Communist presence.

Communist strength was concentrated in central Java, an area too extensive and densely populated for the military to attend to easily. Hence, in the words of one general:

> we decided to encourage the anti-Communist civilians to help with the job. . . . We gathered the youth, the nationalist groups, the religious organizations, we gave them two or three days training, and then we sent them out to kill the Communists.[20]

Popular fury, thus unleashed, shook the islands and inundated the PKI. For the first time that anyone could remember, headquarters buildings of a major Communist party were going up in smoke and flame. The Muslims turned on the PKI with ferocity, but the Hindus on the island of Bali yielded first place to no one in their intense zeal to track down and exterminate Communists. The purge reached the large Chinese community, where numerous anti-Communist Chinese participated in the destruction of the PKI.

The PKI put up some resistance. In central Java, there was an actual massacre of anti-Communists.[21] In general, however, especially considering what was at stake, the resistance of the Communists was half-hearted and ineffective, for which there were several reasons. The Communists well remembered their uprising of 1948, which had been crushed in a matter of weeks. The rank-and-file membership of the PKI was drawn mainly from the lower social classes of Indonesia, not a very warlike group. Java, the geographical heart of Communist strength, was not suited for sustained guerrilla warfare. Most of all, the party was simply inundated by the ferocity and massiveness of the popular uprising against them: the army, the Nationalists, the Muslims, the Hindus, everyone wanted to participate in the decimation of the Communists.

Soon the rivers of Indonesia were choked with corpses in a manner that reminded some observers of logjams. No one knows how many died in the months of vengeance that followed the murder of the generals: the *New York Times* estimated the death toll to be between 150,000 and 400,000; the *Economist* stated that 1 million had died. Whatever the true number, it was one of the most titanic bloodbaths in the sanguinary history of the twentieth century, and left the once-haughty Indonesian Communist party a total wreck. Even Aidit, who had fled Halim Air Force Base along with Sukarno on the evening of October 1, had been tracked down and executed.

THE END OF SUKARNO

Shortly after the failure of the coup and the revelation of the grisly murders of the generals, Sukarno had laughed and engaged in banter with foreign journalists. He also failed to attend the funerals of the slain army leaders and referred to their assassinations as a "ripple in the ocean of the Indonesian revolution."[22] All of this behavior enraged Suharto and other army heads, but they did not move against the president immediately. They appreciated Sukarno's usefulness as a symbol of legitimacy and unity against Indonesia's ever-present and profound centrifugal forces. They wanted to avail themselves of Sukarno's still considerable prestige. If Sukarno could be kept in power nominally, the army would not have to rule the country openly. Moreover, summarily to remove the head of state, the first and only president of independent Indonesia, not to speak of killing him, would set a bad precedent that might one day be turned against the generals themselves.[23] The order of the day therefore was to draw a veil over Sukarno's actions right after (and perhaps before) the coup, and work around him.

Sukarno, however, made this impossible. He had too long been both the leading actor and the imperious director of the drama of Indonesian politics to settle for any subordinate role. He hoped that through charisma, prestige, daring, and his remaining supporters in the military, he could stage a comeback. Thus, in February 1966, Sukarno appointed a new cabinet consisting of pro-Sukarno and pro-Communist elements (Sukarno actually promised to protect and rebuild the shattered PKI). The list of cabinet appointees did not include Minister of Defense Nasution (the one whose daughter had been murdered in the coup) but did include Air Force Chief Dhani, whose involvement in the coup attempt was known to all. The announcement of this unbelievably provocative cabinet brought forth choking indignation within the army and massive demonstrations by students. Sukarno responded by dissolving all student organizations and ordering several universities closed. Instead of calming the situation, these acts provoked even greater manifestations of student unrest. On March 10, Sukarno summoned the leaders of Indonesia's political parties to his main palace and forced them, under threat of arrest, to sign a statement identifying the student protests as part of a CIA conspiracy.[24] The next day, troops loyal to General Suharto surrounded the palace, the cabinet disintegrated, and Sukarno left the city. Later that day, acknowledging the failure of his attempted comeback, and in the face of the continuing student demonstrations, Sukarno signed over to General Suharto power to "take all steps considered necessary to ensure the security, calm, and stability of the government."[25] The first act of the new Suharto cabinet was to outlaw the PKI. (Sukarno had previously denied Suharto's request that the PKI be outlawed because, he inaccurately predicted, such a move would drive them to guerrilla warfare.)

The U.S. government, although greatly pleased with the course events had taken in Indonesia since October 1, 1965, remained relatively discreet while popular wrath destroyed the PKI and the army moved slowly and carefully against Sukarno. Under the new foreign minister, Adam Malik, post-coup Indonesia did not pursue what could be called a pro-Western line, but during 1966, the country did draw back quite noticeably from Mao's Peking. It also reentered the United Nations and brought its disputes with Malaysia to the negotiating table.

In the year following the installation of the Suharto government, President Sukarno continued to show himself unrepentant, and indeed still plotted for a return to his old dictatorship. How far out of touch with the real feelings of his people he had allowed himself to become was demonstrated on March 7, 1967. On that date, the Provisional People's Consultative Congress, the Sukarno-appointed "supreme policy-making body," declared that Sukarno "had failed to meet his constitutional responsibilities" and withdrew all his remaining powers. General Suharto was named acting president, and one year later was installed by the same assembly as second president of the Indonesian republic. Former President Sukarno disappeared almost entirely from the public view and died in obscurity at the age of 68 on June 21, 1970.

NOTES

1. Bernhard Dahm, *History of Indonesia in the Twentieth Century* (New York: Praeger, 1971), p. 1.
2. Joyce C. Lebra, *Japanese-Trained Armies in Southeast Asia* (New York: Columbia University Press, 1977), p. 183.
3. Lebra, *Japanese-Trained Armies*, p. 176.
4. Dahm, *History of Indonesia*, p. 222.
5. Harold Crouch, *The Army and Politics in Indonesia* (Ithaca, NY: Cornell University, 1978), p. 92; Arnold C. Brackman, *The Communist Collapse in Indonesia* (New York: Norton, 1969), p. 48.
6. Donald Hindley, *The Communist Party of Indonesia 1959–1963* (Berkeley: University of California Press, 1964).
7. Dahm, *History of Indonesia*, p. 227.
8. Crouch, *The Army and Politics*, p. 107; Dahm calls the belief that the Generals' Council was preparing a coup "absurd"; *History of Indonesia*, p. 234.
9. Wilfred T. Neill, *Twentieth Century Indonesia* (New York: Columbia University Press, 1973), p. 351.
10. John Hughes, *Indonesian Upheaval* (New York: David McKay, 1967), pp. 114–115; Donald Hindley, "Indonesian Politics," *World Today* 24 (August 1968): 347–349.
11. Dahm, *History of Indonesia*, p. 229.
12. Hughes, *Indonesian Upheaval*, p. 27.
13. Dahm, *History of Indonesia*, p. 225.
14. Crouch, *The Army and Politics*, p. 84.
15. Neill, *Twentieth Century Indonesia*, p. 352.
16. Dahm, *History of Indonesia*, p. 225.
17. Neill, *Twentieth Century Indonesia*, p. 351.
18. Crouch, *The Army and Politics*, pp. 124–125.
19. Dahm, *History of Indonesia*, p. 233.
20. Hughes, *Indonesian Upheaval*, p. 151.
21. Brackman, *The Communist Collapse*, p. 109
22. Hughes, *Indonesian Upheaval*, p. 198.
23. Donald Hindley, "Political Power and the October 1965 Coup in Indonesia," *Journal of Asian Studies* 26 (February 1967):246.
24. Hughes, *Indonesian Upheaval*, p. 232.
25. Hughes, *Indonesian Upheaval*, p. 236.

10

Portugal: The Army and the Liberal Revolution

The foundation of states is a good military organization.

—Machiavelli

When elements of the Portuguese army seized control of Lisbon on April 23, 1974, they put an end, almost bloodlessly, to Europe's oldest dictatorship, a regime that had lasted for half a century. This event also signaled the imminent collapse of Europe's oldest colonial empire. In Portugal, as in France, a protracted colonial war (in fact, a number of simultaneous wars) caused, or brought to the surface, profound dissatisfaction on the part of the army with the policies and arrangements of the civilian regime. Like everything else in the Portugal of those days, the colonial wars and the general distress within large segments of the army developed from the political and social structure laboriously erected and preserved over so many years by Antonio Salazar, de facto ruler of the nation from 1928 to 1968. Even though by 1974 power had fallen from Salazar's own hands and the military coup was directed against his successor and heir, it was nevertheless the Salazar regime and its vision of Portugal that, after so many years, came to its end.

THE COMING OF SALAZAR

Following the assassination of King Carlos and his heir in 1908, the venerable Portuguese monarchy fell almost by default to a modest republican revolt in Lisbon. The republic was very much an affair of the bourgeoisie, with the peasant majority excluded and the working class alienated. The 16-year record of the parliamentary republic is one of unrelieved catastrophe. In its first decade, prices increased twelvefold, while wages lagged far behind.[1] The escudo dropped to its lowest level in history. The honor of the republic was irredeemably besmirched by the famous bank note fraud, which became the "largest state finance swindle in the history of modern western capitalism."[2] The politicians dragged an uncomprehending country into World War I, during which the Portuguese suffered significant casualties. The postwar period witnessed the worst inflation in modern Portuguese history.[3] Economic calamity was matched by political chaos. From 1910 to 1926, only one president of the republic served out his term. One president was assassinated, as was one prime minister. In sixteen years, there were seven general elections, eight presidential elections, ten presidents, and no fewer than forty-five cabinets.[4] The "parliamentary regime of the Portuguese Republicans was the most turbulent and unstable in modern European history."[5] When the military finally stepped in to put an end to this bacchanal in 1926, it was greeted with widespread popular approval.[6]

In April 1926, General Cardona, head of the military government, appointed as minister of finance Antonio Salazar, a man whose books and articles on financial questions had won him respect from friend and foe.[7] Salazar took over the ministries of interior and colonies in 1930, became prime minister in 1932 (which office he maintained until 1968), and after 1936 served also as minister of foreign affairs and of war. The "Salazar regime" was exactly that.

Who was this man who dominated his country so completely for so long?

Antonio de Oliveira Salazar was born in northern Portugal in 1889, of a lower middle-class family; his father was an estate manager. Salazar at first studied for the priesthood, but later turned to law and economics, taking his doctorate in the latter field at the University of Coimbra in 1918. A professor of modest means, a bachelor of austere habits, a Roman Catholic of the school of Leo XIII, concise and simple of speech, fluent in French and understanding English, Salazar was elected to Parliament as a Christian Democrat in 1921. He found life in that raucous assembly not at all to his taste, and soon resigned.[8] Everything that Salazar did or did not do in his long tenure of power must be viewed in the light of his (and many others') unhappy experiences in the parliamentary period, and the conclusions he drew from them. Salazarism was primarily and decisively a reaction to the disorder and demagoguery of the 1910–1926 period. Salazar always believed that during those years the party-parliamentary model had been given a fair trial and had failed resoundingly. "One of the greatest mistakes of the 19th century", he wrote, "was to suppose that the English parliamentary system was a form of government capable of adaptation to the needs of all European peoples."[9] Rejecting such a system as inappropriate to Portugal, Salazar sought to erect a Catholic corporatist structure for his country. Because of his espousal of corporatism, Salazar has sometimes been accused of fascist sympathies; but as he rejected the partisan cacophony of the early republican experiment, so he eschewed fascism's cult of youth and combat and its glorification of the state and the leader. (True, for many years Salazar kept a signed photograph of

Mussolini on his desk, but he put it away when the Italian leader became the ally of Hitler, whom Salazar feared and loathed.) Salazar studiously avoided the limelight; throughout his long tenure of power, he was not involved in any scandal and his modest financial circumstances did not improve visibly. His government has aptly been called "a regime of professors in a discreet dictatorship."[10]

REGIME OF THE PROFESSORS

Quintessentially the civilian, Salazar had nevertheless been placed in power by the army, and the army remained "the backbone of the regime."[11] The softspoken professor of economics was worldly wise enough to lavish attention and financial benefits on the armed forces. He also enjoyed the almost unanimous support of devout Roman Catholics, who had suffered under the republican regime; they would doubtless have supported Salazar anyway, but his signing of a concordat with the church in 1940 solidified behind him the allegiance of what was then a large and powerful group. Later Salazar constructed a sort of political party, the National Union, to serve as a sounding board of public opinion and a channel for government patronage.[12]

The hallmark and style of the regime was well expressed by Salazar himself when he said: "our first care must be to secure and maintain a balanced budget." But Salazar was a builder as well as a budget balancer; a vast public works program, with spectacular bridges, land irrigation, electrification from numerous dams, a doubling of the road network by 1950, and public housing for workers constituted one of the main achievements of Salazar's administration.[13] Kay describes Portugal when Salazar came to power as:

> a bad joke in the European chancelleries, her currency worthless, her army an obsolete remnant, the nation fragmented and beggared. Within a few years, Salazar had balanced the budget, restored the currency, started to build a modern army, constructed thousands of homes. He kept his country out of the Second World War [and] led Portugal into NATO and the United Nations.[14]

Progress continued after World War II. Illiteracy among children fell from 73 percent in 1930 to 10 percent in 1955. Industrial production quintupled between 1933 and 1962,[15] although Portugal did not receive any Marshall Plan aid at all until 1950. During the 1950s, after a quarter-century in power, the Salazar regime still looked good to many observers overseas, especially in Britain. A distinguished British historian wrote in 1955 that Salazar

> had restored order and solvency to his country, given it some useful institutions, steered it past some formidable crises, asserted its prestige, preserved its independence, raised its standards of life. Can any ruler, liberal or illiberal, do more than this for his country?[16]

And the *Manchester Guardian* observed on July 4, 1957, that "Portugal looks from the outside a much cleaner and neater country than when [Salazar] took over."[17]

If Salazar had died in 1945 or 1955, his reputation would also be "much cleaner and neater" than it is today. As MacDonald, Mussolini, Adenauer, and de Gaulle could testify, it is of no little consequence for a politician to know when to retire. But like an aging showman, Salazar remained on the stage too long, repeating his once-popular repertoire again and again while times and tastes changed.

Cracks were appearing in the structure that Salazar had built. For one thing, the government seemed as time went on to look more and more to the political police to protect it from enemies and even critics.[18] Foreign newspapers began concentrating their attention on the activities of the PIDE (International Police for the Defense of the State), to the detriment of the regime's image abroad. Salazar himself admitted that sometimes police abuses occurred in Portugal, but he categorized them as misguided efforts to catch terrorists and thus save innocent lives.[19] Sympathetic foreign observers have maintained that although the PIDE not infrequently overstepped its bounds, allegations against it were overdramatized, especially in the foreign press, and that many of the accusations against PIDE were never proved or had actually been disproved.[20] Even if PIDE had indeed been ferocious in its handling of the regime's enemies, its scope would still have been quite restricted in the 1950s and early 1960s because "opposition, such as it was, remained limited to small groups of students and intellectuals and a handful of middle class activists and military men."[21] Nevertheless, allegations of secret police abuses had a damaging effect on the reputation of the Salazar government: "in practice, the great criticism of his regime has always been that stability was bought and maintained by the suppression of human rights and liberties."[22] Yet accusations of this nature did not prompt the Social Democratic governments of Sweden and Denmark to object when Portugal joined with them in the European Free Trade Area (EFTA), nor did any government ever suggest that Portugal was not fit to participate with the Atlantic democracies in the North Atlantic Treaty Organization (NATO).

A more serious problem for the regime, one that loomed very large as the decade of the 1960s progressed, was the growing belief that it was artificially retarding Portugal's economic development. This was a telling criticism, for the primary claim to fame of the Salazar government had always been that it had rescued Portugal from economic chaos and set it firmly on the road of solvency, stability, and respectability. It is true that "the bitterest detractor of the professor-dictator will not deny that he gave Portugal the only smoothly functioning government it had seen for a century and a quarter."[23] But by 1960, hardly anyone (except Salazar) remembered the days of upheaval and scandal of the 1920s. The later problems of the regime were in fact rooted in its earlier successes; Salazar, by virtue of the very stability in which he took such satisfaction, found himself presiding over and administering the same medicine to a Portugal of the 1960s very different from the Portugal of the 1930s. Salazar as a young man had been a professional economist, but he had learned his economics in another world, before the Great Depression, before World War I. The increasingly rigid application by Salazar of the old once-successful formulas made it increasingly difficult for him to attract capable people to fill the government ministries, especially at the highest levels.[24] Salazar liked to compare the orderly and solvent Portugal of 1962 to the violent and bankrupt Portugal of 1932, but his critics were much more interested in measuring Portugal against her contemporary neighbors; by this yardstick, the Salazar regime came off poorly indeed. As compared with France or northern Italy, rural Portugal was very backward, with low productivity, high emigration, and widespread sickness. Rural life, especially in the southern provinces, was characterized by great landholdings alongside the misery of the landless; the infant mortality rate was twice that of western Europe. As the regime entered its fourth decade, many would have endorsed the conclusion that "although there may be favorable judgments on him in many matters, it was more than time for him to go."[25]

Salazar held on to power until he was finally felled by a severe stroke in September 1968. Portugal had not gone through a major change of leadership in almost forty years, but the system met this crisis with remarkable smoothness. President Thomaz convened what was perhaps the first meeting ever of the Council of State, the body charged with safeguarding the succession. Prime Minister Salazar was released from his office by the council, although this information was not transmitted to him. (Salazar lived until July 1970, a helpless invalid, apparently unaware that he was no longer in authority.) In his place, the Council of State appointed Marcello Caetano.

Born in Lisbon in 1906, Caetano was a lawyer with impressive credentials. Appointed minister of colonies at the age of 38, Caetano had been made deputy prime minister in 1955, a post he resigned to become rector of the University of Lisbon in 1959. Caetano had a reputation as the leader of the "liberal" wing of the Salazar administration, partly because he had resigned his rectorship to protest what he considered unwarranted police intervention in the affairs of the university. In his first months in power, Caetano seemed determined to bring about substantial liberalization of the regime: press censorship was lightened, police activities were less in evidence, even Socialist party leader Mario Soares was allowed to return home from exile (although he was soon sent back again). But not for nothing had Machiavelli pronounced the path of the reformer to be the most difficult. The demands from the leftish elements in Portugal, if Caetano had accepted then, would have amounted to suicide for the regime, whereas conservative elements feared the disintegrating effects of any concessions at all. Hence, within a very short time, almost everyone was disappointed with Caetano. Salazar was gone, an era was clearly coming to an end, change was in the air.

A pressing concern for the new prime minister was African policy. The last years of the Salazar administration witnessed the rise of troublesome guerrilla movements in Portugal's extensive African colonies; the army had insisted, as a condition for acquiescing in Caetano's installation as prime minister, that his government continue Salazar's hard-line position against independence for Portuguese Africa.[26]

WAR IN AFRICA

At the time of the transfer of power from Salazar to Caetano, Portugal possessed Europe's oldest and one of its largest colonial empires. This African domain, dating from the voyages of her intrepid explorers in the earliest years of the sixteenth century, consisted of three territories: Angola with an area of 481,000 square miles (14 times the size of Portugal) and a population of about 4.6 million; Mozambique with an area of 298,000 square miles and a population of 6.5 million; and Guinea with an area of 14,000 square miles and a population of 600,000.

Although the foundations of the empire had been laid in the days of the great seaward-looking monarchs, Portugal's colonial vocation had constituted a fundamental ideal of the republicans[27]; Salazar continued the paternal republican attitude toward Portugal's African subjects, and declared that the African territories were not mere colonies but integral, hence inalienable, parts of the Portuguese nation. Under his regime there grew up "a new, responsible, incorruptible and wholly committed generation of colonial [civil] servants."[28] Viewing African maturation to self-determination as a matter requiring centuries, not decades, Salazar tended to be very skeptical of slogans about democracy in Africa, which he believed masked the raw ambitions of unrepresentative cliques[29]; indeed, well into the 1970s, the colonial liberation movements would reject government offers to hold referenda, apparently fearful that the lack of wide popular support for these movements would become manifest.[30] When Caetano succeeded to leadership, he continued the African policies of all the preceding regimes; the former minister of colonies saw in the empire proof that small and underdeveloped Portugal still "retained a world role and a civilizing mission."[31] Portuguese Africa, moreover, contained a sizable population of European descent, especially Angola, where the general living conditions were much better than in most of the nearby independent African states.[32]

The first serious guerrilla challenge to the Portuguese broke out in northern Angola in March 1961. Until then, to maintain order among 5 million people, Portugal had had to deploy only 9,600 troops, many of whom were black. In 1961, Angola, like Mozambique, was an area on the map, not a nation. Each colonial territory was beset with profound tribal, linguistic, and political divisions. This fragmentation of society accounted for the existence of five major revolutionary groups, each claiming to lead the fight for the independence of Angola. These included UPA, the Union of the People of Angola, under the leadership of Holden Roberto, an African Baptist educated by American missionaries (deeply anti-Communist, Roberto and his movement nevertheless received, through one of those twists so common in southern African politics, the support of the Peking regime); the MPLA, the Popular Movement for the Liberation of Angola, led by Mario de Andrade, a Communist of mixed Portuguese–African descent; and UNITA, the National Union for the Total Independence of Angola, a faction that had split off from Roberto's group and that was headed by Joseph Savimbi. All these factions depended heavily on foreign aid; nonetheless, some central African republics not only failed to give help to these rebel groups but maintained warm ties with the Lisbon government.

The situation in Mozambique, less developed economically than Angola, was politically clearer. Most of the guerrillas in that large territory maintained some sort of allegiance to FRELIMO, the Front for the Liberation of Mozambique, directed by Dr. Eduardo Mondlane, who had been educated in Portugal, South Africa, and the United States. President Nyerere of neighboring Tanzania gave FRELIMO what support he could; Peking supplied it with technical assistance, and leading cadres received training in Algeria and Egypt. FRELIMO launched its first major attacks on Portuguese military installations in September 1964, attacks that were well-prepared and effective. But tribal and linguistic fragmentation complicated the picture in Mozambique: for example, the support of the Makonde tribe for FRELIMO earned that organization the hatred of the Makonde's traditional enemies, the Macua. It would therefore be the grossest distortion to paint either the Angola or the Mozambique guerrilla war as merely the uprising of simple African peasants against intolerable European oppression. In Portuguese Africa as in Algeria and Nicaragua, the leaders of rebellion were educated (often quite well-educated) townsmen. Their life-styles and thought patterns placed them worlds apart from the provincial and unlettered rural masses whose destinies they intended to decide. Their solution to the ethnic and regional fragmentation of the country was to impose unification by systematic violence, including torture and murder, against recalcitrant elements of the native population.[33]

The guerrilla wars in Portugal's African empire were to simmer for thirteen years. The rebels received arms and other assistance from China, the Eastern Bloc, and several North African states. Their respective political headquarters were usually located in the capital cities of neighboring independent states, whose territory served as a sanctuary of sorts. Portugal was far away and poor, with a small population. But the guerrillas faced many obstacles.

Each colony contained rival rebel organizations, often existing in a state of mutual hostility. The guerrilla organizations were usually coextensive with tribal lines, thus automatically ensuring each rebel force the hostility of at least several important tribes. The Portuguese developed village self-defense forces that were large and well-armed.[34] They also eventually fielded an army of 142,000 men, half of whom were black.[35] As one observer described the situation in the Portuguese armed forces, "twelve years after fighting began, in both militia and regular army units, blacks and whites served happily together, eating the same food, both officers and men, and sharing the same barracks rooms."[36] Until 1968, the impact of the fighting in Africa was slight, especially in terms of lives lost. It also produced a stimulating effect on the local economies, and numerous African peasant boys found opportunities to improve their status and living conditions by joining the Portuguese army. By 1974, the guerrillas had been contained, and there was some justification for the belief that they would soon collapse, although assuredly the efforts to defeat them had been very expensive. In the words of one student of the subject, "there was no evident sign of any weakening in Portugal's determination to remain in her overseas provinces, nor was there any evidence that her armed forces could not contain the guerrilla incursions."[37]

A microcosm of Portugal's African problem was provided by Portuguese Guinea. With only 14,000 square miles, much of it deserted or under water, and a population of only 600,000, Guinea was nothing to Portugal economically, but a failure to hold the line here would be enormously encouraging to the rebels in Angola and Mozambique. The rebellion in Guinea was headed by Dr. Amilcar Cabral, a one-time agronomist employed by the Portuguese administration. Cabral founded the PAIGC (African Party for the Independence of Guinea and Cape Verde) in 1952 and retained leadership of the party until his assassination in 1973. The territory of Guinea was small, and Muslim tribes tended to resist the rebels. But PAIGC guerrillas, trained in Russia, China, Algeria, Senegal, and other places, followed the proven tactics of rarely facing Portuguese army units directly; this, along with the inhospitable climate, had over the years weakened the morale of the Portuguese soldiery, black and white.

The situation began to change dramatically in 1968, with the appointment of General Antonio de Spinola as governor and commander in chief of Portuguese Guinea. Born in 1910, son of a civil servant, Spinola entered the army at the age of 18 and became a cavalry officer. His experience included commanding Portuguese volunteers in the Spanish civil war and leading troops against the guerrillas in Angola in the 1960s. Traveling by helicopter or light plane, Spinola paid frequent and unexpected visits to isolated and forlorn outposts, putting new heart into the men. He appreciated the political aspects of guerrilla warfare and, like the French in Algeria, led the army in undertaking programs to improve education and health care for the inhabitants.

His troops won military successes against the PAIGC as well; by 1972, Portuguese Guinea seemed to be more under the control of the central government than ever. Spinola returned to Portugal a hero, receiving a promotion and the country's highest decoration, and was made deputy chief of staff.

Although he had apparently shown the way to victory for the Portuguese in their continental struggle, Spinola was to play a vital role in the overthrow of the regime and the consequent liberation of the colonies. Not long after he had become deputy chief of staff, Spinola published a book, *Portugal and the Future*, which asserted that the African wars could not finally be won by military means alone, and that to win them politically Portugal would have to grant her colonies a form of independence within a grand "Lusitanian Union." Spinola thus challenged the moral basis for Portugal's efforts in Africa (that her overseas territories were truly and inalienably Portuguese) and questioned the army's ability to carry those efforts to success. Under severe pressure from outraged members of the officer corps, Prime Minister Caetano fired Spinola in March 1974.

Some students of the 1974 Portuguese coup maintain that the fundamental cause of the army's action against the regime was the disaffection within the officer corps produced by the long colonial wars.[38] They see the Portuguese army as the victim of "ideological contagion": through talking with their prisoners and reading their books, many Portuguese officers came to feel, according to this view, that the rebels' analysis of African underdevelopment and class division was painfully relevant to Portugal itself. This was especially the case for those officers who came into contact with draftees from that other Portugal, the one beyond Lisbon, where life was as poor and difficult as in a Third World country.

Undoubtedly, some Portuguese officers in Africa came to have a respect, even a sympathy, for their guerrilla adversaries. The colonial wars produced other problems as well. Conditions of protracted guerrilla warfare infinitely aggravated the usual dissatisfaction over the poor equipment, low pay, and miserable conditions of the army in Africa. Another sore point was the continuing failure of the regime and its "political" generals to develop a winning strategy against the rebels: officers feared that the army would be made the scapegoat for a future loss of the empire. These fears were by no means groundless. When military units of "peace-loving" India overran Portuguese Goa in 1961, the Lisbon government ungraciously (and incorrectly) suggested that the army was to blame. And Prime Minister Caetano was heard to remark that he preferred a military defeat to a political retreat in Africa.[39]

All these undeniably grievous aspects notwithstanding, it would be a serious mistake to identify opposition to continuing operations in Africa as the sole or even primary cause of army disaffection from the Caetano regime. Other significant factors were at work that had to do with the African wars only indirectly. Chief among these factors was widespread army indignation at new promotion policies promulgated by the Caetano government; without this provocation it is at least questionable that a successful military coup would have been possible.[40]

THE GOVERNMENT LOSES THE ARMY

Owing in part to a drain on personnel caused by the African wars, as well as to an increasing reluctance of the Portuguese to go out and fight them, the army by the early 1970s was suffering from a shortage of officer candidates. Seeking to remedy this situation, the Caetano government committed a fatal political blunder. On July 13, 1973, it issued a decree law whereby young men of university education were encouraged to enter the officer corps through financial inducements and—most important—provision for quick promotion. In addition, noncommissioned officers would be permitted to become officers after taking some accelerated courses. However advisable these steps may have seemed to the government, they left the regular officer corps (once called by Salazar "the voice of the nation"[41]) appalled and outraged. Their hard-won and deeply cherished seniority was about to be overthrown; one day they might actually find themselves outranked by men whom they had once commanded.[42] The immediate response to the detested decrees was the formation of a secret society of regular officers, the Movimento das Forcas Armadas (MFA). The disgruntled officers prevailed upon General Spinola himself to accept the presidency of the organization. The Caetano government soon found out about the MFA but inexplicably failed to take it very seriously. The anger of MFA members increased when certain officers were arrested by the secret police and accused of antiregime agitation.

The officer corps was tired of the wars in Africa and fearful that the regime's inability to win or to end them was leading up to the scapegoating of the army. It was, however, the new promotion policies of the Caetano government that finally alienated the officers; inexorably this alienation produced a willingness to consider a coup. Once this point had been reached, MFA members could reflect that the Caetano regime faced domestic problems of enormous scope and profound implications, so that an army move against it would be widely welcomed (just as in 1926).

For several years, scores of thousands of Portuguese had been leaving their homes to seek temporary employment in Common Market countries. Their experiences in these more advanced societies opened the eyes of many to the reality of conditions in Portugal, which had the highest infant mortality and illiteracy rates in Western Europe, along with the lowest per capita income and life expectancy. Thus, there was really little room for surprise when, in 1973, for the first time in anyone's recollection, serious labor strife flared in Lisbon. By 1974, only 8 million people were left in the country; fully 1.5 million Portuguese—a third of the entire labor force—had gone abroad seeking work. Half of Portugal's budget was being spent on the military (that is, on the colonial wars), with consequent reductions in expenditures for health, education, etc. Even before the Arab oil embargo of 1973, inflation reached 20 percent annually.

Beset with these mounting difficulties, unable to produce a convincing victory in Africa, lacking the prestige and the "permanency" Salazar had possessed, and having deeply offended substantial segments of the officer corps, the Caetano regime presented to the MFA a more and more irresistible target. A full-blown conspiracy soon developed.

THE ACT

Two conditions of supreme importance confronted the conspirators and shaped their plans and movement. The first was that the great bulk of the Portuguese army was stationed in Africa. Thus, owing to the distance involved and the relative scarcity of air transport, the Caetano regime would not be able to count on any African units, whatever their political dispositions might be, for help in case of trouble at home. The Portuguese troops in Africa were, in Luttwaks' phrase, not "forces relevant to the coup,"[43] a fact that enormously simplified the task and risk of the conspirators. They could concentrate all their attention and their forces on the capture of Lisbon and the key men of the regime; once these relatively uncomplicated objectives had been secured, the coup would be successfully over.

The second condition under which the coup developed was Prime Minister Caetano's inability to grasp the extent of the vulnerability of his regime. For fifty years, political authority in the country had derived ultimately from the support of the army; but Caetano did not comprehend this. It was this failure of understanding that permitted Caetano gratuitously to offend the army with his July promotion policy decrees; this same failure of understanding permitted the coup-makers to confront a regime almost denuded of physical protection. The regime leaders knew from PIDE reports of the existence of the MFA and of the general dissatisfaction within the ranks of the officers. They might have reflected also that the army in Africa would have been of no help to them in case of trouble in Lisbon. In view of these considerations, one would have expected the government to take elementary precautions against a possible coup by maintaining close at hand a carefully chosen, politically reliable elite force, vigorously segregated from the rest of the army and the civil population, a force well-armed, well-paid, and well-watched. But the government neither possessed nor created such a unit, and thereby contributed directly to its own demise.

Meanwhile, the MFA went ahead with its plot, "organized almost entirely by captains and majors, against conservative old-guard senior officers, but later with the open or tacit support of a great many officers of all ranks"[44] April 25, 1974, was selected as the day.

The execution of the coup, when it came, was flawless, a textbook exercise. The plotters had set up their headquarters in the garrison town of Santarem, 40 miles northeast of Lisbon. Santarem was the site of the Cavalry Training School; the cavalry branch enjoyed great prestige in the Portuguese army, and through the school at Santarem had passed many of the country's most senior and respected officers. In the very early hours of Thursday, April 25, a column of twelve vehicles and about 150 men set out from Santarem for the capital. By 3:00 A.M., this advance force was taking over central Lisbon. The ministries of defense, the navy, and the interior all quickly fell into the conspirators' hands. Other units were securing the airport, the television and radio stations, the central post office, and army headquarters itself. The airports at Oporto and Faro were also closed off, thus effectively preventing any government or army figures from flying to the northern provinces or to Guinea in an attempt to rally support for a counter-coup. (Control of the airports also meant that any relief expedition that might set out from Africa for Lisbon could not come safely by air, and thus might as well not come at all.)

Advised that a coup was underway, Prime Minister Caetano and some other high-ranking government officials took refuge in the headquarters of the paramilitary Republican National Guard (GNR). Word came that GNR units from all over Lisbon were converging on headquarters to help resist the coup. Other units also seemed prepared to resist (but without shooting), such as the 7th Cavalry Regiment and the 2nd Lancers (with whom the aged president, Americo Thomaz, had sought shelter). But the expected reinforcements failed to arrive at GNR headquarters. As the hours passed, information reached Caetano that the coup-makers were receiving the assistance or the surrender of units throughout central Portugal. After several hours of a tense standoff, General Spinola himself was admitted at about 5:40 P.M. into the GNR building; before the hour had struck, the announcement was made that Prime Minister Caetano had handed over his powers to the general, thus preserving the appearance at least of legal continuity. By late evening, all real resistance in the capital city had ceased. A few hours later (April 26), the PIDE prison on the coast outside of Lisbon surrendered to paratroopers under MFA command. The only real violence had occurred (in the Budapest pattern) when some panicky members of the PIDE opened fire from the upper windows of their Lisbon headquarters on the crowd gathered below, killing three and wounding several; one secret policeman was killed as he attempted to escape from the building.

Thus the system fashioned by Salazar came to its end in a manner reminiscent of the fall of the Romanovs: after so many years, in so few hours, with so little blood shed.

Within a year the Portuguese had elected a constituent assembly. One of the first acts of this body was to grant independence to the African colonies, consigning to their fate the thousands of European and Asian settlers, the many Africans who had worn the Portuguese uniform, and the countless tribesmen who had never supported, or had actually resisted, the guerrilla bands who were now their masters.

NOTES

1. Hugh Kay, *Salazar and Modern Portugal* (London: Eyre and Spottiswoode, 1970), p. 31.
2. Stanley Payne, *A History of Spain and Portugal*, vol. 2 (Madison: University of Wisconsin Press, 1973), p. 571.
3. Payne, *A History of Spain and Portugal*, p. 571.
4. A. H. De Oliveira Marques, *A History of Portugal: From Empire to Corporate State*, 2nd ed., vol. 2 (New York: Columbia University Press, 1976), p. 162; Payne, *A History of Spain and Portugal*, pp. 559–569.
5. Payne, *A History of Spain and Portugal*, p. 572.
6. Payne, *History of Spain and Portugal*, p. 663.
7. Oliveira, *A History of Portugal*, p. 211.
8. Oliveira, *A History of Portugal*, p. 211.
9. Kay, *Salazar*, p. 66.
10. Kay, *Salazar*, p. 84.
11. Howard J. Wiarda, *Corporatism and Development: The Portuguese Experience* (Amherst: University of Massachusetts Press, 1977), p. 122.
12. Wiarda, *Corporatism and Development*, pp. 118–119.
13. Oliveira, *A History of Portugal*, p. 196.
14. Kay, *Salazar*, pp. 6–7.
15. Kay, *Salazar*, p. 344; Payne, *A History of Spain and Portugal*, p. 677.
16. Quoted in Kay, *Salazar*, p. 333.
17. Quoted in Kay, *Salazar*, p. 84.
18. Wiarda, *Corporatism and Development*, pp. 178–179.
19. Kay, *Salazar*, p. 77.
20. For example, Kay, *Salazar*, takes this position.
21. Payne, *A History of Spain and Portugal*, p. 672.
22. Kay, *Salazar*, p. 65.
23. Charles E. Nowell, *Portugal* (Englewood Cliffs, NJ: Prentice-Hall, 1973), p. 153.
24. Wiarda, *Corporatism and Development*, p. 210.
25. Nowell, *Portugal*, p. 168.
26. Wiarda, *Corporatism and Development*, p. 256.
27. Oliveira, *A History of Portugal*, vol. 2.
28. Kay, *Salazar*, p. 213.
29. Kay, *Salazar*, p. 413.
30. Jonathon Story, "Portugal's Revolution of Carnations: Patterns of Change and Continuity," *International Affairs* 52 (July, 1976): 417–434.
31. Ben Pimlott, "Socialism in Portugal: Was It a Revolution?" *Government and Opposition* 7 (Summer 1977): 339.
32. Payne, *A History of Spain and Portugal*, 682.
33. Neil Bruce, *Portugal: The Last Empire* (New York: John Wiley, 1975), p. 80.

34. Bruce, *Portugal: The Last Empire*, p. 66.
35. Bruce, *Portugal: The Last Empire*, p. 66.
36. Bruce, *Portugal: The Last Empire*, p. 73.
37. Bruce, *Portugal: The Last Empire*, p. 63.
38. See, for example, Pimlott, "Socialism in Portugal"; G. W. Grayson, "Portugal and the Armed Forces Movement," *Orbis* 19 (Summer 1975): 335–379.
39. Pimlott, "Socialism in Portugal", p. 339; Antonio Rangel Bandiera, "The Portuguese Armed Forces Movement: Historical Antecedents, Demands, and Class Conflict," *Politics and Society* 6 (1976): 1–57.
40. This is the position of Philippe C. Schmitter in his "Liberation by Golpe," *Armed Forces and Society* 2 (Fall 1975): 5–34.
41. Michael Derrick, *The Portugal of Salazar* (London: Sands, 1938), p. 148.
42. Bandeira, "The Portuguese Armed Forces Movement."
43. Edward Luttwak, *Coup d'Etat: A Practical Handbook* (Cambridge, MA: Harvard University Press, 1979).
44. Bruce, *Portugal: The Last Empire*, p. 10.

Conclusions: Armies and Revolutions

To draw conclusions from events in one time or place and apply them to another is a perilous undertaking. But perhaps the danger is lessened if the conclusions are offered not as ironclad laws but rather as stimuli to the reconsideration of questions that may have been forgotten or prematurely dismissed.

Perhaps the most fundamental conclusion of this book is this: the success or failure of a revolution is intimately connected with the government's appreciation of the military dimensions of political power. This is as true for reformist and parliamentary and "enlightened" governments as it is for dictatorships.

WAR AND REVOLUTION

Lenin said: "Revolution is impossible without a nationwide crisis."[1] From the revolutionary point of view, the ideal crisis is one that renders the army unable and/or unwilling to defend the regime. The most effective instrument for producing such a situation of paralysis in the army is a losing war. Defeat in war contributes to the revolutionary situation in at least three ways: (a) it decreases the credibility of the regime leaders; (b) it increases economic deprivation and social tensions; and most of all, (c) it shatters the army both physically and psychologically.

True enough, military defeat does not *guarantee* a successful revolution. The Russian uprising of 1905, which flared in the circumstances of Russia's unexpected and ignominious defeat at the hands of the Japanese, is a case in point. Revolutionary outbreaks in the great cities of Russia were severe, but most of the army (only a part of which had actually faced the Japanese) stood firm and the regime survived. The big, crucial difference between the Russia of 1905 and the Russia of 1917 was that in the former case the army was still relatively small, professional, and cohesive. Neither did the approaching total collapse of Germany in 1944–1945 and Japan in 1945 produce even an attempted revolution (no doubt owing partly to the Allied policy of unconditional surrender: Why run the risk of opposing the regime? The whole nation was going to pay anyway).

Nevertheless, in spite of these cases to the contrary, the evidence is overwhelming that a nation about to suffer defeat after a bloody confrontation with a foreign power is ripe for revolution. In modern times, we can immediately think of the collapse of Napoleon III after the disaster of Sedan; the fall of the venerable Romanov, Habsburg, Hohenzollern, and Ottoman empires; the suicide of the Third Republic in 1940 and the arrest of Mussolini in July 1943. It is unlikely that a Portuguese army that was clearly winning in Africa would have overthrown the Caetano regime. Even the vaunted discipline and tradition of the army of the kaisers was not proof against the confusion and bitterness of wartime defeat: the two weeks before the proclamation of the armistice in 1918 saw mutinies within the navy and even among picked Jaeger battalions sent to suppress Republican demonstrations in Berlin, with officers stripped in the streets of their epaulettes and insignia. Events throughout Germany in those days recalled scenes in St. Petersburg a scant year earlier.

China provides another and gigantic example of the defeat-into-revolution scenario. One must never lose sight of the fact that Mao was at the end of his rope by the mid-1930s: the now highly romanticized Long March was in fact a Long Retreat, an attempt to escape the conquering armies of Chiang Kai-Chek. Between the Long March and the Communist occupation of Peking the Japanese invasion occurred, providing Mao the scope in which to perfect his guerrilla tactics *and* build a regular army. No Japanese war, no Maoist victory.

War can be the obvious and immediate catalyst of revolution, or it can ignite a fuse that takes years to reach the powder keg: The march on Rome in 1922 and the overthrow of Farouk in 1952 are unimaginable without the defeat (in the Italian case a totally subjective one) each country had endured four years previously. Students of Bolivian politics attribute the upheaval of 1952 in that country mainly to the disastrous reverses of the Chaco war against Paraguay almost a generation before.[2]

Let us further reflect that from Tokyo in 1941 and Rome in 1940 to Berlin, Vienna, St. Petersburg, and Constantinople in 1914, to Paris in 1870, and even to Charleston and Montgomery in 1860, leaders deliberately took the path of war because they had convinced themselves that such was the only choice available not for their aggrandizement but for their survival; all were swept away by the very wars they themselves unleashed. (In the waning days of the Civil War, the Confederate leaders offered freedom to any slave who would fight for the Southern cause. Those who had begun the war to continue slavery would now end slavery to continue the war! And war consumed them, confederacy and slavery both.)

In light of all this, prudent statesmen must reflect upon the cogency of Mussolini's dictum: "Today the war, tomorrow the revolution." Sometimes war cannot be avoided: the case of Israel comes to mind, along with Serbia and Belgium in 1914, China in 1937, Poland in 1939, the USSR and the United States in 1941, and South Korea in 1950. Clearly, however, the consequences of even a victorious war cannot be foreseen; hence, war can never be the *preferred instrument of a truly conservative statecraft.*

REVOLUTION WITHOUT WAR

Unsuccessful wars are clearly the antechamber of revolution. But what lessons can we derive from those numerous instances, including several considered in this book, in which the armed forces had not been defeated in war yet were unable to protect the regime? Specifically, what about Cuba, Nicaragua, Hungary, and Iran?

At first glance, all of these cases seem to invalidate the principle advanced by several distinguished authors that a government in control of an army undefeated in war is invulnerable to revolution. But peculiar circumstances in at least three of these instances becloud such a conclusion.

In the fall of Batista, we have not so much the victory of the revolutionaries as the collapse of the regime. In the end, Castro owed his triumph less to the few victories that rebel columns scored over isolated Batista detachments and garrisons than "to the forces of decay gnawing at the Batista army from within and without."[3] Batista's army was in fact an army in name only. Failure to appreciate this basic fact would cost Ernesto Guevara his life, and a whole generation would elapse before there was another successful Latin American revolution.

In Nicaragua, Somoza's Guardia Nacional was certainly hard-pressed, but never defeated. With all due regard for the fighting qualities of the Sandinistas, one cannot deny that the combat came to an end through negotiations directed by a foreign power, followed by Somoza's flight from the country. Nobody can be at all sure what would have happened if the negotiations had failed; that is, if the Guardia had felt it had no choice but to continue fighting.

Both the Hungarian Communists and the shah were in control of extensive security establishments backed up by powerful armed forces undefeated in war. Until the actual crisis was upon them, those predicting that either of these regimes was about to face a mortal challenge were few indeed. In both revolutions, it seems clear that what at first might have been no more than dangerous but transitory mass demonstrations turned onto the path of implacable revolution because the crowds were fired upon by security forces. It became immediately obvious that the Hungarian regime did not in fact possess the loyalty of the bulk of its army, hence the necessity to employ foreign troops who had both the strength and the will to kill civilians (at least armed Hungarian ones). In Iran, the initially loyal army eventually disintegrated because the shah permitted his soldiers to fire upon the crowds but did not have the stomach to order the Budapest-type repression necessary to put an end to the rebellion. The mullahs, in the name of the 1,000-year-old struggle between the true religion and the barbarian West, could demand the shedding of blood. But how could the shah, in the name of liberal reforms, have countenanced massacres of his own subjects within sight of the royal palace? Thus, the Iranian army spilled enough blood to stimulate the frenzy of the mobs but not enough to quench it.

The fall of the shah is the most severe challenge to the dictum that a government with the allegiance of its armed forces cannot be overthrown. In light of these Iranian events, we may want to refine this principle slightly, to the effect that a government is probably immune to successful revolution as long as it possesses (a) the loyalty of its armed forces, and (b) the conviction that it has the moral right to use whatever amount of lethal force might be required. Experience suggests that these characteristics may become incompatible, especially over the long run. That is, for a government to require its troops to use lethal force against civilians is politically perilous (to say nothing of the ethical aspect). A government confronted with such a mortal situation faces a triple task with regard to its troops: it must (a) preserve them from external contamination, (b) work against internal discontents, and (c) exercise great care in the choice of units actually to be sent into the capital city to confront civilian mobs. (But bear in mind that a government lacking the skill to avoid such a confrontation will most likely lack the skill to win it.)

First, troops should never mingle with the civilians they may have to confront in the near future. In a revolutionary situation, securing the capital city is of paramount importance. This will often require that troops remain *outside* the city, preferably at work on obviously useful projects, until or unless they are needed to suppress disorders that have outgrown the police. One might think that everyone, or at least experienced politicians whose careers and even lives might be at stake, would understand that sustained contact with a tumultuous or even a murmuring civil population is a bath of corrosion for military discipline, yet in the crucial summer of 1789, the Paris garrison did not even have its own barracks, but was quartered in rented living space in civilian houses. Political indoctrination, no matter how systematic, cannot be relied on to effectively counteract the spread of disaffection from civilians to soldiers, as the sudden collapse of the Hungarian army illustrates all too well. From Paris in 1789 to St. Petersburg in 1917 to Budapest in 1956 to Tehran in 1978 (and to Manila in 1986), one sees the folly of asking soldiers to control, injure, and perhaps kill civilians with whom the day before they may have been talking, drinking, dancing, or praying. But if it becomes evident that through some grave mischance contact with civilians has indeed undermined the morale of the troops, the government must immediately imitate the course taken by Adolphe Thiers in Paris in 1871: get the troops out of the city fast, away to a place where their discipline and morale may be rebuilt, even at the cost of temporarily giving the city over to the control of the revolution. *Those who lose the capital, but save the army, may return.* Neither the Tsarist nor the Kerensky governments sufficiently appreciated the power of this Parisian precedent, to their fatal cost.

From the viewpoint of protecting the government, the St. Petersburg–Tehran scenario is the worst possible: calling out troops — especially conscripts — to confront civilians, forbidding the use of lethal force for an extended period, then ordering the troops to open fire.

Although protecting their morale from outside contamination is essential, the government faced with potential turmoil in its capital city (or anyplace else) must also take heed of the physical and emotional needs of its soldiers. Twenty-five hundred years ago, Sun Tzu wrote in his book, *The Art of War*: "Pay heed to nourishing the troops!" Here once again, one might think: "But how obvious!" Yet from Sun Tzu's time to our own, the path is littered with the wreckage of regimes that failed to heed the implications of this simple precept. Miserable living conditions for the common soldiers — bad food, low pay, little or no medical care, and inadequate equipment — notably characterized the armies of the tsar and of Chiang Kai-Chek. In the Tsarist case, men were sent into the lines to face the mighty Germans without proper weapons, or without *any* weapons. Among Chiang's forces in the 1940s, several generals pocketed monies allocated for food while the common soldiers went hungry or extorted goods from civilians. Thus, these corrupt Nationalist generals were among the most effective propagandists and recruiting agents for Mao's Red forces.

But soldiers need more than bread and bullets. They need leaders they can respect. The armies of the tsar exhibited a great gulf between officers and enlisted men; so did the armies of the shah and of Louis XVI. In the French army on the eve of the Great Revolution, enlisted men endured overly strict discipline and harsh punishments; and no one not a member of the nobility, no matter how intelligent, dedicated, or brave, could hope to rise above the rank of lieutenant. The events of February 1917 were in part the consequences of the excessive subordination of Russian enlisted men to their officers. Mao, on the other hand, ceaselessly emphasized that the officer must win the respect of his men through deeds of endurance and courage. Officers, he insisted, must share the discomforts and dangers of their men, and *must be seen* to share them. Simple logic, bolstered by the unfortunate experience of so many regimes (and the counterexample of Mao's victorious forces) suggests that officers must not so far separate themselves from their men that the latter come to look upon them not as their leaders but as their jailers. If government leaders have been so incompetent as to neglect the lessons of all this experience and fear an approaching tumult within the precincts of the capital, timely pay raises and promotions may become their best weapons.

Another lesson on this subject of morale can also be derived from the Algerian war. One must absolutely prevent the torture of prisoners, no matter what the provocation or justification may seem to be, because it damages the image, and the self-image, of those who use it. Here, as with Mao's insistence that prisoners be well-treated and then released, we have one of those happy instances in which empirical evidence undeniably vindicates the best moral and religious sentiments of the race.

Finally, in preparing for a potentially sanguinary confrontation between troops and civilians, the authorities should take great care to make use of units that differ from the civilians racially, linguistically, ethnically, religiously, or, at the very least, regionally. This is an especially crucial consideration when troops must confront mobs led by religious figures. Here we have the invaluable old principle of *divide et impera*, known and used by every successful imperial power from Rome to Moscow. After he seized power, Lenin left turbulent St. Petersburg and ensconced himself within the thick walls of the Kremlin, guarded from his Muscovite subjects by foreign troops—namely the 4th Latvian Rifles; to this day, the Politburo sees to it that soldiers are sent to serve outside their ethnic area. The Soviets, to their cost, forgot this principle or at least felt unable to implement it in the early months of the Afghanistan war; an all the more remarkable lapse because the Soviets also provided, in their remorseless crushing of the Hungarian workers and students, one of the most convincing examples of the successful use of ethnically diverse troops against rebellious civilians. (It is sometimes observed that if Hungary were an island, the revolution of 1956 would have succeeded; but if Hungary were an island, a Communist regime would not have come to power there in the first place.)

PEASANTS, GUERRILLAS, AND SOLDIERS

The Hungarian, Iranian, and both Russian revolutions are all examples of the Western Model of revolution, which begins with dramatic events in the capital city, like the Great French Revolution that is the prototype.[4] Now it is time to turn from the problem of mobs in the capital city to the challenge of guerrillas in the countryside and to see what conclusions we may want to draw from the Algerian, Chinese, Cuban, and Nicaraguan cases.

Because of the almost universal contemporary tendency to trace all revolutions, successful or not, back to deep socioeconomic causes, we confront today

the pervasive belief in both Communist and noncommunist countries that revolutions occur because some government, or group, or class, or race is blocking a needed and probably desirable change in social organization. . . . The very occurrence of revolutionary violence establishes a prima facie judgment in our minds in favor of the rebels and against the authorities.[5]

That revolutions "erupt spontaneously out of conditions grown socially and economically intolerable—and can only erupt out of such conditions—is a very important propaganda weapon in the hands of sympathizers with revolutionary warfare."[6] Nonetheless, did Trotsky not say that if poverty were the cause of revolution, the world would be wrapped in revolutionary flames all the time? Every society created by human beings has contained at least some politically alienated members, and the capacity for political alienation seems to increase directly with education. That is, those who are most deeply alienated politically are usually those most removed from the world of the peasant.

There have always been distinguished students of revolution who have challenged the proposition, so blithely assumed in our own day, that every, or almost every, revolution represents a spontaneous popular movement. When Chalmers Johnson insistently distinguishes between "rebels" and "professional revolutionaries" one recalls Pareto's concept of "counterelites."[7] As one student of Algeria states, "the revolution was not born in the hearts of the peasantry and proletariat, nor was its ideology directly derived from their deepest concerns."[8] When the Castro brothers were in the Sierra, they promised the Cuban people not Communist dictatorship but Western democracy; only later did it become evident that the principle of Fidelista rule would be that "a select core of intellectually superior and proven revolutionaries has to lead the masses."[9] Che Guervara's ill-fated Bolivian expedition merely carried to extremes the principle that any peasant masses can be organized for revolution by their intellectual and social superiors.

The social backgrounds of Lenin, Trotsky, Zinoviev, Mao, Ferhat Abbas, the Castro brothers, Guevara, Ho Chi Minh, and most of the Sandinista leaders illustrate the middle- and even upper-class origins of many revolutionary movements, which turn to the proletarians or the peasants to find the necessary numbers. It is this social gulf between the leaders of revolution and those who are led, perhaps, that accounts for the phenomenon that de Tocqueville observed a century ago: the common people support revolution because it promises to get the state off their backs, but in fact every revolution in modern times (from 1789) has *resulted in the strengthening of the state*[10]; that is, the intelligentsia, having won the support of workers and peasants by promising equality and liberty, use their new political power to establish a degree of social control over the common people far more pervasive and efficient that that which preceded it. However we may morally evaluate the policies of this or that revolutionary regime, we may be sure enough that the masses who lent their decisive support to the revolution did not get what they had expected (consider the fate of the "Land to the Tiller" slogan in Communist-ruled peasant societies).

When we turn from the Western Model of revolution to the countryside (Eastern) version, it nonetheless becomes clear that the overthrow of governments has to do with the degree of success achieved by elements of the urban intelligentsia in forming and dominating an alliance with the peasantry.

In most peasant societies, harsh conditions often reflect the difficulty of the struggle against the forces of nature. These harsh conditions may be aggravated by certain peasant social practices (such as having an excessive number of children or consuming economic surplus in frequent festivals) and by exploitative aspects of the society's economic structures. But by no means does it inevitably follow that peasants are natural revolutionaries; far from it. The peasant, with his village, his farm and his family, is peculiarly vulnerable to organized violence and displays a profoundly pacifist attitude under the guise of religious fatalism. He tends to perceive political struggles as quarrels of city men. As a general principle, peasants rise in rebellion (that is, bring the danger of violence on their exposed world) only when they have been provoked beyond endurance, either by the depredation of marauders, as in China in the 1930s, or the insatiability of exploiters, as in pre-1910 Mexico.[11] In situations in which a revolutionary intelligentsia organizes guerrilla warfare, the peasants normally seek to remain aloof. If this is not possible, they will prudently lean to the side that seems most likely to win. (The general public in Western societies is usually unaware of these conditions, because journalists, especially Americans, are much more likely to have frequent contact with alienated urban intellectuals than with peasants, whose language they cannot speak, literally or figuratively. Consider the shah's regime, which, with all its faults, was committed to land reform, popular education, and women's emancipation, yet was successfully depicted in much of the American media as hardly different from the Somoza or Amin dictatorships.)

Because of the natural passivity and pacifism of the peasants, and their resulting tendency to support the side that seems likely to win or most able to harm them, it is absolutely crucial to the government's survival to convince the peasants that *it can provide them with physical security*. At the most elementary level, blind reprisals against the inhabitants of guerrilla-infested areas — the kinds of campaigns practiced by the Japanese and by the Somoza government — create sympathizers and recruits for the guerrillas, and are thus stupidly self-defeating. Soviet actions in Afghanistan, the deliberate destruction of the whole civil population over vast areas of the country, flagrantly violate this principle; but the relative size of the two countries and the determination of the outside world to act as if Afghanistan did not exist may allow Russian tactics to succeed, in the sense of bringing guerrilla activity to an end ("they made a desert and called it peace").

Beyond refraining from wholesale assaults on the civil population, the government must demonstrate that it can protect the civilians from the guerrillas.

First, it is essential that no village once occupied by government forces ever be allowed to fall back into guerrilla hands. Under this rubric, early French anti-guerrilla efforts in Algeria were very poor: the army would move into a village, stay for a short time, and then leave, exposing any cooperative elements to instant punishment. Consequently, in the early years of the revolt many people in rural areas supported the revolution "through fear of reprisal from their nationalist rulers-to-be."[12]

The occupation of a village or district by government troops should not be comparable to the descent of a plague of locusts. The guerrillas will not normally molest the peasants unless they are in unfriendly country and wish to make an example; the level of behavior of government troops should not fall too far below that of the guerrillas. Providing for the physical needs of the troops will not only help keep up their morale but inhibit them from destroying that of the civilians among whom they find themselves.   Governments must also develop methods whereby civilians can provide information about guerrilla activities without fear of being betrayed. "Counterinsurgents seem unaware of how commonly the police of a defending power are penetrated by the revolutionary party and therefore how dangerous it is to an informant to have his name in a police file."[13] Similarly, British intelligence in India found its numerous native sources drying up after World War II, when it began to seem that British power was coming to an end.

When we consider the question of what kinds of troops to use in rural anti-guerrilla campaigns, we arrive at principles completely opposite to those applicable to urban situations. In the city, the troops that confront civilians should be as different from them as possible; in the countryside, government soldiers should be as *similar* to the local population as possible. The principal weapon in guerrilla warfare is intelligence, that is, information about the enemy. To keep the guerrillas from having a monopoly of intelligence in a given area, the government must win the allegiance or at least the cooperation of the peasantry. Therefore, government soldiers should be natives of the contested area. Ideally, they will be recruited from the very villages that the government is trying to clear and hold; at least, many of them should come from the local district (a successful guerrilla operation will be recruiting its fighters along exactly these lines). Local recruitment means that the government troops will know and be known by the peasantry, which should facilitate both the gathering of intelligence and the maintenance of proper behavior standards among the soldiers. It also means that the troops will be familiar with the terrain in which anti-guerrilla operations are carried on. The presence of locally recruited soldiers also implies to the peasants and guerrillas that the government will not abandon the area.

It follows from this that the government should avoid using foreign troops in the countryside. Exceptions to this rule could include anti-guerrilla campaigns in very small areas (in which the campaign can be won without the sympathy of the civil population) or societies with deep ethnic or religious divisions in which the presence of foreigners would not be gravely provocative per se.

REVOLUTION IN THE UNITED STATES?

"Perhaps the most important and obvious, but also the most neglected fact about great revolutions is that they do not occur in democratic political systems."[14] If we consider the nature and condition of the regimes whose downfall we have been examining in this volume, it seems almost certain that events in the United States in the foreseeable future will not invalidate this observation. The Tsarist regime was illegitimate to almost the entire educated class in Russia and had involved the country in a devastatingly unsuccessful war. The Hungarian Communists, rejected by their people, distrusted by their allies, and abandoned by their own police, had no legitimacy whatsoever. The young Chinese Nationalist regime had not even established its hold over all of the country before Japan shattered it. Batista and Somoza both headed governments that relied almost entirely on apathy and coercion and notably lacked the modern technology necessary to fight guerrillas successfully. The shah represented a new dynasty, one that was the object of religiously generated hatred. Many people saw him as too closely aligned with a foreign superpower; worse, his vision of a westernized Iran was offensive to many Iranians and incomprehensible to most of the rest. President Sukarno associated himself with a movement that sought to murder the army command. To expatiate on how utterly remote all these situations are from that of the United States would be excessive even for a college professor.

But even if we conclude that the United States is relatively safe from revolution, what about a military coup? Certain elements in American society continue to view the military with unease and even suspicion—the "Seven Days in May" syndrome. But of the three cases we have examined of actual or threatened military takeover—Portugal, Brazil, and France—the first two arose in circumstances totally alien to the United States. The Portuguese army removed a regime for which it had been, however discreetly, the principal bulwark for half a century. The Brazilian army displaced the most poorly advised president in the country's history, one who, amid widespread public demand for just such a military intervention, had openly questioned the national constitution of which the army had traditionally been the supreme interpretor. Even then, huge strata of the Brazilian armed forces were disinclined to support the coup, and were overcome mainly by their reluctance to fire on brother soldiers.

If there is any case among those we have studied that might seem to have any relevance at all, however remotely, to the future domestic politics of the United States, it is the revolt of the French army against the Fourth Republic. In its view, that army had been shamefully permitted to suffer military defeat in one cruel guerrilla war and was about to suffer repudiation by the politicians after it had been victorious in another. Granted both the U.S. army's traditional reverence for constitutional processes and the common sense of common citizens, it is highly improbable but not inconceivable that a protracted and controversial military intervention overseas, combined with a belligerent anti-army reaction at home, could call forth the dread specter of an "American Algeria."

CONCLUDING THESE CONCLUSIONS

Whatever we think about the real causes of revolution, perhaps most of us might agree that its success or failure often has some of the dimensions of an automobile accident. That is, under certain highway conditions, a certain number of accidents will occur; it is clear, however, that in any *particular* accident, human decisions at any number of points might have prevented or altered the outcome. The causes of a revolutionary outbreak are not accidental, but the causes of its success at time *x* often seem to be. If Nasution and Suharto had been murdered along with the other generals, we would no doubt today be benefiting from numerous learned disquisitions explaining the historic inevitability of the triumph of communism in Indonesia. Consider the possibilities if the popular President Quadros had not resigned and the Brazilian army had not thereupon been confronted with an accidental president who lacked both political skill and a political base; if the shah had not had to battle cancer as well as mullahs or had been more concerned with his hold on the throne than with his place in the history books; if Wrangel instead of Denikin had commanded the advancing Whites or if Pilsudski had been able to take the long rather than the short view. What if Kerensky, after he escaped from the Winter Palace, had been able to gather up three battalions of well-drilled young men under a few score officers with a minimum of professional competence and pride? What if in St. Petersburg in February 1917 some government official had decided to get together and keep together in one place just 2,000 reliable troops? We do not necessarily argue that, for example, tsarism would never have fallen, but that, given certain relatively minor changes in its security arrangements, it need not have fallen in February 1917. The revolution of 1905 did not arise by accident, but the military defenses of the regime held; the day of reckoning was thus put off for a full twelve years. If the crisis of February 1917 had been overcome, and the revolution put off from one season to another, from one year to another, for an additional twelve years, it is very difficult to imagine a successful Bolshevik coup led by Lenin, and very easy to imagine a world vastly different from the one in which we live.

NOTES

1. V. I. Lenin, "Left-Wing Communism: An Infantile Disorder," in Lenin, *Collected Works*, vol. 3 (Moscow: Progress Publishers, 1966), p. 85.
2. James M. Malloy, *Bolivia: The Uncompleted Revolution* (Pittsburgh, PA: University of Pittsburgh Press, 1970); Robert J. Alexander, *The Bolivian National Revolution* (New Brunswick, NJ: Rutgers University, 1958).
3. Edward Gonzalez, *Cuba Under Castro: The Limits of Charisma* (Boston: Houghton-Mifflin, 1974).
4. Samuel P. Huntington, *Political Order in Changing Societies* (New Haven, CT: Yale University Press, 1968).

5. Chalmers Johnson, *Autopsy on People's War* (Berkeley: University of California Press, 1973), p. 5.

6. Geoffrey Fairbairn, *Revolutionary Guerrilla Warfare: The Countryside Version* (Harmondsworth, England: Penguin, 1974), p. 71.

7. Vilfredo Pareto, *I sistemi socialisti* (Turin, Italy: U.T.E.T., 1963).

8. George T. Kelly, *Lost Soldiers: The French Army and Empire in Crisis, 1947–1962* (Cambridge, MA: MIT Press, 1965), p. 152.

9. Harvey F. Kline, "Cuba: The Politics of Socialist Revolution," in Howard J. Wiarda and Harvey F. Kline, eds., *Latin American Politics and Development* (Boston: Houghton-Mifflin, 1979), p. 452. On the necessity for the revolutionary elite to hide their true plans from their followers, see Abraham Guillen, *The Philosophy of the Urban Guerrilla* (New York: Morrow, 1973).

10. Alexis de Tocqueville, *The Old Regime and the French Revolution* (New York: Anchor, 1955).

11. John Womack, *Zapata and the Mexican Revolution* (New York: Vintage, 1969).

12. Kelly, *Lost Soldiers*, 154–155

13. Johnson, *Autopsy on People's War*, 41.

14. S. Huntington, *Political Order in Changing Societies* p. 275.

Select Bibliography

Arendt, Hannah. *On Revolution*. New York: Viking, 1963.

Andreski, Stanislav. *Military Organization and Society*. Berkeley: University of California, 1968.

Barnett, A. Doak. *China on the Eve of Communist Takeover*. New York: Praeger, 1963.

Batista, Fulgencio. *Cuba Betrayed*. New York: Vantage, 1962.

Bell, J. Boyer. *The Myth of the Guerrilla*. New York: Knopf, 1971.

Bradley, John. *Allied Intervention in Russia, 1917–1920*. Lanham, MD: University Press of America, 1984.

Brinton, Crane. *Anatomy of Revolution*. New York: Vintage, 1960.

Bushnell, John. *Mutiny and Repression: Russian Soldiers in the Revolution of 1905–1906*. Bloomington, IN: Indiana University Press, 1985.

Carver, Michael. *War Since 1945*. New York: G. P. Putnam's Sons, 1981.

Chaliand, Gerard, ed. *Guerrilla Strategies*. Berkeley: University of California Press, 1982.

Chamberlin, William Henry. *The Russian Revolution, 1917–1921*. New York: Macmillan, 1935.

Chassin, Lionel M. *The Communist Conquest of China: A History of the Civil War, 1945–1949*. Cambridge, MA: Harvard University Press, 1965.

Chorley, Katherine. *Armies and the Art of Revolution*. Boston: Beacon, 1973.

Crouch, Harold. *The Army and Politics in Indonesia*. Ithaca, NY: Cornell University Press, 1978.

Cuzan, Alfred G., and Heggen, Richard J. "A Micro-political Explanation of the 1979 Nicaraguan Revolution," *Latin American Research Review*, Summer, 1982.

Daniels, Robert V. *Red October: The Bolshevik Revolution of 1917*. New York: Scribners, 1967.

De la Gorce, Paul-Marie. *The French Army: A Military–Political History*. New York: George Braziller, 1963.

Deutscher, Isaac. *Trotsky: The Prophet Armed*. New York: Oxford University Press, 1954.

Dunn, John. *Modern Revolutions*. Cambridge, England: Cambridge University Press, 1972.

Eastman, Lloyd E. *The Abortive Revolution: China under Nationalist Rule, 1927–1937*. Cambridge, MA: Harvard University Press, 1974.

Eckstein, Harry (ed.). *Internal War*. Glencoe, IL: The Free Press, 1964.

Ellis, John. *Armies in Revolution*. New York: Oxford University Press, 1974.

Fairbairn, Geoffrey. *Revolutionary Guerrilla Warfare: The Countryside Version*. Harmondsworth, England: Penguin, 1974.

Florinsky, Michael T. *The End of the Russian Empire*. New York: Collier, 1961.

Footman, David. *Civil War in Russia*. New York: Praeger, 1962.

Forbis, William H. *The Fall of the Peacock Throne*. New York: Harper and Row, 1980.

Godechot, Jacques. *The Counter-Revolution: Doctrine and Practice*. New York: Fertig, 1971.

Goshal, Baladas. *The Role of the Military in Indonesia*. Madras, India: University of Madras Press, 1980.

Graham, Robert. *Iran: The Illusion of Power*. New York: St. Martin's, 1980.

Grayson, G. W. "Portugal and the Armed Forces Movement," *Orbis*, Summer, 1975.

Green, Jerrold D. *Revolution in Iran: The Politics of Countermobilization*. New York: Praeger, 1982.

Guevara, Ernesto. *Guerrilla Warfare*. New York: Vintage, 1969.

Guillen, Abraham. *The Philosophy of the Urban Guerrilla*. New York: Morrow, 1973.

Hindley, Donald. *The Communist Party of Indonesia, 1951–1963*. Berkeley: University of California Press, 1964.

Hindley, Donald. "Political Power and the October 1965 Coup in Indonesia," *Journal of Asian Studies*, February, 1967.

Hughes, John. *Indonesian Upheaval*. New York: David McKay, 1967.

Huntington, Samuel P. *Political Order in Changing Societies*. New Haven, CT: Yale University Press, 1968.

Johnson, Chalmers. *Autopsy on People's War*. Berkeley: University of California Press, 1973.

Johnson, Chalmers. *Peasant Nationalism and Communist Power*. Stanford, CA: Stanford University Press, 1961.

Johnson, Chalmers. *Revolutionary Change*. Boston: Little, Brown, 1966.

Johnson, John J. *The Military and Society in Latin America*. Stanford, CA: Stanford University Press, 1964.

Katkov, George. *Russia 1917: The February Revolution*. New York: Harper and Row, 1967.

Katkov, George. "German Foreign Office Documents on Financial Support to the Bolsheviks in 1917," *International Affairs*, April, 1956.

Kecskemeti, Paul. *The Unexpected Revolution*. Stanford, CA: Stanford University, 1961.

Kelly, George T. *Lost Soldiers: The French Army and Empire in Crisis, 1947–1962*. Cambridge, MA: MIT Press, 1965.

Kenez, Peter. *Civil War in South Russia, 1918: The First Year of the Volunteer Army*. Berkeley: University of California Press, 1971.

Kenez, Peter. *Civil War in South Russia, 1919–1920. The Defeat of the Whites*. Berkeley: University of California Press, 1977.

Kiraly, Bela. "Hungary's Army: Its Part in the Revolt," *East Europe*, June, 1958.

Knox, Sir Alfred. *With the Russian Army, 1914–1917*. London: Hutchinson and Co., 1921.

Ledeen, Michael, and Lewis, William. *Debacle: The American Failure in Iran*. New York: Knopf, 1981.

Lenin, V. I. *Collected Works*. Moscow: Progress Publishers, 1966.

Lieuwin, Edwin. *Arms and Politics in Latin America*. New York: Praeger, 1960.

Liu, F. F. *A Military History of Modern China, 1924–1949*. Princeton, NJ: Princeton University Press, 1956.

Luckett, Richard. *The White Generals*. New York: Viking, 1971.

Luttwak, Edward. *Coup d'Etat: A Practical Handbook*. Cambridge, MA: Harvard University Press, 1979.

Mandel, David. *The Petrograd Workers and the Soviet Seizure of Power*. New York: St. Martin's, 1984.

Mao Tse-Tung. *On the Protracted War*. Peking: Foreign Languages Press, 1954.

Mao Tse-Tung. *Selected Military Writings*. Peking: Foreign Languages Press, 1966.

Marcum, John. *The Angolan Revolution. Vol. 1: The Anatomy of an Explosion, 1950–1962*. Cambridge, MA: MIT Press, 1976.

McAleavy, Henry. *The Modern History of China*. London: Weidenfeld and Nicolson, 1968.

Millet, Richard. *Guardians of the Dynasty*. Maryknoll, NY: Orbis, 1977.

Nolan, David. *FSLN*. Miami, FL: University of Miami, 1984.

O'Ballance, Edgar. *The Algerian Insurrection, 1954–1962*. Hamden, CT: Archon, 1967.

Osanka, Franklin Mark. *Modern Guerrilla Warfare*. New York: Free Press, 1962.

Paret, Peter. *French Revolutionary Warfare from Indochina to Algeria*. New York: Praeger, 1964.

Pareto, Vilfredo. *I sistemi socialisti*. Turin: U.T.E.T., 1963.

Parsons, Anthony. *The Pride and the Fall: Iran 1974–1979*. London: Jonathan Cape, 1985.

Pepper, Suzanne. *Civil War in China*. Berkeley: University of California Press, 1978.

Perez, Louis A. *Army Politics in Cuba, 1898–1958*. Pittsburgh, PA: University of Pittsburgh Press, 1976.

Pipes, Richard, ed. *Revolutionary Russia*. Cambridge, MA: Harvard University Press, 1968.

Pomeroy, W. J. *Guerrilla and Counter-Guerrilla Warfare*. New York: International Publishers, 1964.

Porch, Douglas. *The Portuguese Armed Forces and the Revolution*. London: Croom Helm, 1977.

Pye, Lucian. *Guerrilla Communism in Malaya*. Princeton, NJ: Princeton University Press, 1956.

Pye, Lucian. *Warlord Politics*. New York: Praeger, 1971.

Rubin, Barry. *Paved with Good Intentions: The American Experience and Iran*. Harmondsworth, England: Penguin, 1980.

Ruiz, Ramon Eduardo. *Cuba: The Making of a Revolution*. New York: Norton, 1968.

Russell, D. E. H. *Rebellion, Revolution, and Armed Force*. New York: Academic Press, 1974.

Schapiro, Leonard. *The Russian Revolutions of 1917*. New York: Basic Books, 1984.

Schmitter, Philippe C. "Liberation by Golpe," *Armed Forces and Society*, Fall, 1975.

Schram, Stuart. *Mao Tse-tung*. Harmondsworth, England: Penguin, 1966.

Schram, Stuart. *The Political Thought of Mao Tse-tung*. New York: Praeger, 1963.

Schwartz, Benjamin. *Chinese Communism and the Rise of Mao*. Cambridge, MA: Harvard University Press, 1951.

Seton-Watson, Hugh. *The East European Revolutions*. New York: Praeger, 1956.

Sheridan, James E. *China in Disintegration*. New York: Free Press, 1975.

Skidmore, Thomas E. *Politics in Brazil, 1930–1964*. New York: Oxford University Press, 1967.

Stempel, John D. *Inside the Iranian Revolution*. Bloomington, IN: University of Indiana, 1981.

Stepan, Alfred. *The Military in Politics: Changing Patterns in Brazil*. Princeton, NJ: Princeton University, 1971.

Story, Jonathon. "Portugal's Revolution of Carnations: Patterns of Change and Continuity," *International Affairs*, July, 1976.

Sukharov, N. N. *The Russian Revolution 1917*. New York: Harper, 1962.

Talbot, John. *The War Without a Name: France in Algeria, 1954–1962*. New York: Knopf, 1974.

Tang Tsou. *America's Failure in China, 1941–1950*. Chicago: University of Chicago Press, 1963.

Thomas, Hugh. *The Cuban Revolution*. New York: Harper and Row, 1977.

Tokes, Rudolph. *Bela Kun and the Hungarian Soviet Republic*. New York: Praeger, 1967.

Trotsky, Leon. *The History of the Russian Revolution*. New York: Simon and Schuster, 1936.

Trotsky, Leon. *Military Writings*. New York: Merit, 1969.

Trotsky, Leon. *My Life*. New York: Grosset and Dunlap, 1930.

Vali, Ferenc A. *Rift and Revolution in Hungary*. Cambridge, MA: Harvard University Press, 1961.

Volgyes, Ivan, ed. *Hungary in Revolution, 1918–1919*. Lincoln: University of Nebraska Press, 1971.

Whitson, W. W. *The Chinese High Command: A History of Communist Military Politics, 1927–1971*. New York: Praeger, 1973.

Wolf, Eric. *Peasant Wars of the Twentieth Century*. New York: Harper and Row, 1969.

Wolfe, Bertram D. *Three Who Made a Revolution*. New York: Dell, 1964.

Womack, John. *Zapata and the Mexican Revolution*. New York: Vintage, 1969.

Zeman, Z., and Scharlau, W. *The Merchants of Revolution*. New York: Oxford University Press, 1965.

Zinner, Paul E. *Revolution in Hungary*. Freeport, NY: Books for Libraries Press, 1962.

Index

About the Author

Anthony James Joes was born in Philadelphia and received his Ph.D. from the University of Pennsylvania. A professor of politics and director of the International Relations Program at St. Joseph's University, his major research interests include the subjects of revolution, nationalism, and dictatorship. He is the author of *Fascism in the Contemporary World* (1978), *Mussolini* (1982), and contributor to *Political Parties of Europe* (1983). His articles have appeared in *Comparative Political Studies, Orbis, Presidential Studies Quarterly, Transaction/Society*, and *Worldview*. He is currently working on a book about the fall of South Vietnam.